ADVANCE PRAISE FOR

THE FIELD HOUSE

"I just finished this lovely book and feel richer for it. Meticulously researched and deeply felt, *The Field House* is a compelling hybrid of biography and memoir. An exploration of the life and legacy of novelist-poet Rachel Field, it is interwoven with personal reflections that reveal the influence of Field's work ethic and passion on the biographer's life. This book is also a meditation on the nature of creativity and a love letter to a house on Sutton Island in Maine once owned by Field and now by Wood. For both writers, the house became a touchstone and a haven, a place to reflect and rejuvenate and create."

- #1 *New York Times* best-selling author Christina Baker Kline

"*The Field House* lures readers to 'a long-abandoned, wood-framed house on an island off the coast of Maine.' When author Robin Clifford Wood buys a summer cottage belonging to famed poet and award-winning author Rachel Field, Wood is haunted by Field's sudden death, her untold stories. Discovering treasures and clues Field left behind, Wood weaves a stunning and intimate portrait of a once-prized American writer and poet who deserves to be remembered."

—Barbara Walsh, Pulitzer Prize–winning writer and author of *August Gale: A Father and Daughter's Journey into the Storm* and *Sammy in the Sky*

"This elegant hybrid of biography and memoir introduced me to Rachel Field and Robin Clifford Wood, whose lives, separated by generations, uncannily twine. Compelling, instructive, inspiring, and beautifully written. I was greatly moved."

—Monica Wood, award-winning author of *The One-in-a-Million Boy*, *When We Were the Kennedys*, and *Any Bitter Thing*

"Robin Clifford Wood's biography of Rachel Field is a beautiful and thorough history of an artist and writer with important connections to Maine. In *The Field House*, Wood doesn't back away from the complexity of Field's life: self-doubt, aspirations, flaws, triumphs, unrequited loves, and final losses. And yet this book is also a clear-eyed survey of the literary world of the 1920s and '30s, Maine island life, and a woman who, transcending gender roles and notions of physical beauty, offered the world a gift that, because of Wood's deeply personal book, will hopefully never be forgotten."

—Jaed Coffin, author of *Roughhouse Friday* and
A Chant to Soothe Wild Elephants

"I highly recommend Wood's enchanting *The Field House*, her intensely personal reckoning with the life and work of the nearly forgotten author Rachel Field . . . Field left plenty of evidence for her biographer to explore—in archives across the country, and in the Maine island cottage they both called home in a curious twist of fate that enabled this charming and heartfelt narrative."

—Megan Marshall, Pulitzer Prize-winning author of
Margaret Fuller: A New American Life and
Elizabeth Bishop: A Miracle for Breakfast

"Robin Clifford Wood has combined immense archival material and keen insights to create a detailed and enchanting biography of Rachel Field. The author's skillful use of granular sources, paired with her sophisticated wordsmithing, has produced a book that is both informative and lyrical. Readers will also appreciate the author's parallel discussion of the writing process itself—an articulate discussion that will undoubtedly seem familiar to anyone who has ever struggled to discover and tell a story. This is a delight to read."

—historian Jacalyn Eddy, author of *Bookwomen: Creating an
Empire in Children's Book Publishing, 1919–1939*

"This fascinating book about the life of Newbery Medal-winning author Rachel Field lives at the intersection of seamless research and rich personal reflection. Robin Clifford Wood offers such insightful, knowing details about Field's writing life and her personal attachment to Maine, that we come to feel we are reading the account of a close friend. Wonderfully executed, *The Field House* renders Field's extraordinary life with great empathy and beautiful, lucid prose."

—Susan Conley, critically acclaimed author of *Landslide*, *Elsey Come Home*, *The Foremost Good Fortune*, and *Paris Was the Place*

"This wonderful book—based on meticulously thorough, devoted research—is a lovingly tender, wise, and judicious account of Rachel Field and her world. Its unusual blend of memoir and biography helps to illuminate the life, even as a poignant dialogue between the author and her subject unfolds. Truly, a tour-de-force!"

—Benson Bobrick, award-winning author of *Angel in the Whirlwind* and *Wide as the Waters: The Story of the English Bible and the Revolution it Inspired*

THE
FIELD HOUSE

THE

FIELD HOUSE

A Writer's Life Lost and Found
on an Island in Maine

Robin Clifford Wood

SHE WRITES PRESS

Published 2021
Printed in the United States of America
Print ISBN: 978-1-64742-045-1
E-ISBN: 978-1-64742-046-8
Library of Congress Control Number: 2020917547

For information, address:
She Writes Press
1569 Solano Ave #546
Berkeley, CA 94707

She Writes Press is a division of SparkPoint Studio, LLC.

Book design by Stacey Aaronson
Circular inset silhouette on the cover reproduced from Rachel Field's original illustrations

All company and/or product names may be trade names, logos, trademarks, and/or registered trademarks and are the property of their respective owners.

Names and identifying characteristics have been changed to protect the privacy of certain individuals.

To my mother, who opened my heart.

To my husband, who opened my wings.

Oh, you won't know why, and you can't say how
Such change upon you came,
But—once you have slept on an island
You'll never be quite the same!
—RACHEL FIELD,
"IF ONCE YOU HAVE SLEPT ON AN ISLAND"

Silhouette illustration by Rachel Lyman Field,
from The Pointed People

Contents

Prologue

In 1994, my husband and I purchased a long-abandoned wood-frame house on an island off the coast of Maine. In the 1920s and '30s it had been the summer house of author Rachel Field, on the island that inspired all her most successful work—the poetry, plays, children's books, and novels that took her from struggling writer to Newbery medalist, National Book Award winner, then rising Hollywood success. At the peak of her renown she died suddenly and unexpectedly, leaving so many stories untold, including her own. When I first walked into the island home that had been her magical place, her muse, some of those stories reached out tendrils, looking for a place to attach themselves. I felt their presence in the flutters of my heart but didn't know at the time what it meant.

Many people know the sensation of entering an old house and feeling something of its history in the air. It whispers from the corners, buzzes indecipherably in the motes of dust illuminated by a ray of sunlight through wavy glass. The building retains some indefinable quality left behind by its former inhabitants, some of their energy lingering in the atmosphere.

On an island with no roads, only footpaths and wooden wheelbarrows, the leavings of former inhabitants are not just figurative. Rachel's weighty wooden sleigh bed is still there in the room where she slept. The old wicker chairs in front of the fireplace creak under my weight, as they creaked under hers. Her Scottie-dog trinkets and paraphernalia wait expectantly, pointy ears on alert, on shelves and in drawers. I sit on the front porch—the "covered piazza," as Rachel called it—and I contemplate the same view of Seal Harbor and Acadia National Park's rocky-top mountains across an expanse of sea called the Eastern Way. That same view inspired Rachel's creative work, her joy, and her loneliness.

Rachel's life was not easy. It was not all fairy houses and moonglow, or silver streaks of rain on city streets, or soaring gulls alighting gracefully on the barnacled rocks of an island off the coast of Maine, even though her work is alive with all those wonders. It wasn't a life of deep deprivation either. Her family had enough means to get by and the social status to be accepted into most echelons of the stratified society of her time. The difficulties in Rachel's life were more situational and internal. First, there was her physical presence. Many who knew her effervescent spirit on the page were shocked to meet Rachel for the first time, for she was not the elfin sprite they expected but a woman of imposing stature and heavy, masculine features. Her warmth quickly eclipsed superficial impressions. She had a lightness about her, something open and engaging that made people feel like an old friend at her kitchen table. Nevertheless, her exterior self caused her a lifetime of rue.

I also sensed that her story was weighty with much deeper disappointments, even before I'd begun my research. There were shadows of loss, heartbreak, secrecy, a sister gone mad, an "improper" marriage, infertility, a child who seemed to disappear—so many unanswered questions. But Rachel's story, I was certain, held more than anything a prodigious share of redemption and hopefulness. I was certain not only because of Rachel's work but because I inhabited her space.

I explored every inch of Rachel's old house and discovered treasures. I studied a map of Paris that she brought back from Europe in 1920, browsed through a stack of magazines in the attic that arrived new when she was here, and brushed my fingertips across the faded stitches of her initials, embroidered by her own hands into an old linen dishtowel. This house that I settle into every summer is saturated with Rachel—her life, her spirit, her secrets. Why has no one told her story? Were those legions who loved her simply too undone by the ache of her loss to record the bright light that her life shed here on Earth? Was the weight of tragedy or the burden of untold secrets too great an obstacle? Why was this delightful woman, this vibrant spirit, consigned to the vaults of oblivion? No one had stepped up to share Rachel Field's life story, but something told me it was time, and I'd been chosen to take on the task.

I tried to stick to the story, Rachel's story, but I fell into a not uncommon trap for biographers. Something happens during the writing of a biography that feels a lot like falling in love. Some argue that this is true of the best biographies, because without a degree of passion, biography can feel overly clinical, flat. On the other hand, how can you write an accurate history if you carry that kind of bias?

You can't. That is what I concluded at last, after the first eight years of stuttering progress. Try as I might to divorce my relationship with my subject from the writing of her life, I failed. It didn't help that I resided for days on end amongst her things, warmed by her fireplace, immersed in that fantastically drenched atmosphere of pine scent, salt air, pounding surf, and keening gulls.

One of Rachel's characteristic practices was to open her books with an apology. Even after winning multiple awards for her writing, she never lost her amazement that people liked her books well enough to keep buying them. So she warned her readers—anyone who might expect more than her humble scratchings could accomplish—not to overestimate her ability. I understand the inclination, so I am following Rachel's lead.

What follows is an account of the life of Rachel Field, written by someone who never met her, yet learned to love her. I did not succeed in hiding my devotion to my subject in this biographical tale, and I hope you'll forgive me for that. On the other hand, neither did I hide the times that she disappointed me, which were few, but real. I have done the best I could to tell all of the truth I could discover, but part of that truth is certainly refracted through the lens of a deep and abiding affection.

Because I had the advantage of the internet, I was able to find caches of Rachel's personal history and correspondence that no one had pieced together before. In addition to browsing several private collections of Rachel Field paraphernalia at the invitation of their owners, I spent many hours studying and photographing archive collections in Maine (the Cranberry Isles, Portland, Augusta); Massachusetts (Cambridge, Stockbridge, Springfield); Connecticut (New Haven); New York (Poughkeepsie); Washington, DC; Louisiana (New Orleans); and California (Beverly Hills, Los Angeles). I visited her former homes in several states, her college campus, and the hospital in California where she died. I had long conversations with Field family historians and other Rachel Field enthusiasts who had blazed the beginnings of many trails that I was grateful to follow. After ten years of hunting, I have uncovered almost all the mysteries that I set out to solve. The greatest mystery, however, is always at the core of a human's animated being, inaccessible to all, sometimes even to the person herself.

Rachel Field died in her forties, much too young. She had seen many successes in her writing life and quite a few, if belatedly, in her personal life. She had also suffered deeply, made sacrifices, felt profound inadequacy, and had her fathomlessly generous heart broken. No one I know has ever exceeded Rachel's capacity to infuse souls with delight. I hear it in the bright-eyed musicality of her voice on an old radio-show recording. I see it in her plays, poetry, and prose, but also in her letters and in the letters friends wrote to and about her. A great many people loved Rachel in life. She was a sensible, practical, hardworking New Englander, but she also gave abundantly of herself—her counsel, her connections, her financial support, her prolific correspondence, and her meticulously hand-crafted gifts.

I have seen the products of Rachel's giving, held the hand-sewn books and rugs in my hands, turned the pages of her letters sideways so I could read her marginal words of affectionate parting. I even have her recipe for fish chowder. I never had the good fortune, however, to witness her face in animation, to see her blue eyes light up and recognize me as a friend. It would be logical to assume that our relationship is one-sided, but that is not so. Rachel Field gave me many gifts. One of them was a reminder to embrace life with the heart of a child and the soul of a poet. Another was the inspiration to write. This book is my gift to her.

Author's note:
Given the casual nature of personal correspondence, some of Rachel Field's letters and her friends' letters contain inconsistencies in syntax, punctuation, or spelling. To preserve authenticity I have retained all correspondence as originally written.

Dear Rachel Field,

Your island home continues to stand against the ravages of time, tides, and winter storms—with a bit of help. That rustic 1898 structure of wood that you called "the Playhouse" is still there on the craggy northeastern cliffside of Sutton Island. I've been taking care of it with my husband for about twenty-six years now, and our four children know all its secret spaces, its boxes of old junk in vast metal chests in the attic, the creepy outdoor stairway that melts into woodsy blackness at night, the wonderful old kitchen filled with open pantry shelves, a pegboard shopping list that includes alum, lamp wicks, and lard, and the enormous woodstove that we are determined to restore to use again one day. Your house is still well loved, and it is still filled with you.

That's how I got to know you so well, really—it was that house. Maybe you are still lingering there, waiting to catch one more glimpse of that particular blue you wrote about: in the harebells that grow out of cracks in the rocks, in the September sky, or in the sea on just the right kind of day. I read about your blue in your poetry, and I looked for it, wishing I could know if I had found exactly the right one. Then I thought maybe that wasn't the point. It was the looking that was important, so I keep on going.

You see, that's the kind of thing you have done for me. That's why I started reading more of your books, your poetry (my favorite), your plays, your novels, everything. Then that wasn't enough, so I tried to learn more about you. I got a lot of information from the Great Cranberry Island Historical Society and the registry of deeds in Ellsworth, Maine. I found two women, now elderly, who knew you when they were little girls. One thing I noticed was how many people become more animated when they begin to talk about you, whether they knew you in person or only in print. A light kindles in their eyes like imagination, or anticipation, or a sense of wonder. Did you know that there are people who have moved to Maine specifically because of you and your writing? Come to think of it, maybe you played a role in my decision to make Maine my year-round home, so that our trips to Sutton would take just over an hour instead of half a day. I spoke for hours on the phone with one woman on the West Coast who was so enthralled with your story that she had delved deeply into your personal history—although nowhere near as deeply as I delved, in the end.

Once I started looking, I found there were many mysteries about your life, shadowy bits of rumor and unconfirmed speculation. How did you die? Newspaper reports were vague. Was there a secret shame around your death? What about your sister? It appeared that you had a sister, but her presence in your life seemed to end abruptly in the 1920s. What happened to her? No one seemed to know for certain if you were able to bear a child. Did you adopt? Some stories indicated that you did, but what happened to that child? Who was the man you married? Why did you marry so late in life, and why was the marriage kept so quiet? Was there a scandal, something inappropriate? My mind was abuzz with questions.

That West Coast woman who spoke to me at such length on the phone loved your book Hitty best of all. She was one of hundreds of doll enthusiasts who still pay annual tribute to your adventurous doll heroine to this day. I thought you would be amused to know that. She was the first one to tell me I could view some of your personal records; they were available to the public. She also said she sometimes felt so overcome with connection to you that she wondered if a part of you had come to life inside of her. Wow, I thought, she's obsessed. That was before I started to feel a little bit the same way.

There is another thing I thought would mean a lot to you, so I'm writing to tell you about it. After you died—so abruptly, so unexpectedly, at the pinnacle of success and happiness in so many parts of your life—I think the world trembled a little bit. Your loss was no small thing, and maybe you even resisted it somehow, lingering stubbornly to take care of the unfinished business of your life. Maybe you even sought help from the living, from someone like me, to finish telling your story. I spent hours in the archives at your old alma mater, in Radcliffe's Schlesinger Library, reading piles of condolence letters to your grieving Arthur. Here is a selection:

I met your wife so seldom, and yet she meant so much—it was always exhilarating, so pleasurable to meet and talk with her. So much vitality and warmth, indeed our world is the poorer. We shall not look upon her like again. I wonder is it any comfort to know that so many countless people share your grief.

I have been thinking of you and of little Hannah all night, ever since the radio message came through. Never have I been so profoundly shaken. Rachel who had so much to live for, who meant so much to so many people. I had such a happy letter from her, not four weeks ago. She was so deeply happy with you and Hannah, she had accomplished so much and now this last wish that she had wanted so passionately for so many years, the cup quite brimming over and I know that is *how she felt it. . . . No one, I think, had a fuller life. Fate was generous to her in all but this and I can almost hear her saying, "well I suppose it is too much for any one person." But to us—I just cannot realize this world without her.*

I felt cut in two when the most unexpected sorrow of all leapt out at me from the air, just a week ago today. . . . I have been trying since then to draw near to you in sympathy, but I have been numbed and stunned, and no words would come to me. It has been dear and gracious Rachel herself who has released me from this dumb imprisonment in sorrow. Today my heart turned over when I saw, which I had never again hoped to see, the dear, gracious, generous rounded handwriting on an envelope which dropped at the door.

When I arrived in the Schlesinger research room, I was only curious, but after reading these letters, I was in thrall. Who could this person have been, I wondered, to have elicited this kind of impassioned, visceral grief in so many people across the country and across oceans? That was when the seeds of my own obsession sprouted. I sought out every archive I could think of that might have records of you and your life—in Maine, Massachusetts, Connecticut—and that was only the beginning. I contacted Field family descendants and learned more about your highly accomplished relatives. Then I went to the heart of Field family history, your first childhood home in Stockbridge, Massachusetts, where your story begins.

Yours sincerely,
Robin Clifford Wood

o n e

The Illustrious Field Family

In the town cemetery in Stockbridge, Massachusetts, is Rachel Field's gravestone, seamed by a crooked scar across its middle where it was once broken and repaired. Though it reads "Rachel Field Pederson," there is no other sign that Rachel ever had a husband or daughter. She was laid to rest with her parents and siblings, the Matthew Dickinson Field family. Within a few hundred feet are monuments of varying degrees of grandeur commemorating dozens more Fields and Field family descendants. For better or for worse, Rachel was descended from an illustrious family of great historical prominence in the nineteenth century, and their influence on her life was inescapable. This undated poem from one of Rachel's notebooks is playful but prophetic:

MY EPITAPH

A-field she went and knew right well
Grass, daisies, berry and blue-bell;
Now their same roots do cover she
Who still in death a-Field must be!

In Laura Benét's tribute to Rachel in the March 1942 issue of the *Horn Book Magazine*, she recalls an anecdote about Rachel's childhood. William Thomas Manning, who would later become the Episcopal bishop of New York, was one of many prominent summer residents of Stockbridge. He observed young Rachel as a child, playing on a Stockbridge lawn during a birthday party. "His eyes singled her out with pleasure and he turned to her mother, saying: 'You have a brilliant, splendid child. She will do you honor.'"

To do honor was an expectation that weighed on Rachel by virtue of both her mother's and father's family lines. She resented that expectation, feeling for many years that she would never measure up, and she chafed against haughty social elitism throughout her life. Nevertheless, she was fascinated by stories and personal histories, including her own. All of her novels and much of her poetry include elements of history, often her own family history, including conflict around the breaking of social barriers. In that sense, Rachel's ancestry pushed and pulled upon her psyche throughout her lifetime in both positive and negative ways.

Rachel was named for her maternal great-great-grandmother, Rachel Lyman, wife of Noah Atwater, an influential minister in western Massachusetts. Rachel's conflicting feelings toward her heritage—dismissive on the one hand and sentimentally attached on the other—are evident in this letter of thanks for a silver porringer that was sent to her baby daughter, Hannah: "Well, you've endowed her and how she will treasure it and use it always even after porridge days are over. I never had one, being the last of five and named for a great-great-grandmother I had no such things—a rather battered coffin handled soup spoon and a funereal Watts' hymnal were my only legacy from my departed namesake, so I feel

I'm being richly rewarded now in your gift to Hannah." The Atwaters certainly left their mark on Rachel, but it was the Field family that weighed in most powerfully in the world of Stockbridge, Massachusetts.

When Rachel Lyman Field was born on September 19, 1894, her family was living in New York City. (There are rare references to uncertainty over whether Rachel was born on September 18 or 19, including one from Rachel herself. The vast majority of sources use the nineteenth, so this book will do the same.) Rachel was the fifth child born to Matthew Dickinson Field and Lucy Atwater Field, but one of only two to survive beyond childhood. One son and a daughter died in infancy, and another daughter, Katharine, died at age five. Rachel's surviving older sister, Elizabeth, was born in 1891. Their father, Matthew Dickinson Field, was a physician specializing in mental health. Matthew battled a heart condition for much of his life. His grief over the loss of his children visibly weakened him. His suffering was particularly profound after five-year-old Katharine's death in 1892. A colleague reports that Matthew took a trip to Europe in the hopes of regaining some of his strength. Though his health improved, he never fully recovered. Matthew Field did not live to see Rachel's first birthday.

In spite of his absence from her life, descriptions of Dr. Matthew Field indicate that he passed on some distinct genetic characteristics to his youngest child. Descriptions of his physical presence and his character echo many of the same traits that people later described in Rachel:

> Dr. Field had an ardent, generous nature, and his warm grasp of the hand, direct glance and bright smile inspired

a trust and confidence which were never disappointed. His devotion to his friends was unbounded, his quick sympathies responded instantly and lavishly to the appeal of one in trouble;—in innumerable instances time, strength, skill and money were freely given, even at great personal sacrifice, to assist an unfortunate professional brother or other needy friends. . . . While reserve was not easy to his frank, impulsive nature, he was rarely heard to utter a harsh criticism even of persons uncongenial to him.

Rachel's father had a "buoyancy which rose above every difficulty" and was rife with "ability, energy, strength of character, and rare sweetness of spirit." Rachel was an apple that did not fall far from the tree.

Shortly after her husband's death, Lucy Atwater Field packed up her household and her two young daughters and moved to Stockbridge, Massachusetts, where the roots of her own and her husband's families were deeply woven into the fabric of the community. For the next nine years, Rachel and her sister lived with their mother, aunt, and Atwater grandparents in a world that was both a bucolic paradise and a bastion of lofty ancestry, tradition, and ponderous expectation. Though Rachel said in later years that she felt little emotional connection to Stockbridge, the impressions made on young Rachel by those early years never disappeared from her writing: the transcendent beauty of fields, woods, and streams; the love of stories in a household where reading aloud was a daily ritual; and the ever-present reminder that she was descended from a grand line of elite ancestors who had changed the world.

In the early 1800s, Rachel's great-grandfather the Reverend

David Dudley Field moved with his wife, Submit Dickinson Field, to his new position as pastor for the Congregational church in Stockbridge. The descendants of this union, beginning with their ten offspring, had such an impact on nineteenth-century American history that one historian refers to them as "the Kennedys of the 1800s." Though history primarily highlights four of the Reverend Field's sons—David Dudley Jr., Stephen Johnson, Cyrus West, and Henry Martyn—these four were by no means the only ones of his children to display intelligence, initiative, innovation, charisma, and creativity. Amongst them, Rachel's great-aunts, her great-uncles, and her grandfather all left a profound impression upon the politics, law, science, religion, and circulation of ideas during their historical period.

David Dudley Field Jr. (1805–1894), the oldest of the ten children, worked for most of his life on legal reforms that widely influenced the codification of both US and international law.

Emilia Ann Field (1807–1861) was educated at three seminaries before marrying a missionary, the Reverend Josiah Brewer. They moved to Turkey for nine years, where they founded and administered a seminary for girls.

Emilia's younger brother Stephen Johnson Field (1816–1899) came to live with them in Turkey as a teenager before returning to the United States for college. Stephen later became the longest-serving Supreme Court justice in history (a distinction he held until William O. Douglas took the number one position). Emilia and Josiah Brewer's son David Brewer also sat on the United States Supreme Court, serving alongside his uncle for eight years.

Another of the ten Field children, Jonathan Edwards Field (1813–1868), was actively involved in law and politics in Michigan, where he took part in the drafting of the constitution of Michigan for its admission to statehood. Later he served as a state senator in Massachusetts.

Matthew Dickinson Field (1811–1870), Rachel Field's grandfather, was a self-taught engineer, mechanic, and entrepreneur. He started a paper business near Stockbridge, which served as inspiration for the mill in Rachel's last novel, *And Now Tomorrow*. Matthew also spent time in the mid-1800s building railroads and suspension bridges in the South, but they were destroyed during the Civil War. He was elected to the Massachusetts state senate and became an instrumental partner in the project to lay the first telegraph cable across the Atlantic Ocean, headed by his brother Cyrus West Field.

Cyrus (1819–1892) is arguably the Field brother who had the most permanent and far-reaching impact on the world of the late nineteenth century. Another driven soul who found great success without formal education, Cyrus left home for New York City at age fourteen to make his way in the world. His business talents led to great financial success, which allowed him to retire at age thirty-two. It was around this time that Cyrus got the notion of a transatlantic cable that would carry messages across the ocean in minutes, rather than the weeks that it took for a ship to make passage. After years of failed attempts, ridicule, and lost investments, he finally succeeded and gained worldwide fame. There are several biographies of Cyrus, one of which was written by his brother, the minister, correspondent, and family historian Henry Martyn Field (1822–1907).

Henry and his sister Mary Elizabeth (1823–1856) both became published correspondents from Europe during their travels abroad. Mary, sadly, both was widowed and died young, but Henry, a minister by profession and an avid traveler, produced a lifetime of writings about European and domestic affairs. In addition, he wrote extensive chronicles of Field family history. In many ways, her great-uncle Henry was the most influential Field family member in Rachel's life. This was partly due to the fact that Henry was the only member of his generation who lived beyond Rachel's early childhood. She writes in the introduction to one of her novels: "I can just remember Great-Uncle Henry as a small, elderly man with a vague smile, whose mind had a disconcerting way of wandering off without warning into labyrinths of the past where a matter-of-fact seven- or eight-year-old might not follow."

Although Rachel had an apparent interest in her ancestry, it was an interest based largely on stories, poetic fancy, and artifact. She writes with pleasure about her two-year-old daughter wearing a dress from Madeira, a gift from her father that both she and Elizabeth had worn. In a poem titled "Family Pew," Rachel waxes nostalgic, comparing her own childhood with those of her ancestors: "I wonder if my Great-grandmother felt / Air half so keen and sweet with salt and bay / On such a summer Sunday as she knelt / In this old pew and heard the Parson pray?" Similarly, her poem "Grandmother's Brook" considers a childhood memory recounted to her by her grandmother: "Sometimes I ask her:—'Is it there, / That brook you played by,—the same, to-day?' / And she says she hasn't a doubt it is— / It's children who change and go away."

When it came to genealogy and conspicuous achievement, however, Rachel was uninterested. In a letter to a friend after the success of her novel *All This and Heaven Too*, she tells of the flood of letters asking questions about Field family history. She refers with some dismay to her deficiencies as a family historian: "It's a judgment on me, I guess, for family relationships have always bored me and I refused to listen when they were explained to me in my youth and now I wish I had listened."

The converse to Rachel's love for family stories was her insecurity in the face of the family's reputation and her dismay at her physical inheritance. She felt a constant sense of inadequacy in the face of Field family accomplishments and expectations. Rachel may have appeared to others to be "a splendid, brilliant child," but she saw herself to be deficient. She bemoaned her large frame and strong facial features, which were said to be much like her father's. She wrote to a friend, in describing her newly adopted daughter, "You can see she has the kind of nose I could never have given her, a darling little turned up petal—not the Field variety, praise be!"

Rachel's performance in school was neither splendid nor brilliant in her early years, and she rebelled against the burden of family legacy. In a letter to a college friend, she apologized for having been a poor conversationalist at her friend's home on a recent visit: "Please tell your father that I do not always sit about like a log of wood, but logic and wisdom always reduce me to a wondering puppy—you see I'm not truly a Field at all—for they 'hadda da brain,' and I 'no gotta one.' But, even without it, I like the people I like, and you are one of them!" Even at age thirty-seven, she wrote to a friend, "I send you this rather sad looking four leafed clover for future luck—But it came from the Field-Estate, so too much mustn't be expected of it."

The legacy of Rachel's ancestry gave her two points of strength: stories to ponder and something to push against as her developing ego battled to assert itself during those first tender years. Amongst the fields and Fields of Stockbridge, Massachusetts, both plentiful, the seeds of great success were planted in the heart of Rachel Field.

One of the most fruitful seeds planted in Rachel's heart grew from her great-uncle Henry—or rather, from the story of his first wife, the infamous Henriette Desportes. Rachel's great-aunt Henriette, though they never met, was the source of the utmost fascination for young Rachel. In the mid-nineteenth century, Mademoiselle Desportes had been the object of international fascination for her involvement in a dramatic scandal of murder and intrigue that had a significant impact on French politics and the French royal family. Henriette's departure from France was an effort to escape the specter of scandal that loomed over her, in spite of her legal exoneration in the case. Henry Field had met Henriette during his travels in France, and after she came to the United States, they married. It was Henriette's true story, part of Rachel's family history, that turned into Rachel's most successful novel and feature film, *All This and Heaven Too*. The introduction to her novel is in the form of a letter written to her great-aunt:

Dear Great-Aunt Henrietta,
Although I never knew you in life, as a child I often
cracked butternuts on your tombstone. There were other
more impressive monuments in our family lot, but yours
for some unaccountable reason became my favorite in
that group erected to the glory of God and the memory
of departed relatives.

Rachel's sister Elizabeth remembers in her memoir how Rachel used to linger amongst the Field family monuments in the Stockbridge cemetery, particularly singling out the brown stone (the others are all white) of her great-aunt.

Rachel goes on in her introductory letter to talk about lying awake in the same bed that had belonged to her great-aunt Henrietta, thinking about her past and

> trying to piece together from scattered fragments of
> fact and hearsay all that you spent so many years of your
> life trying to forget.
>   I have grown up with your possessions about me. I
> know the marble-topped mahogany bureau that matches
> your bed; the pastel portrait you made of the little girl
> who became your adopted child; I know the rosewood
> painting table that held the brushes and paints and
> crayons it was your delight to use; I know your silver
> forks and spoons with the delicately flowing letter D on
> their handles. On my hand as I write is a ring that was
> yours, and I never take out a certain enamel pin from its
> worn, carnelian-studded box without wondering if it may
> not have been some bit of jewelry tendered as peace-
> offering by the Duchesse after one of her stormy
> outbursts. Strange that these intimate keepsakes should
> survive when I have never seen so much as a word in your
> handwriting.

It is telling that Rachel's most profound ancestral interest was in a family member who was not blood related. Something about this woman, who had no family whatsoever, resonated with Rachel Field. Rachel admired her aunt Henriette's independent courage, her charm, wit, and intelligence, and her air of dignified reserve. In analyzing her aunt's portrait, Rachel betrays her own youthful vexations over her physical appearance. She talks in her letter of Henriette's "too large and firm a mouth," which "must have been a trial to you in your youth." Poignantly, Rachel also felt a connection to Henriette's inability to bear children, a pain shared by Rachel decades later. This personage from Rachel's family tree captured her imagination and admiration more than any other, and Rachel mused over the fact that her great-aunt's simple gravestone offered neither biblical verse nor summation of the drama of her life.

Rachel wondered, "Why is there no hint of the destiny which was reserved for you alone out of a world of other human beings?" The fact so perplexed Rachel that her early working title for Henriette's story was "Omitted Epitaph."

A few steps away, today, sits Rachel's own stone. Though Rachel might have preferred that her stone be elsewhere, among other people or places that held more of her heart and soul, perhaps she might take some consolation in the parallels between her own simple grave and that of her greatly admired great-aunt. Nowhere on her stone is there any hint of the destiny and fame which were reserved for Rachel alone. It reads, simply:

Rachel Field Pederson

1894–1942

Dear Rachel Field,

    The first time I stood in the town cemetery in Stockbridge, in front of your simple tombstone, I experienced a shudder of grief. You left that place behind, and yet it claimed you in death. The family and loves of your adult life—all far from Stockbridge—were nowhere to be found there, erased from your history. Where were they? I had no idea. Why weren't you with them? Why weren't you buried on your treasured Maine island? Why was there no reference, somewhere on this stone, to the profoundly alive person that you were?

    Perhaps, though, you would appreciate the parallels between your understated stone and that of your great-aunt Henriette. The first time I read your letter to her at the beginning of your book All This and Heaven Too, I caught my breath. You knew that same feeling that I know! You are aware of that sense of connection to someone in the past through the artifacts that they left behind. Could there be a form of intercourse that transpires between the spirits of the living and the dead? Could a piece of furniture or a trinket on a shelf be the conduit through which those connections are made? Or maybe could it be a homely utensil that two separate hands grasp across time, thus sharing some indefinable pulse of life?

    A Sutton Island neighbor of mine told me that when she was in grade school, she once had to memorize and recite a poem. She chose "My Inside-Self," not realizing that it was written by you, a fellow Sutton Islander. Once she discovered your identity and your island connection, my neighbor embraced a lifetime sense of sisterhood with you. It is amazing how many people I met who experienced a similar personal resonance with you and your work. As I lived with your unfolding story and surrounded myself more and more with your life's echoes, I felt that connection with growing insistence.

I went to Stockbridge to give a talk at a national conference about your Hitty doll and about you. It may sound funny, but I was becoming known, at least in some circles, as a Rachel Field expert. I spoke in the library across the street from your house, that same library where you read St. Nicholas magazines and dreamed of writing your own stories. I wandered around the town of Stockbridge to get a feel for the spaces you rambled through as a child, visited the church with the Field family pew where you sat and fidgeted, gazing at the swaying trees out the window. I read newspaper interviews in which you talked about your childhood, and I browsed through your earliest journals in archive collections, wearing protective white gloves as I leafed through the brittle pages. In all these ways, the child Rachel came slowly to life in my mind.

Your childish loves and trials resonated with me even more deeply than your adult life. Childhood is more eternal than adulthood; its essence is far less altered by the vicissitudes of society and culture. Your descriptions of childish forays into fantasy and rapt absorption in books could have been my own story. My heart went out to the young girl, rife with insecurity, who so keenly felt the betrayal of her physical appearance, the girl who couldn't read until the age of ten and felt herself to be so inadequate. And yet, there was that fire of drive in you too. You were a formidable child. I sometimes wonder how you would have taken on the world if you'd been born a hundred years later, when women were more able to stretch their wings without reproach.

In learning about your early years, I also began to understand your fraught relationship with your only living sister. It was hard for me not to resent her disdain toward you, but she is a part of your story too, and she provided me with some invaluable background material. In my more forgiving moments, I feel a profound sorrow for Elizabeth Field; in other moments, her bitter jealousies infuriate me. For better or for worse, her story is inescapably bound up in yours.

Always sincerely,
Robin C. Wood

two

Inside-Self and Outside-Self

The town of Stockbridge, Massachusetts, has taken great pains to preserve its historic authenticity. Its town center is a charming array of buildings and storefronts that still evoke the quintessential New England town of the early twentieth century. Strict ordinances disallow changes to Main Street, ever since Norman Rockwell painted his ambitious *Stockbridge Main Street at Christmas* in 1967. Though it was painted a few decades after Rachel Field's Stockbridge childhood, much of the flavor of historical Stockbridge remained in the 1960s. Even today, one can get a sense of how the town appeared when Rachel lived there as a child from 1895 to 1906. The library, churches, an old country store, and the Red Lion Inn look much as they have for over a century.

Rachel Field and Norman Rockwell, both born in 1894, share an unexpected connection to Stockbridge. On Rockwell's 1967 canvas a particular white colonial house can be seen on the same lot where it sits today, looking very much as it has for a century or more. In the 1970s, Rockwell's artistic works went into a trust in the custodianship of the Stockbridge Historical Society, whose home at that time was the Old Corner House, the white house in Rockwell's painting. For twenty-four years, the building housed the first Norman Rockwell Museum. That same house happens to be the home in which Rachel Field grew up.

It was known as the Dwight house in 1895 and was already over a hundred years old when the recently widowed Lucy Atwater Field moved in with her two young daughters, her parents, and her sister Katharine Atwater—Aunt Kitty. They moved in as renters from the Dwights, one family amongst the multitudinous relatives who were a perpetual presence in Rachel's life. Thereafter, Rachel and her family lived under the eye of the soberly dressed "Auntie Dwight," whose portrait hung in the back parlor, putting a face to some of the family stories that Rachel and Elizabeth heard so often from their mother. Another family portrait hung in their dining room, about which Rachel wrote this poem:

GREAT-UNCLE WILLIE

High on our dining-room wall,
Smiling and little and neat,
For years Great-Uncle Willie
Has watched us sit and eat.
Breakfast, dinner, supper,
Parties and afternoon tea—
I can't help thinking sometimes
How hungry he must be!
But he never looks reproachful,
Though cruel it must seem
To be a family portrait
On days when there's ice cream!

For nearly ten years, the two young girls lived, played, and formed their earliest impressions of the world amidst bucolic New England beauty and tradition.

The most detailed depiction of life for the two Field girls in turn-of-the-century Stockbridge is in Elizabeth Field's book, *A Stockbridge Childhood.* Elizabeth wrote it in 1947, five years after Rachel's death. In order to put Elizabeth's narrative into its proper perspective in the context of her sister's life, it is important to understand something of Elizabeth herself. Elizabeth Field's life followed a vastly different path from Rachel's, and their relationship bristled with an undercurrent of tension and resentment, mostly one-sided. Rachel envied her sister's fair-haired, delicate beauty, the kind one finds in storybooks. Elizabeth's jealousy of Rachel went much deeper, and lasted a lifetime.

Elizabeth never married nor had much of a social life, two facts which pained her. At some point in her adulthood, she suffered from a mental illness which preceded many years in a sanatorium in North Carolina. Rachel paid some share, if not all, of the cost of her sister's care over time, in addition to supporting her mother and aunt for most of her life. Rachel never discussed Elizabeth's condition publicly. On the rare occasions when she made reference to her sister in personal letters, she did so discreetly. In the 1920s and '30s mental illness was an exquisitely delicate and private matter, something to keep hidden from view. Elizabeth's health improved eventually, but not until shortly before Rachel's death.

Elizabeth does not dismiss Rachel entirely from her Stockbridge history, but her younger sister is strikingly absent from most of her narrative. She makes small, grudging references to Rachel's literary career, and her bitterness and jealousy toward her sister are evident from the first page. In the prologue to her book Elizabeth writes that it had long been her wish to bring her hometown of Stockbridge to life in her memory: "This wish has persisted even while facing the hard fact that I was not a type for conspicuous accomplishments, though these gifts had in some degree been conferred on other members of my family." In another part of the book Elizabeth gives this lukewarm acknowledgment of Rachel's blockbuster best-selling novel and film, part of which recounted some of the history of their Field ancestors in Stockbridge: "In . . . *All This and Heaven Too* Rachel Field tried to recreate the married life of our French great aunt-in-law, a portion of which was spent in Stockbridge." Later she refers to a family anecdote that Rachel included in her novel. "My sister put this story in the second part of her book but I did not care for the way she wove it in."

Notwithstanding her bias, Elizabeth's accounts of her Stockbridge days are an invaluable part of the record of her own and her sister's early lives. She had an exceptional memory for detail (very like Rachel's), which paints a vivid picture of those early influences on her life and her sister's. In conjunction with recollections in Rachel's writings, letters, and interviews, Elizabeth's book creates a lively picture of Rachel's childhood world.

"The world of Stockbridge just before the turn of this twentieth century was very like the nineteenth century English novel," writes Elizabeth. "The automobile had been invented but had not yet appeared in Stockbridge where tally-hoes [horse and buggy] were still in vogue." There was no electricity, only two known typewriters, and no private telephones; daily activities consisted largely of domestic duties, walking outdoors, and visiting. An annual boat parade, guest lecturers, local dramatic performances, fairs, sewing circles, parlor games, and especially hikes around the local woods and hills are all remembered with great fondness in the book. The simplicity and beauty of Stockbridge life attracted many summer visitors seeking escape from the bustle of the city. It was (and still is) a popular retreat for artists, intellectuals, and citizens of great wealth and prominence. The likes of Herman Melville, Henry Wadsworth Longfellow, and Nathaniel Hawthorne (who was once a dinner guest at the table of David Dudley Field) all wrote warmly of the unrivaled beauty of the surrounding area.

"Like many other towns," writes Elizabeth, "our village was affected by the inflow of immigrants from Europe as well as the Chinese laundrymen and the Eastern pack peddlers who often came walking through the country in native costumes trying to sell trinkets from their home countries." Rachel used to tell a story of one memorable day when she ran in fright from a group of gypsies who were passing through town; Rachel got herself tangled in the barbed wire of a fence. A smiling gypsy extricated the frantic child and set her down on the ground. After she got over her hysteria and he was gone, Rachel realized that she was fascinated by the exotic man who rescued her. She never forgot his flashing smile and his twinkling spiritedness.

The child Rachel spent a great deal of time outdoors, where she played with See-Saw, the family fox terrier, or watched squirrels gathering nuts from the strawberry box that her grandfather had nailed to a tree in their backyard. She embraced the beauty of her environment with a poet's sensibilities.

BLUE

There at the old wood's edge
I saw a bluebird fly.
And its wings beat bright against
The paler blue of sky;
They seemed to burn a way
Into the sky and me,
Till my heart stood still in a hush
Of ecstasy.
I watched that bluebird fly,
And knew with a queer dull pain
That nothing now can ever seem
So blue to me again!

In summer Rachel spent hours playing and exploring near her home. In winter she and the other children in town went coasting down hills or tied their sleds to the backs of wagons for a ride. Christmastime, forever one of Rachel's favorite times of year, saw trees decorated with strings of popcorn and handmade ornaments. The magical excitement and subsequent discarding of a Christmas tree held poignant associations for Rachel throughout her lifetime. January was a dreadful time of year, she once wrote, largely because of the "Christmas trees in ashcans along the curbs."

Rachel Field as a toddler (circa 1897 or 1898), posed on a sled during a childhood winter in Stockbridge, Massachusetts

Sundays were church days, when no sports were allowed. Aunt Kitty went to the Congregational church down the street. She sang the praises of the simple beauty of the white church with its graceful spire, which caught the fancy of young Rachel. Rachel, however, was obliged to attend the darker and more solemn Episcopal church with her mother and Elizabeth, who preferred the more somber building. Rachel sat dutifully in the family pew at St. Paul's and often visited family monuments in the cemetery nearby. She "had decided ideas," however, reports Elizabeth, and once proclaimed defiantly that she would one day belong to the Congregational church ("but of course she would be married in the Episcopal," Elizabeth writes). Although Rachel's poem "Family Pew" indicates a coastal Maine setting, it gives us, perhaps, a picture of how Rachel might have experienced her own days in church on a Sunday morning, longing to be out and away.

Once a week Rachel and her sister looked forward to feeding lumps of sugar to the big horses that pulled Mr. Dunham's grocery wagon, full of supplies from nearby Pittsfield. Rachel spent plenty of time, too, at the library across the street from her home, where her "stone deaf" grandfather was known to fall asleep for an afternoon with See-Saw in his lap. "Miss Well, the librarian, would have to wake them up at closing time." It was in that library that Rachel was first introduced to *St. Nicholas* magazine, where some of her own earliest publications appeared years later.

Through a narrow basement window of their white clapboard home, Rachel would gaze at the world from a bug's-eye view while she sat in the workshop that she had fitted out for herself. Perhaps it was here where she assembled her first book at age seven or eight. It was a sheaf of papers lovingly cut out, with one edge sewn together. She decorated the cover with roses and forget-me-nots and carefully printed her name and the letters B-O-O-K. That was the extent of the book; she never made a mark on its clean white pages. She often cited that first book in interviews. "Perhaps it was my best book, who knows?" she quipped to one interviewer. The longer she considered the immaculate blank pages in front of her, the more uncertain she became about marring their perfection with her uncertain hand, so she left it as it was. "The experience gave me a certain reverence for blank paper. It is just as well when you begin to write to make sure that you have a something worth recording. I have often thought that I should like to keep that first book of mine on my desk, as a warning."

One thing Rachel was not doing in her basement workshop was reading. Rachel did not read until she was nearly ten years old, even after she learned how to print words. "Literally, I wrote before I could read," she would recount. As she told one interviewer, "I liked to print, because I liked to draw. But I heard so much grown-up reading aloud that I lazily refused to learn to read myself until I wanted to for purposes of my own when I was over ten years old."

Rachel also loved her dolls. "I had dozens—one old one I called the Empress Eugenie—and I liked to make paper ones," she told an interviewer. "You see, I liked to make things with my hands." Rachel sat for hours, cutting out paper dolls behind a sofa in the parlor while listening to an adult read children's stories aloud. There were also stories she heard from family members about the colorful history of Stockbridge and New England— from the Indian legend of Monument Mountain to the shipboard romance and hurried wedding of a family ancestor and the hundred-year evolution of a local family who started as slave owners, became abolitionists, and later hosted a luncheon to honor Booker T. Washington. It was a household rich with stories both factual and fictional. The worlds conjured by those stories and the brave characters of her youth, who faced life with such courage and panache, all became as much a part of Rachel's life as her own backyard.

Some of Rachel Field's most popular poetry, plays, novels,

and verse were particularly cherished for their vivid evocation of the heart and imagination of a child. Intriguingly, in a 1931 interview she confessed that she did not get her ideas through spending time with children: "All I really know about children is what I can remember about myself from my own childhood." What she remembered, though, she remembered in intricate detail.

Perhaps I have the sort of memory that holds impressions; a "camera memory." Anyway, I have many pictures in my mind, many impressions that I have carried since my childhood. I was always able to take in details. I loved old houses, and I never entered one for the first time that I did not get an exact picture in my mind of at least one of the rooms. I would know just where the windows were, how the furniture was placed, the position of a rug on the floor, what ornaments were on the mantel.

In addition to a fine memory for detail, Rachel had a healthy relationship with fairies, elves, and other magical beings all through her life. Her words in one interview could well refer to her own experience as a child:

Children live in a world of make-believe, not all of the time, but some of the time. It is a world they can pass into and out of on a moment's notice, or without any notice at all. And who knows that it is not just as real as the matter-of-fact world in which their elders live?

Come to think of it, don't we all of us, all our lives, live much of the time in a world of our own creating?

The interviewer asked Rachel if she believed in elves, fairies, and gnomes like the ones that appear so often in her children's verse and stories. She responded:

Not so much in them as about them. I was willing to accept them as real characters in some of the stories I loved. When the story was finished the characters vanished, just as characters that now come to life out of the pages of a good novel are gone as soon as some other interest takes the place of the novel. As a child I could pop out of Elfland into the kitchen as quick as a wink. A moment after a fairy tale had held all my attention I could be just as deeply entranced in the cook and what she was getting for dinner, and whether or not she was going to let me stir up something to bake in her nice hot oven.

While her imagination took everything in, Rachel's hands always kept busy, a habit she took into adulthood. Even in her thirties she spent hours hooking rugs or cutting out silhouette pictures while she listened to her mother and aunt read aloud by the fire in the evening.

It was not only her home life that fed the imagination and creativity of young Rachel. In the little school that she attended from age four through nine she spent many more hours listening to literature read aloud. Although there was a public school near their house in town with a playground and a big bell that rang the children in to class, Rachel and her sister walked up nearby Yale Hill to a private school run by two single women—a family cousin, Miss Brewer, and her colleague, Miss Byington. The Field girls' daily walk took them past a blacksmith shop, a house where bees were kept, and a wide meadow through the woods along a babbling stream that fed two nearby sawmills. Their school bell was a delicate tea bell, and their education both more refined than that offered in the public school and rather unconventional. Elizabeth Field writes of their Stockbridge education: "Compared to Henry Adams' methodical curriculum in the Boston schools . . . the desultory information which I acquired in this community of western Massachusetts would seem like a patchwork quilt in contrast to an oriental rug." However, she goes on, "if education also means the bringing out of one's power to appreciate the wonders of this earth as 'a thing of beauty which is a joy forever,' then one could never cease being grateful for a childhood spent in Stockbridge."

There were generally only nine or ten children in the school. They spent time each day listening to the Bible, poetry, great literature, morality tales, and other things read aloud by their teachers. In a weekly break from their individual work, they spent time memorizing and reciting lines. The two teachers put a particular emphasis on seeing to it that every child spoke English not just correctly but beautifully. This lesson bore fruit in Rachel, whose lyrical voice and articulate diction were often praised later in life by her peers. Once, in her thirties, Rachel won a contest on a radio show called *Rise and Recite*, which featured celebrities who took part in a traditional schoolhouse version of a recitation contest. A recording of the show includes Rachel's enchanting voice. Her speaking is professionally perfect, yet carries a warmth and a musical quality that seem to betray a twinkling smile of delight behind each phrase. It is no wonder that she would quickly take to the stage with such success in her youth.

Nevertheless, at age six or seven, she was still struggling her way through those early days of academia. School days were filled with genteel rituals: "At the end of each day after we had put on our outer wraps we returned to our desks and waited till Miss Brewer had wound her small music box, and then we marched around the desks till the signal to leave and as each child reached the door it was the rule to turn around and say, 'Good morning, Miss Brewer.'"

Though Rachel bemoaned some aspects of her early school days, she treasured others. She particularly loved going into the room of Miss Byington, her favorite teacher because she taught them drama and poetry. Miss Brewer's room was the more cumbersome one, filled with the dreary parts of schoolwork that were more of a plague to Rachel. Could it be, though, that Miss Brewer's music box, at least, planted a seed of enchantment in Rachel's heart? She was an avid collector of music boxes throughout her life. She had an extensive collection of them in her New York apartment and incorporated music boxes into several of her stories and poems, including "The Old Music Box," published in *Child Life* magazine in the spring of 1931: "It's not the tunes that it can play, / But something else. I can never say / . . . But always under the tinkling part, / You can hear it beating like a heart, / Or the tick of tiny fairy clocks / Hidden away in the music box."

During much of her life, Rachel felt that she was a disappointment to her line—she called herself "lazy," and struggled in school with any subject that did not capture her interest. The math and science parts of school plagued her from the first, and her slowness to read became somewhat of an embarrassment. Neither was she able to tell time until she was twelve years old. She was by no means the only Field to make a success without a brilliant academic career, however, as history eventually proved. In a

1932 letter she recounts a visit to Miss Brewer, her "90 year old cousin who used to teach us school." Typically self-disparaging, she adds, "God knows she never managed to teach me anything to speak of." Then Rachel goes on, "She looked just the same to me except she had taken to her bed and she had forgotten that I wasn't one of her favorite pupils."

One thing that Rachel had an uncanny talent for was memorization. She was able to repeat a poem word for word after hearing it only once. This skill became particularly providential when her school put on plays. Every Friday the children put on some kind of "entertainment" for the parents, and sometimes they performed more lengthy dramas. One educational piece was called "The Congress of Berlin." Every child played the part of a foreign nation, and Elizabeth recounts this amusing version of what may have been Rachel's first appearance on the stage, somewhere around the turn of the century:

> Karl Bidwell took the part of Montenegro, and the part of Servia [*sic*] was taken by my little sister Rachel whose chief remark was "I have borne the burden and the heat of the day and my reward has been small." We Balkan states sat at a small side table. My part was to run in late all out of breath shouting, "Oh, the Turks, the Turks, they're after me! Give me refuge! I am Greece." Then when some of us at our small, detached table tried to express opinions, Germany interrupted with "Silence, children, or you will be sent supperless to bed."

During the winter of 1903–04 the children took on the daunting task of performing Shakespeare's *The Merchant of*

Venice. The cast consisted entirely of children under the age of thirteen, including Elizabeth as Portia and Rachel as Shylock. Rachel and Elizabeth each wrote of this experience, and a hint of sibling rivalry is evident in both versions, though the women's differences in confidence and temperament are equally apparent. After her visit to her aging teacher, Rachel reports that old Miss Brewer "reminisced at a great rate about our production of *The Merchant of Venice,* saying how beautiful my sister looked as Portia, but she insisted that I got <u>the</u> most applause—and she reminded me of how Mollie Punderson's brother Frank, who was the little Judge in the trial scene, went to sleep and nearly ruined the scene!" Elizabeth's version of the event has none of Rachel's lighthearted humor. It reveals a lifetime of insecurities, compounded by her perception of having lived perpetually in the shadow of her younger sister:

> The time the *Merchant of Venice* was played at Miss Brewer's School I was given a certain satisfaction which has lasted through life from playing Portia at the age of twelve. In the jewel casket scenes there were enough beaux to satisfy for years to come, while in the court scene even though my younger sister had the talent to play Shylock, I was for once able to stand up to her in an argument and to be cheered by the rest of the school with "A Daniel come to judge us, yea a Daniel."

Another significant event in Rachel's young life, one whose impact carried well into her adulthood, was when her school put on a play based on Kate Douglas Wiggin's *Rebecca of Sunnybrook Farm.* Rachel was nine years old when she was given the part of one of her favorite fictional heroines. "I don't suppose I shall ever feel quite so proud, or happy, or so full of responsibility again," Rachel recounted in a 1934 interview. "I wasn't altogether a novice. I had played Shylock in our school productions of *The Merchant of Venice* that winter, and I had reveled in it (especially scraping the dagger on my shoe, whereby wearing out my second best pair) and felt myself already on the way to becoming a great actress." She had heard the book read so many times that she nearly had it memorized (although she still wasn't able to read it for herself). After Miss Byington converted it into a play, Rachel had every part by memory in no time.

She became somewhat concerned, she told the interviewer, when she realized how little she looked the part of Rebecca. "Judging by looks," she thought, "I ought to play Emma Jane, for she had been as round and freckled and red-haired as I. That meant I must act like Rebecca, and make the audience forget I wasn't slim and dark and dashing." Rachel threw herself into the role, ending up covered in bruises from repeatedly rehearsing the scene where Rebecca falls off a porch into a bed of lilac bushes. It was not only parents but many community members who came and paid twenty-five cents apiece to watch the quaint staging of "Rebecca." One audience member was a summer resident, New York publisher R. R. Bowker, who played a role in Rachel's early professional life and never stopped addressing her as "Rebecca." The school's performance was a fundraiser that made twenty-five dollars to donate to some worthy cause.

Rachel recalled:

I remember more especially how wonderful it seemed when the audience laughed in the funny parts and clapped; and how at the end, after we all bowed in front of the two sheets that did for curtains, someone handed me a big bouquet of white daisies with a pink peony in the middle. Not even when I saw my first one-act play given behind real footlights, or when I held the first book I ever wrote in my hands, have I been quite so surprised and pleased.

Charisma notwithstanding, Rachel had a lifetime of angst over her physical appearance. Perhaps her remark about playing Rebecca gives a hint to what drove this powerfully vibrant personality to perform in life as well as she did. Since she despaired of ever looking the part of the spritely, elfin spirit that inhabited her, she determined that she must act the part, in order to show the world the Rachel she wanted it to see, the Rachel who, like many of her buttoned-down characters, held "a hidden fairy tune in the bottom of [her] heart."

The following poem may be brief, but it represents a weight on the life of a growing girl that helped to mold the adult she became:

MY INSIDE-SELF

My Inside-Self and my Outside-Self
Are different as can be.
My Outside-Self wears gingham smocks,
And very round is she,
With freckles sprinkled on her nose,
And smoothly parted hair,
And clumsy feet that cannot dance
In heavy shoes and square.

But, oh, my little Inside-Self—
In gown of misty rose
She dances lighter than a leaf
On blithe and twinkling toes;

Her hair is blowing gold, and if
You chanced her face to see,
You would not think she could belong
To staid and sober me!

In the Stockbridge Library there is a copy of *The Pointed People*, Rachel's first book of poetry, published in 1924. Inside the first page Rachel inscribed it to "The Stockbridge Library from an ex-next-door neighbor—with best wishes. Rachel Field 1931. For Stockbridge verses see pages 8, 15, 47, 61." Two of those poems were "Great-Uncle Willie" and "Blue." Before we leave Rachel's Stockbridge childhood behind, here are the other two, both illuminating glimpses into the heart and spirit of the budding young writer:

Almost

There are things you almost see
In the woods of evening—
Fairies as thick as fireflies,
Elves leaping in a ring.

There are things you almost hear
When no one passes by—
Stirring of seeds in good damp earth,
Stars marching through the sky.

THE QUIET CHILD

By day it's a very good girl am I;
I sit by the fire and sew,
I darn the stockings and sweep the floors
And hang the pots in a row.
But, oh, by night when the candle's out
And my bedroom black as pitch,
I've just to crackle my thumbs to turn
Into a wild bad witch.

Nights of storm and nights of stars
Are all the same to me—
It's up on my broom and straddle the wind
As it whips my pigtails free.

Over the chimney pots to go,
Past the jumbled lights of towns,
With the hosts of good black trees beyond,
And dim sheep-sprinkled downs.

No one knows when morning comes
And I'm back in bed once more,
With tangled hair and eyes a-blink
From the sunshine on the floor—
No one knows of that witch who rode
In the windy dark and wild—
And I let them praise my sober ways,
And call me a quiet child!

It would be years before Rachel finally established peace between her inside and outside selves. In the meantime, her writing skill would become an increasingly important tool for navigating the difficult times ahead.

Dear Rachel,

Bruce Komusin was one of those people whose life was transformed by you, even though he never met you. He was largely responsible for the Rachel Field and Hitty corner in the Great Cranberry Island Historical Society museum, just across the way from Sutton Island. His collection of your works was probably one of the biggest in the country. It was Bruce who gave me the recording of your voice on Rise and Recite, and for that I will be forever indebted to him. To hear your sweet voice, your gentle laugh, and your beautiful elocution was one of the pinnacle moments of my years studying your life. Bruce's recording brought you to life as nothing before ever could, and I think I began to consider you a friend right around that time.

Since your presence in my life has been so important to me, Rachel, it seems that I should share some things with you in return. I'd love to tell you a little bit about myself as a child. I always had a lot of pluck, a bit of unbridledness that was gently, and perhaps inadvertently, squashed over time. Some said I was too bossy. I was known to burst into my parents' bedroom, startling them breathlessly from a sound sleep, with news that was earthshaking only to me. I'd arrive home from school with big GUESS WHATS, or implore everyone to "come see this!" I was compassionate and sincere, and people liked me, but I was aware that I was also somehow inappropriate, and I was very sensitive. So I became self-conscious.

My successes in life were often tinged with doubt. One day my fourth-grade teacher announced my stellar grade on a spelling test (unlike you, I excelled more in academics than in charisma) and called me forth to receive it. As I walked, blushing, back to my seat, another girl disdainfully murmured "show-off" as I passed. My blush deepened, and I felt as much confusion as I did shame.

I always loved to sing. In seventh grade, I got into an audition-only middle school singing group, but only after I was rejected in the first round of auditions. The teacher liked me; I was sweet. So she took me in after the fact. I always felt vaguely apologetic for my performances after that. I was never MVP of any sports team or high school class president, as my older siblings were, but on their coattails I received kind attentions that always felt undeserved. At the end of my high school years, I was accepted into Yale University. I felt sure it was only because my dad was an alumnus—or maybe because the dean of admissions thought I was sweet and sincere and felt sorry for me, standing there dripping wet in his office, late for my admissions interview on a torrential autumn afternoon. I got into an audition-only singing group at Yale too. Once again, however, it was only after I didn't get in the first time around. I was always the afterthought, the sympathy gesture, not quite as good as people wanted, but oh well, why not?

I wanted to be a writer starting when I was a wee thing. I spewed forth writings as my great-aunt, great-grandfather, and great-great-grandfather had done before me. But I don't remember anyone taking it seriously. I was never disparaged, but I wasn't encouraged either. No helicopter mom for me— quite the opposite. Mom loved me terrifically, of that I was always certain, but I was generally left to play and discover and make do on my own with my siblings or cousins or friends.

My boisterousness was not my mother's way at all, nor

really my father's. Sometimes I wondered where it came from. I spent a lot of my life feeling vaguely apologetic about my explosive nature—I had a temper and a physical streak, and when I was young, I was prone to hit. I felt uncouth, not quite acceptable, if kindly tolerated.

Somewhere in all this, an inclination to know the rougher side of life pushed itself to the forefront of my longings. I wanted to be a boy, as my mother had when she was a child. I wanted to jump out of airplanes, go rock climbing, climb to the tops of trees, swim to the bottom of the lake, get dirty and scratched and maybe even bleed. Those were the times when I felt truly alive. Since there was such an undercurrent of disapproval toward that kind of behavior in my privileged cultural echelon, I was attracted to a less genteel class of society, but at the same time I wasn't. I felt uncomfortably awkward around and repelled by unsophisticated, less cultivated people. I think I felt the disapproval, the distance, between my family and those "others," and surely I took some of that prejudice into my own heart.

Into my adulthood, the urge to write was always there for me, always haunting me with its pull. I just felt that I had nothing to say worth hearing. Having children was so much more patently acceptable, and as it turned out, I adored being a mom. So that's what I did. But the longing to write never stopped appearing in my journals. I ached to write, to be published, to write a book—but no, there's Robin, being grand and silly again.

So maybe that's part of where my attraction to you came along, Rachel. I saw in your life the same pull toward crossing social boundaries, but you were also clearly imbued with the *prejudices of your higher-class ancestry and family, even when you didn't want to be. You had spunk and pluck and vivaciousness. I've thought a lot about that scene you recounted about your interaction with the gypsies—you were both drawn to and repelled by them. You always had a tinge of insecurity and inferiority going on. For you, writing became the thing to latch on to, the thing that made you feel worthy and proud. For me, it was motherhood. But I'm getting ahead of myself.*

In appreciation,
Robin C. Wood

three

Beauty, Loss, and the Emergence of a Poet's Heart

During Rachel's second decade, Lucy Field took active steps toward enriching her daughters' education beyond the capabilities of Miss Brewer and Miss Byington. In 1904, Lucy and her sister Kitty, who was to be a beloved member of their household for life, left Stockbridge with the two girls and moved to 384 Union Street in Springfield, Massachusetts. Lucy hoped that her children might be better served by the highly reputed schools and larger community of Springfield.

Rachel's older sister enrolled at a small private school, the MacDuffie School for girls, but no records indicate that she graduated. Public records from that period indicate that Elizabeth Field spent a great deal of time in volunteer work, especially sewing for the Hampton Club and the YWCA, giving sewing instruction for girls and, later on, rolling bandages for the war effort. Rachel, on the other hand, was drawn to the realm of books, writing, and theater, which may explain why Lucy chose to enroll Rachel in Springfield's public schools. Although Rachel still faltered in some academic realms, her astute mother, who Rachel always said should have been a teacher, likely saw an innate talent in her younger daughter, a seed that needed cultivating. The contrast between the two girls, which had already preyed upon the psyche of Elizabeth, grew even greater as Rachel's education led her further along the path toward "conspicuous accomplishments."

The dreamy musings of a poetic soul continued to thwart Rachel's attentions to schoolwork, as exemplified in her poem "Rebellion in September." The poem repeatedly juxtaposes the sort of educational fare with which the speaker is meant to be filling her head with the natural wonders she might see out the classroom window: *"Five and twelve make?* Oh dear me, / How the red leaves shine on the maple tree."* Rachel continued to be confounded by mathematics, algebra, and geometry, but her skills in drawing and composition soared. During her ten years in Springfield, Rachel developed several creative passions that carried through to adulthood. She grew in confidence, creativity, independence, and ambition.

It was also during this period that Rachel began her lifetime practice of filling notebooks with poetry. Later in life she would meticulously mount clippings of her published poems onto the pages of homemade books. In less formal notebooks, from both girlhood and adulthood, her pages of poetry are accompanied by scribbled lists of rhyming words in the margins, editorial notes ("Needs work!"), and occasional artistic doodles. To my mind, Rachel's poetry is her finest work. Whether she writes about childlike fantasy, playful observations, or the penetrating raptures and aches of the human heart, her voice is deeply personal and genuine.

At the same time, writing was never a frivolous activity for

Rachel. Even as a teenager, she kept careful, dated transcriptions of her work in a cloth-covered book in which she wrote *"Nolite Tangere"* ("touch not") on the first page. Since math continued to frustrate her (perhaps, she once confessed, because she used to spend math class reading about Robinson Crusoe behind the cover of her desk), she turned to words to find success. Rachel was both ambitious and practical, and met her self-perceived handicaps with a fierce determination to excel in spite of them.

Once, in 1936, an interviewer asked Rachel which of her works she most enjoyed writing. She smiled, wrote the interviewer, as she replied, "I don't know as I could say I 'enjoyed' writing any of them. The enjoyment is in the experiences and the research and the feelings out of which the book grows. The writing of it is just plain work. But I think I care most for my poetry."

Unfortunately for the adult Rachel, poetry could not provide a livelihood. For Rachel the teenager, however, poetry brought early success, public accolades, and a sense of identity amongst her peers. Rachel suffered the usual complement of rejection letters from magazines, but she gained early recognition as a poetess in her community. In 1911, Rachel wrote a Christmas poem that was published in the *Recorder*, Central High School's school newspaper. That was the first of several of her poems to appear in the *Recorder*. Later, some of her poems were accepted for publication in Springfield's *Sunday Republican* and in the nationally distributed children's magazine *St. Nicholas*.

Rachel's high school yearbook offers some insight into her public persona during the delicate years of adolescence. Photographs show a heavyset, large-framed girl who towered over many of her peers—the epitome of that weighty "outside-self" which so contradicted the sprite-like "inside-self" of Rachel's soul.

But Rachel's spirit was formidable, and it came through in her writing, particularly her poetry. Through poetry, Rachel gained recognition and acceptance in the social world of her peers. Rachel was active in debating clubs, drama, and the school paper. She was art editor of the yearbook her senior year. Though she was not included in the ranks of the "popular crowd," she appeared to have been liked and admired. Rachel was named class poet, and her poem was selected as the class of 1914's class poem, immortalized in her senior yearbook.

THE PNALKA

RUTH EVANS   94 Abbe Ave.

General

Glee Club (3) (4), German Club (3) (4),
German Club Play (4).

MIRIAM H. FIELD   17 Douglas St.

General

Contributor to Calendar (4).

RACHEL L. FIELD   384 Union St.

General

Pierides (3) (4), Pierides Play (3), *Recorder*
Staff (3), Winner Board of Trade Essay Contest (3), Candy Committee (4), PNALKA Staff
(4), Phillip's Debate (4), Class Poet (4).

MILDRED FISK   110 Holland Ave.

General

German Club (3) (4), German Club Play (3),
Pierides (3) (4), Pierides Play (3), Senior Play
(4), Candy Committee (4), PNALKA Staff (4).

*Rachel Field's high school senior year photograph in the 1914 issue of
The Pnalka, Central High School's yearbook, Springfield,
Massachusetts*

53

Poetry served Rachel in a less public way as well. In her note-books are several poems dedicated to a dear girlhood friend, Sheelah Kilroy, who died in 1911 at the age of thirteen. There is no indication that Rachel attempted to submit these poems for publication, but they are an outpouring of her grief and incredulity over this tragic, premature loss. Through her private poetry, Rachel explores the mystery of death and the confounding juxta-position of beauty and tragedy. Though these sentimental girl's poems, such as "Her Message," lack the depth of her adult work, they are the first illustrations of many themes that reappeared in Rachel's work for the rest of her life: grief, loss, the search for consolation, and a reverence for beauty.

HER MESSAGE

Do you see her touch in the daisied fields,
Or the flowers along a grass grown street?
By orchard trees, and flower stemmed brooks
Do you mark the prints of her vanished feet?

In the wind's soft call, hear you not her voice?
By the water's edge her lost laughter gay,
In the golden gleams of the dusky woods
Does the light of her smile not cheer the way?

Her face you see not here as once?
Look! On every hand breathe signs of her.
She lives and speaks to your heart again,
All nature is her messenger!

Rachel adds in pencil at the bottom of the page, "Why do they say that she is dead?"

In addition to poetry, the world of theater enthralled Rachel throughout adolescence. Opportunities to attend live performances were among the most cherished events in her life. She also became a voracious and passionate reader of books. In a 1931 essay for *Child Life* magazine, Rachel extols the wonders of books in the lives of young people. She talks about her own favorite childhood books, dog-eared and ratty from multiple readings and still on her shelf as an adult: Hans Christian Andersen's fairy tales, especially *The Little Mermaid*; *My Wonderful Visit*, by Elizabeth Hill; Kate Douglas Wiggin's *Rebecca of Sunnybrook Farm*; Frances Hodgson Burnett's *Sara Crewe*; and *Lorna Doone*, by R. D. Blackmore. These books opened up entire worlds in which her young imagination could lose itself.

She recounts one particular childhood memory. For some forgotten infraction, young Rachel was forbidden one evening to attend a theatrical performance with the rest of her family. It was a book that rescued her. She had hoped up to the last minute for a reprieve, that she would, in the end, be allowed to accompany the rest to the show, but to no avail:

I remember as if it were yesterday the sound of that door closing and of how I went listlessly into my room and over to the bookshelves. It was "Heidi" that I reached for and took down. Although I had read it many times before, it took only a few minutes of turning the printed pages and I was on the steep mountain side with Heidi and the Blind Grandfather, with Peter and all the goats. As I read I knew that the end of the world had not come.

No matter what happened, I told myself, there would always be books.

In the upper corner of the article is a note, handwritten by Rachel's mother: "Every word is true!"

In another essay recalling her childhood, Rachel tells of her thrilling first encounter with the author of *Rebecca of Sunnybrook Farm*, Kate Douglas Wiggin, with whom she carried on a friendship for some years afterward. Of course Rachel had always loved the novel, having played the title role in her proudest moment on stage. Unbeknownst to Rachel, after her nine-year-old self's performance as the heroine of Wiggin's famous book, her mother wrote to Ms. Wiggin all about the children's production, and included a snapshot of Rachel in costume, pink parasol and all. In midsummer, a reply from Wiggin arrived for Rachel. Rachel goes on to describe the letter:

> It was written, if I remember rightly, on blue paper with a little design of a weather vane shaped like a quill-pen at the top, and "Quill-cote-on-Saco, Hollis, Maine" printed underneath. That was the name of her summer place where she had grown up as a child, and it was the scene of Rebecca's own Riverboro. All this she wrote out in the letter, and she asked my mother to come and see her there, and to bring me along, too. I wish I had that letter now, but it has gone the way of the snapshot. From the day of its arrival, however, I counted Kate Douglas Wiggin as someone I really knew.

Rachel's story continues. Notwithstanding the one woeful night of missing an outing to the theater, the most rapturous moments of Rachel's life centered around theatrical performances. "The Court Square Theatre had become for me a sort of modern Olympus where gods and goddesses moved in enchanted places. . . . It didn't matter about failing in tomorrow's arithmetic, or not knowing 'future indicative tense' while one was there."

When Rachel was about thirteen years old, living in Springfield, she learned that a new, professional stage production of *Rebecca of Sunnybrook Farm* was to be performed at Springfield's Court Square Theatre. "I lived from play to play, and I still reckon up early happenings by calculating—'that was the year before I saw *Peter Pan*,' or 'it was the winter *Polly of the Circus* came,' or 'that was just after I waited at the stage door to see Maude Adams after *The Jesters*.' And so, that was the fall that I went to the opening performance of *Rebecca of Sunnybrook Farm*." Rachel's recounting of the ensuing events read like something out of a novel, and in fact she included them in a highly autobiographical manuscript for a novel that was never published, called *Islanders All*.

As a rare treat, Rachel was allowed to attend opening night of the performance, an adventure that kept her out until midnight for the first time in her life. She had written a letter to Kate Douglas Wiggin, reminding her that Rachel, at age nine, had been the very first stage Rebecca. Rachel knew that a response was unlikely from a busy author on opening night, so she was thrilled to receive a very gracious reply from Ms. Wiggin, regretting that she could not make the time to meet the many young people who wrote to her. Nonetheless, Rachel did not give up. Upon arrival with her mother at the theater, Rachel saw a woman at the back who she was sure must be the author.

"I'm sure it is," I insisted. "Let's ask her."

My mother hesitated.

"But we don't know," she said. "Why, we've never even seen a picture of her. What makes you think so?"

"I don't know," I said, "except she looks as if she'd written it."

In spite of her mother's uncertainty, Rachel hurried to introduce herself and, indeed, had a breathless conversation with the idol of her imaginings for several minutes before the show began.

Even this great triumph was not enough to satisfy Rachel. She desperately wanted to see the show again, though she knew her family would consider it frivolous. One school day when she knew there was a matinee, Rachel skipped out of school after the lunch hour and sneaked into town, where the show was in intermission between the second and third acts. The theater owner, who knew Rachel, invited her to go in and see the rest of the show. Rachel looked around, saw Kate Douglas Wiggin sitting alone at the back of the theater, and boldly sat next to her. Here is Rachel's account of their visit:

> There were still some minutes before the footlights came on and the theatre went dark, so we talked together. I told her all my favorite parts in the play, and where I thought our Stockbridge production had been better. She seemed interested and led me on. Her eyes were bright and twinkling, and her hair was auburn and curly under her hat. I felt completely at my ease, and she tactfully asked no questions about my being there alone with a bundle of school books under my arm. I wish I could re-member all we talked about. But I do recall that I told her

I was having difficulty deciding whether to be an actress, or an author. I wonder now that she didn't laugh at my seriousness.

"But if I do become a writer," I said with finality, "then I am going to write plays for other people to act."

Four years later, in 1911, Rachel did, in fact, write a play that was performed by some of her high school friends at the Springfield Women's Club. It was a morality play titled *Everygirl*. Seeing it performed, she once told an interviewer with her usual humility, was the only time in her life that she truly felt like an author. Two years later, in 1913, *Everygirl* was published in *St. Nicholas* magazine, earning her thirty dollars. She sent a copy to Ms. Wiggin to share the successful beginnings of her career as a writer.

The check from *St. Nicholas* was not Rachel's first, however. In another memorable moment from her high school days, Rachel won an essay contest that was open to three area high schools. The Springfield Board of Trade awarded her a check for twenty dollars (the equivalent of $530 in 2020). For a young woman who had experienced a longtime nagging feeling of deficiency in certain areas, this was a momentous event. It too is fictionalized in her unpublished novel, *Islanders All*.

Throughout her life, Rachel repeatedly said that her greatest writing inspiration came from her own personal observation and experience. Her fictive children were based on the muse that was her own childhood self, whom she remembered vividly. It is not unreasonable, therefore, to imagine that we can experience Rachel's moment of triumph in the essay contest by reading the following scene from another unpublished manuscript titled *The House of Make-Believe*. The award recipient is "Johanna," and she hears her name announced as the winner of the Municipal League's essay contest.

> Johanna sat perfectly still in her place while the assembly hall burst into wild applause.
>
> "Get up, get up!" Alice was urging her above the noise, "Didn't you hear him say to?"
>
> "I can't!" Johanna heard her own whisper as she shrank back.
>
> "You've got to! Can't you see he's looking for you? Everybody's looking!"

Finally "Johanna" is guided up to the podium, where she spends the bulk of her time in the limelight terrified that her new shoes will squeak on her way back to her seat. It is just the kind of detail one can imagine lingering in Rachel's memory.

Books, theater, and writing all grew in importance for Rachel as she moved through late childhood and adolescence. Another of her growing interests was history. Tales of life in earlier days and the hidden stories contained within ancient relics and artifacts had always intrigued her. In a 1929 interview, Rachel recalls one particular history teacher from her Springfield days with gratitude:

> We moved to Springfield after a while, and I went to high school there. I am glad of it, for I think I had the best history teacher in the United States. I would not take anything for having had Dr. Jessie M. Law as my teacher in English and American history. She taught me to love history, and made it real and vital. Teachers always meant a lot to me, one way or another, when I was a child. I

think they nearly always mean more than either they or the children themselves at the time realize.

Rachel surely supported her class's decision to dedicate their senior class yearbook to Dr. Law. Rachel's fascination with history would later become an essential ingredient in her most successful works.

Rachel possessed one more creative talent that her mother saw fit to cultivate beyond the reaches of Springfield's schools. Her penchant for art and drawing had always been strong, so Lucy Field made arrangements. In 1910, Rachel completed her elementary studies at State Street Grammar School and was to attend Central High School in the fall. That summer, Rachel was sent to study art with some cousins at their cabin in Maine. It was a visit that would stir a sea change in Rachel's heart from which she would, happily, never recover.

Dear Rachel,

One evening when I was at Yale, studying at a remote desk high in the stacks of the Sterling Memorial Library tower, a boy called down the row of books to where I was sitting and asked me the time. I was buried in whatever it was I was reading, sitting on a creaky wooden chair, leaning over an ancient little desk in front of a leaded glass window. It was my favorite place to study when I wanted to immerse myself in a kind of romantic illusion—that I was part of an ancient tradition of scholars, engaged in the toil of opening shuttered windows in my brain to discover truth and wisdom. (I know you never thought of yourself as a scholar, but your love of history and artifact and romantic connections to the past makes you one in my book.)

I imagine I blinked once or twice before I could focus on that boy who asked his question from down there at the end of the book-lined passage. I was likely lost in thought, a place I love to be lost. I've always felt a strong attraction to libraries, especially that musty, papery smell of hidden promise as you walk down rows and rows of books stacked to the ceiling on either side. When I wanted to leave all distractions of the present world behind and enter a sort of sacred cerebral space, that's where I liked to go.

It so happened that it was five minutes to closing time when this boy asked me the time. A short time later I packed up my things and walked out, and there he was, leaving at the same time—apparently that was no coincidence, but he didn't tell me that until years later. Each floor of Sterling's book-cramped stacks had a massive metal-lined door that you had to haul open when you left, a fire door to contain potential disasters. When you exited the stacks, the door closed ponderously behind you with a weighty, reverberant, metallic click that echoed up and down the stairwell. I was always stirred by that sound, and waited for it before I'd begin my descent. I suspect I did the same that day, but probably surreptitiously, since that boy and I had already begun a friendly chat.

We hit it off. I was cautious at first; he was disarmingly persistent, in an unconventional way. He spent summers working on an apple farm, he said. Soon, he started showing up at the dormitory suite I shared with several roommates. Rather than ask me out, he'd do things like pry off our doorknobs so he could use them to teach us all how to juggle. He always left something behind—a hat, a football, a book— so he had a reason to come by again.

The reason why I'm telling you about Jonathan is because he is the one who introduced me to Sutton Island. In 1979, the first summer after we started seeing each other, he invited me to visit his family on an island off the coast of Maine. I was eighteen, only a few years older than you were when you first arrived on Sutton, and I responded to that magical place just as you did. I began to fall in love during that first visit, with both boy and island. They have both been constants in my life for over forty years now. Once I had slept on that island, I'd never be quite the same.

In shared island appreciation,
Robin

four

If Once You Have Slept
on an Island

No one knew, least of all Rachel herself, how her life would be altered by her introduction to the Maine coast. "From the year that I was fifteen," Rachel wrote in 1934, "I have been going each summer to a small, beautiful, wooded island off the coast of Maine and I suppose that it, more than any one other thing in my life, has helped me with my writing. For it means roots and background to me. It creeps into nearly everything I write and I never want to be anywhere else when summer comes 'round." Roots and background were essential forces throughout Rachel's life, but the roots and background of her Stockbridge ancestry faded out of sight once she discovered Maine.

> One doesn't have to be born in a place to have roots there. I think one root struck down into Maine soil on my first visit to the State. It was when I was fifteen years old, the most impressionable age. I shall never forget how I was stirred by my first view of the Maine coast, coming into Rockland in the early morning light. I felt an uplift

as at no other place, in the firs pointing skyward, the glisten all around me, the old ships from distant ports at the wharves. These things still stir me.

Though she never rejected her family heritage, it was typical of Rachel's unique spirit that she discovered and set down roots of her own making in a brand-new state. In a poem called "Taking Root," she contemplated the alchemy that made this possible: "If I should sit the summer through / And never move or stir, / Could I take root on this pasture slope / With the bay and juniper?"

This fanciful girl whose heart was filled with the rapture of a romantic imagination had conjured a picture of Maine in her mind long before she first crossed its borders. Two of Rachel's favorite childhood books, both published in 1903, were set in Maine: *Rebecca of Sunnybrook Farm,* and Elizabeth Hill's *My Wonderful Visit.* It is no wonder that Rachel was drawn to the heroines in both books; they exude the same vivaciousness and romantic imagination as Rachel herself. Each book also portrays with delight the beauty of farm, field, and woods. Rachel writes this in her introduction to a 1921 edition of Hill's book:

> It was some years after the coming of the book that I actually saw the State of Maine which forms so authentic a background for this unforced and genuine story of a little girl's first visit to her cousins in the country, but as soon as I saw those woods and farms I recognized how truly and simply Elizabeth Hill had described them. Even now when I walk in especially lovely, eerie wooded places I am reminded of Lucy's explanation of why she liked the woods better than any other place;—"Because they're so

greenery and whithersoever." I knew exactly what she meant by that. I still do.

Rachel had thoroughly internalized the character of Rebecca of Sunnybrook Farm, of course, when she played the part on stage in Miss Byington's production. "Rebecca was a thing of fire and spirit," writes Wiggin, and Rachel was the same. The character of Rebecca won hearts with her straightforward charm, her unbounded storytelling, and an elfin spirit. The same can be said for Rachel Field, who was fully primed to fall in love with Maine before she had ever laid eyes upon it.

RUTH FEIS AND Prentiss Taylor, two longtime friends of Rachel's, exchanged twenty years' worth of letters with Rachel during her lifetime, and many more with each other after Rachel's death. Both were determined to collect and preserve memories of their cherished friend, and we are the richer for their efforts. In her research into Rachel's early life, Ruth Feis met a woman who was on Sutton Island in the summer of 1910. Mrs. Whittemore "gave a pleasant and helpful picture of Rachel that first Sutton summer, from which I can see the beginnings of her passion for bunchberries, blueberries, the grey rocks, the white gulls, and the blue water!" No doubt Rachel's first island-inspired poetry came out of her pen that very summer, and it continued to flow for years to come.

Sutton Island is a small member of the five Cranberry Isles, scattered just off the southern edge of Mount Desert Island along the coast of Maine. Even today there are no roads on Sutton Island, only root-strewn, spruce-needle-y footpaths along which people tote their belongings in wheelbarrows. It is accessible only by boat, and in Rachel's first years on the island they had no electricity. The name of the cottage where she stayed with her cousins was "Bunchberry Bungalow," an apt storybook title for a small cabin perched on the rugged, northeastern shore, looking out to sea. Still today, on a shelf in the tiny living room of Bunchberry Bungalow, is a guestbook, over a hundred years old. In an entry from August 1, 1910, you can read the youthful swoops of a fifteen-year-old's signature: *Rachel Lyman Field.*

The north side of the island is bounded by rocky cliffs and promontories sculpted and scoured by the relentless surf. On the south side, the lee side, meadow grasses and blueberry fields slope more gently to the shore. Wildflowers abound, berries flourish, and in the island's interior, in the shadows of thick spruce forests, are bright-orange chanterelle mushrooms and deep, spongy carpets of vibrant green moss. Berry picking and mushroom gathering became lifetime loves of Rachel's. Although the foraging was ostensibly intended to provide food for dinner, one friend describes how Rachel decoratively arranged her baskets of provender, even adding a few flowers for good measure.

During that fifteen-year-old summer, Rachel's skills as an artist improved. She learned to produce beautiful watercolor miniatures like her uncle's. In future summers, she was able to sell scenes of local landscapes painted on dinner cards at the Jordan Pond House, an inn on Mount Desert Island. In the course of time, Rachel developed a charming style of her own in hand-colored pen-and-ink sketches and silhouette cutout pictures, both of which appeared as illustrations in her own and in others' books. Beyond any technical skill acquired, however, the most profound effect of that first Sutton summer was an indelible imprint on her artist's soul. This island became Rachel's creative muse.

For several years Rachel returned to Sutton Island during the summers with her mother, aunt, and sister as renters of Bunchberry Bungalow. The friendships that she forged with her island neighbors grew fast and endured forever. Rachel not only became deeply attached to the island, the landscape, the particular character of tide and wind and fog; she also grew to love the people of Maine. Over time, the rhythms of local speech, the lore and legend of the sea and seafaring folk, all captivated the heart and imagination of Rachel Field. The spirit of the region inspired not only poetry but Rachel's first book of nonfiction, *God's Pocket*; two award-winning children's books, *Hitty, Her First Hundred Years* and *Calico Bush*; and her award-winning first adult novel, *Time Out of Mind*.

By her second trip to Sutton Island, Rachel had already claimed it as her own. In a carefully indexed notebook of her writing, there are two unpublished poems from the summer of 1911. The first was written on July 2, when she was sixteen, the second in late September, shortly after her seventeenth birthday:

SUTTON ISLAND

Have you heard of Sutton Island
    with its wide expanse of sea,
Where the waves are dashing ever
    in their mad excess of glee—
Where dark fir trees bow forever
    to the blue above, below,
And the mountains o'er the waters
    cast a hazy, purple glow?

In the dim woods of that Island
      lights and shadows, dancing gleam,
And the little paths so winding,
      must indeed for fairies seem!
In the cool and shady hollows
      grow the scarlet berries gay,
And on gray cliffs grim and rugged,
      dainty harebells gently sway.

There the far and dim horizon,
      deepens to a hue of blue,
And we gaze with growing wonder,
      at this ever changing view.
Now there may be other places
      quite as beautiful to see,
But on fir clad Sutton Island
      is the place where I would be!

MY ISLAND

It lies so far from noisy crowds—
Away from the citie's [sic] din
Only the sound of wind and waves
Borne on the breezes thin.

Only a tiny bit of land,
Covered with spruce and pine
But I love it best in all the world,
This Island I call mine.

Rachel was twenty-seven years old in 1922 when a house came up for sale on Sutton Island. It was only a short distance from Bunchberry Bungalow, along the same rugged northeastern shore, and in spite of worries over the financial burden, she bought it. She called it "the Playhouse," and it was her cherished haven for nearly twenty years. Sadly, no old guestbook remains in Rachel's house, which suffered years of neglect and ungoverned explorations. Books and records in other island houses, however, shed a cheerful light on Rachel's island life over the years.

Rachel's name appears repeatedly as a visitor in the Bunchberry Bungalow book, along with those of her mother and aunt, her sister, many cousins, and familiar friends who reappear time and again. "A literary evening enjoyed by all," reads one entry next to the names of the Field family. "Swordfish party on the beach with Lucy and Kitty," recalls another. "Tea and parcheesi" was on the schedule for another day. Rachel's drawing of her beloved Scottish Terrier, Spriggin, appears in 1927. "The electric cable came to Sutton" is recorded in 1931, a landmark event which surely facilitated island housekeeping. In 1935, Rachel signs for the first time as Rachel Field Pederson, with the signature of her new husband, Arthur, alongside. Their last visit to Sutton Island is recorded on the page where Rachel and Arthur signed the book in August 1938.

Rachel Field and Spriggin on Sutton Island (circa 1929)

In the homes of other island friends are guestbook entries from Rachel—hand-drawn tributes, poems, and an illustrated payment from Rachel to the Sutton Island water company. A few photographs remain—pictures of Rachel with her ever-present Scottie dog, swimming in the tide pool, or picnicking with a crowd of friends on neighboring Gott's Island.

Sutton Island filled a space in the soul of Rachel Field that no place had entered before. Sutton was not only the poetic muse that inspired so many of her greatest literary creations, it was also the outer expression of her most natural self. The island was a place of raw, rugged nature in all its unfettered glory. Rachel felt a kinship with all of the island's moods—the rhythms of the tides, the soughing of wind in spruces, the weighty gloom of foggy nights and tolling bells, the brilliant blue of sea, sky, berries, and harebells. In a 1925 letter written from Sutton Island, Rachel writes, "I am truly most myself here—the self I was intended to be."

Rachel's Playhouse, which sits just on the verge of a rocky outcropping facing north, is made up of four wood-frame buildings on brick piers, connected by elevated walkways: the main house overlooking the sea, a freestanding kitchen and pantry building, a three-room annex, originally used as servant quarters and later for guests, and a large, square room with windows on all four sides, known as "the studio." The studio was a long-ago laundry room, which still has a few old-fashioned hand irons, a woodstove, and a large soapstone sink. In early days, according to the first owner's writings, all the island staff liked to meet and relax together in that big room during their break times. It was back in the former laundry room, warmed by the old wood stove, where Rachel toiled away at her writing every day, occasionally pondering a mountain ash tree outside her window. She sometimes wrote in longhand, but an old typewriter was her usual tool of choice. Although in days of old the house had had live-in staff, Rachel's only paid help came from old Jim Sprague, a caretaker who helped with supplying firewood, turning on the water, and occasional odd jobs.

Island life was not for lovers of leisure. Even the logistics of transportation were complicated, involving various combinations of car, boat, and rail over the years. Rachel often spent all or most of a day "motoring" to Bar Harbor, Bangor, or Portland to meet incoming guests. Doing the never-ending "marketing" off-island involved a great deal of walking and lugging of supplies. One island guest penned this wonderfully descriptive account of a visit with Rachel on Sutton Island:

After the motorboat had chugged us across Northeast Harbor to Sutton, Rachel would insist on trundling the luggage up to "The Playhouse," as she called her cottage, on a huge wheelbarrow. None of the friends who visited her there will forget the combination of Maine spruces and sunshine and Rachel's warm laugh. Tall and vibrant, pushing back her auburn hair as she talked, her gray-blue eyes sparkling, she vehemently refused any help in pushing the wheelbarrow, and we made our way to "The Playhouse" in its wake.

No wonder Rachel declared that Sutton Island influenced her writing more than anything in her life until her marriage. Carpeted with moss and bunchberries, hollowed into little pools over which harebells hung in fragile security, it had a charm which reached a climax in her little house. With that creative gift of hers, she was always translating the charm of the island into different forms, and the walls and shelves of "The Playhouse" breathed Sutton Island in every nook and cranny. Sometimes it would be an arrangement of berries and flowers; sometimes a hooked rug designed by herself and picturing some characteristic Sutton Island scene—perhaps the sea gulls whose swooping beauty enchanted her, or a lighthouse whose stones knew the secrets of the Maine coast. Often her subject was a dog, for she loved dogs with a devotion which never faltered through a succession of them. . . .

Sometimes before breakfast we would gather on the porch to watch the curtain of mist roll up from the Fels estate across the water; then would follow breakfast in our kimonos, with coffee and toast made over the living room fire and carried to the porch steps to be enjoyed with sunshine and memorable talk. Spriggin, waiting patiently near, was never disappointed in her expectation of bits of toast, liberally spread with the cranberry jam from Sutton Island's or Cranberry Island's own berries. The jam was a specialty of Rachel's Aunt Kitty, whose fine cameo profile was bent over its manufacture that summer.

But if breakfast was fun, it was nothing to the spell of the evenings when Mrs. Field would read aloud. Reading aloud had always seemed to me something reserved for invalids or blind people until Rachel's mother taught me its possibilities. She would choose one of Sarah Orne Jewett's stories, or some bit of neighborhood history such as "The Story of John Gilley," and in her voice and inflection the spirit of Maine and Massachusetts would spring to warm life. During the reading Rachel would be designing a new rug, perhaps, throwing covetous glances at my lisle stockings. When it came to her hooked rugs, no material was safe, and she would look hopefully for signs of wear and tear in any article of clothing. When she had claimed the garment, Aunt Kitty would cut it into the strips Rachel used in her rugs. The tan of lisle stockings was a great favorite of hers, hooked in artfully to make the roofs of fine cottages or the undersides of mushrooms nestled at the foot of a tree.

The main house had a deep front porch overlooking the sea and a large, wood-paneled living room. Off the living room were two bedrooms, one for Rachel's mother and aunt and the other for Rachel. Rachel's room was dominated by a large wooden sleigh bed. Like most of the furniture, the bed came with the house, left behind by the departing owners. The Worcester family that sold the house to Rachel in 1922 had been her island friends for years, which may be why she never erased the family's penciled growth-chart lines on a doorframe, tracking the heights of the Worcester children through the first decade of the 1900s. During the summer of 1918, some of those children played parts in an island production of *Three Pills in a Bottle*, one of Rachel's most successful plays, directed by Rachel herself.

Once Rachel owned her own home, her attachment to the island grew all the more. The island fed her spirit in the best of times, and it enfolded her during her years of discouragement. The "roots and background" that gave Rachel's life such a solid foundation were crucial supports that buoyed her up. Even during her last years in California, when Sutton was too far for a summer visit, she cherished her island connections both in friends and in memories. In 1939, from her Hollywood home, she wrote to an island friend, "Trust you to bring the Island closest! We were so happy to have your letter and as mother and Aunt Kitty were with us when it came we all shared the news. You made me smell the fir balsam and sea-weed and the spiciness of berries ripening in the sun."

Rachel Field housed an irrepressible optimist's spirit that found the best in many people and places in the world. Nevertheless, there was no place in her life that ever captivated her childish sprite, her poet's heart, and her womanly roots like this island off the coast of Maine. "No other place," she wrote, "has my heart so completely."

Dear Rachel,

I have to confess to you that Sutton Island was not my first heart home, as it was yours. I had long since attached myself to a similarly enchanted place in New York State's Adirondacks. You would appreciate the fact that my great-grandfather first purchased the land around Big Wolf Lake, so I had deep ancestral roots there. Since it is a deep blue lake, far inland amongst the mountains, you might think that Big Wolf is completely unlike Sutton Island. I never would have expected it, but part of my first attachment to Sutton was its similarity to my cherished childhood paradise in the Adirondacks. The old Adirondack camp buildings are filled with many generations' worth of relics from the past—rusty woodstoves, heavy flatirons now used as doorstops, well-worn brickwork in aged fireplaces, a pump house built over a well, horsehair-stuffed mattresses, ancient wagon wheels, meat grinders, a washboard, early-twentieth-century magazines stuffed in the corners of closets, and heavy-lidded bins filled with musty wool paraphernalia from some long-ago time. Outdoors, there are root-strewn, pine needle-y paths that wander through quiet forests, where you are rebaptized every year—a full immersion in the scent of balsam. You explore woods and water all day, often stumbling upon some dappled hollow, or a bubbling spring, or a sunny glade that feels like your own secret discovery. Time and change don't work there as in other places; it is the essence of life in suspension.

Doesn't that all sound familiar? That's why, even though I had never been an ocean girl before, Sutton Island still felt deeply familiar to me. Like you, I started putting roots down into the rocky soil of Sutton the first time I set foot in that island world. I also got a thrill on two occasions when Big Wolf and Sutton Island merged together in ways that felt strangely portentous. First, I found your island poem tacked onto a wall in my great-aunt's cabin on a small island in Big Wolf Lake. Your island poetry reached far away from any ocean, right into my family's world of mountain and lake. Second was the time my mother found one of your novels on a shelf at Big Wolf with my great-grandmother's name written in it. Mom gave me the book for Christmas, knowing what a treasure it would be for me to link these two special places, my mother, and you. It wasn't the first time that a strange connection between your world and mine created an electric shiver of wonder that started at the base of my spine and sparkled down to my fingertips.

The big difference between us is that you invited Sutton to fill your creative being, and you worked doggedly to express all that it had to say. You listened to that passionate call to write. In my case, the loud voice of uncertainty drowned out that call. I stumbled into teaching for a few years at a boarding school, because Jonathan, that boy from the library, tendered me a marriage proposal that came with a job offer. I said yes to both. We started married life as teachers in the small New Hampshire town of Meriden.

I let life lead me, rather than taking life in hand. The boarding school needed a French teacher, so I taught French. Then they needed a Spanish teacher, so I taught Spanish. They needed a swim coach. I knew how to swim, so I coached the swim team. Eventually they agreed to let me teach an English class, where I thought my truest inclinations lay. Halfway through my one year as an English teacher, a student who had been in my classes before said,

"Mrs. Wood, you should probably stick with Spanish."

It certainly wasn't all discouragements. I loved hiking in the fall through yellow-leafed woods, engaging young people in dinner conversation, and learning to be married, raise a dog, and share a home for the first time. And still there was that flutter of desire, the jolt that reared its head in its old familiar way and urged me to write. I dabbled in writing, got a feature story into the local Valley News, but nothing felt certain.

Then I got pregnant. Suddenly, my fingernails grew unhindered. My appetite became sensible. I was like a starving person sated at last. I was producing something beautiful and important. My path was clear.

Anna's birth caused a seismic shift in my heart's attentions. It wasn't mother love instantly, just awe and a sense of intense responsibility. I needed time to get to know her and this new kind of relationship, but love grew quickly, like a fire. When Anna was a few weeks old, I went to pick her up at day care, since I was back to teaching part-time. A two-year-old gazed up at me, turned, and ran back into the room crying, "Anna's mom is here!" I froze. I am Anna's mom. I tried on this new identity, and my body flushed with heat. I was finding a new passion.

My contentment wasn't perpetual, however. There was still plenty of time to ponder the future of Robin, who was not Anna's mom. Where was she going?

We moved to a new state, new town, new house. I did some substitute teaching. I studied Spanish, pondered a master's degree, and took a writing class. I got pregnant again. My mother, who knew what it was to raise five children, was somewhat distraught at the speed with which my new family was increasing in size.

"Well, just take a little longer before you have a third child," she said.

About a month later I gave her a call.

"Hey, Mom, you know how you said to wait before a third child?"

"Yes?"

"Well, it looks like my third child will be here sooner than we thought." Twins were on the way.

There was no more room for pondering. When Nellie and Sam were born, there was no period of acquaintance necessary; I felt instantly like their mom. A few months later Jonathan's medical training required that we move again, to another new state, new town, new house. I gave myself, heart, body, and soul to my children—being with them, surrounding them with a cocoon of love, comfort, security, curiosity, challenge, delight. It was exhausting, exhilarating, and strangely liberating. There were no agonizing questions about what I should be working toward. Every day when I got up in the morning, I knew exactly what I had to do, which was so satisfying that three years later I went ahead and had a fourth child, Tessa.

Jonathan and I continued to come to Sutton. His family had a house near the Hessenbruchs' grand home, where you were a regular visitor in your time. There, we settled into the serene pace of island living every summer. Watching Anna, Nellie, Sam, and Tessa make the island their home rekindled our own sense of magic about the place. They built fairy houses out of moss, shells, and bark, or on rainy days, blanket forts on beds and under tables. They leapt from rocks into the icy green water, played daylong games of Capture the Flag in

a pack of scuff-kneed, barnacle-scraped cousins, beachcombed
for sea glass, painted rocks, played flashlight tag, got scared of
the dark, swatted mosquitoes, made collections of urchin shells,
and watched the giant yellow moon rise up over Schoodic
Point. They ran with a wheelbarrow to the town dock to fetch
supplies dropped off by the mail boat before the seagulls
scavenged the hamburger, sang songs as they washed dishes,
toasted marshmallows over the fireplace. They even put on a
couple of plays in the woods with a pack of childhood friends
and invited all of our island neighbors to attend. Unlike your
friends the Worcester children, they did not have the
playwright as director, but they still managed highly energetic
and entertaining productions.

In 1993, fourteen years after my first introduction to
Sutton Island, word came to us that there was a house for sale
up the shore a ways, and we hurried to arrange a visit.

Rachel, I believe you left something behind in that
magical house. Lingering wisps of your creative energy float
like ocean mists around the walls and doorways. I felt it the
first time I walked across the creaky old front deck and stepped
inside. You know, many others have found inspiration in your
house—the poet Hortense Flexner; her husband, a Saturday
Evening Post cartoonist named Wyncie King; the Oscar-
nominated composer Laurence Rosenthal. It is an artist's
house, and I think it is your buoyant legacy that stirs the hearts
of those who tread its wooden floorboards with the desire to
create. I felt that desire instantly, and I feel it still.

I carried my own desire to write from childhood, but I
couldn't find my way to see it through. Motherhood thrilled me
to distraction for many years while the call to construct words

on the page sat patiently in the wings. From the moment I first stepped into your precious house, I think your characteristic enthusiasm began to work on building me up. Who knows, maybe you sought me out even earlier than that, and led a certain boy down a certain aisle in the stacks of the library tower in Sterling Memorial, so that I could eventually find my way to your island and your poor, neglected house. Maybe you needed something from me, so you laid before me your muse, your inspiration. In it lay hidden your gifts to discover— confidence, persistence, optimism, and a poet's reverence for beauty.

Ever grateful,
Robin

five

Special Student

Rachel's writing became her ticket to a future that would not otherwise have been hers. In the early 1900s, Radcliffe College, in Cambridge, Massachusetts, occasionally admitted a particular category of applicant. These applicants failed to meet the usual requirements for admission, but they had a unique, outstanding specialty. Their title was "special student," and though they attended classes, they were not eligible for a degree. The policy was discontinued some years later, but thankfully for Rachel, it was still in place when she finished high school in 1914. Rachel's skills in writing stood out, and she was accepted into Radcliffe's writing program as a special student in 1914.

MAY IN CAMBRIDGE

How could I learn philosophy
Or read great books of history,
When May came into Cambridge town,
Sending the petals drifting down
From tall horse-chestnut trees alight
With flower-candles, waxy white?

Although she remained keenly aware of her deficiencies in other areas of intellectual pursuit, Rachel honed her skills and gained confidence as a writer during her four years at Radcliffe. She also forged friendships with intelligent and independent women, many who helped support and nourish Rachel's strength and independence as she crossed the threshold into adulthood.

In 1943, a year after Rachel's death, Radcliffe College's class of 1918 celebrated their twenty-fifth reunion. To honor Rachel and another literary classmate who had died prematurely (Ruth Burr Sanborn), members of the class of 1918 held an evening tribute for the two women. The printed program talks of the unusual spirit and drive of their two classmates, neither of whom was deterred in their hopeful endeavors by the "black and bewildering" cloud of World War I that hung over the United States during their four years in college. We get a glimpse into Rachel's life at Radcliffe through the eyes of those who knew her:

The thought of Rachel at Radcliffe evokes a memory vital with warmth and color. And time, for whom she had a strange, personal feeling, was kind to her in that he changed her very little. As the years passed her red hair darkened only slightly, her eyes remained as blue as chicory flowers and her voice never lost the young, eager, woodwind quality that made listening to her such a delight. . . .

She entered into college life as ardently as she did everything. She knew very well what she wanted—it was to learn to write—and English 5 under Professor Copeland and English 47 under Professor George Baker gave her what she had come to find. In her high corner room in Eliot Hall where the winter sunsets across the hockey-field were things to remember, she began her work. There, too, her active fingers painted and drew and clipped silhouettes of dancing elves among leafy branches, predecessors of those that were to adorn her books in later years.

That energy, warmth, and determination which had already won hearts, leading roles, and essay contests continued to impress friends and teachers at the college level.

George Baker's class in playwriting, known as "the 47 Workshop," was a prestigious program. In virtually every biographical write-up of Rachel Field, Baker's class is cited as the source of Rachel's early literary training. Indeed, by the time Rachel left Radcliffe, she had written several plays and published a volume of six of them.

In 1918, the spring of her senior year, one of her plays, *Three Pills in a Bottle*, was given the first position in Baker's 47 Workshop publication of plays for that year. Professor Baker wrote the introduction to that volume, and made this explanation of his course in playwriting: "The fundamental principle of The 47 Workshop— and to this it has held steadily throughout its history—has been that everyone from director to stage hands must cooperate in putting the play upon the stage as the author sees it."

Professor Baker's student playwrights were required to be present at all rehearsals and were involved in every aspect of the production of their plays. So Rachel's involvement with the theater expanded dramatically during her work at Radcliffe.

Three Pills was so successful that for decades following its publication it was performed an average of once a week, year-round, in community theaters all over the country. No version of the play, however, had quite the allure of one particular production during the summer of 1918 by a small theater company on Sutton Island, directed by the playwright herself. Several of the performers were Rachel's neighbors, the Worcesters. Rachel describes the production in a letter:

> I've been busy the last two weeks, coaching the seven little girls (17 years to 9) to give "Three Pills." The play came off last Wednesday and I am still a wreck from rehearsing every morning from 8:30 to 11 or sometimes longer, and being author, coach, prompter, producer, first stage carpenter, etc. Then just as the 70 people who had been invited were beginning to arrive the Scissors' Grinder fell ill with mumps and I had to do the part on 15 minutes' notice.

In spite of her successes and her ambitious energy, Rachel continued to doubt herself. She often felt that each success was, perhaps, only a lucky break and might be her last. She also felt a growing weight of responsibility to help support herself and her family financially. During the summer of 1917 Rachel took her first job, doing editorial work at *Publishers Weekly*. She had decided that it was time to leave school behind and stay in the workforce when Professor Baker appealed to her to return to Radcliffe for one more year. In June of that year she agonized over the decision of whether to return to school or not. In a letter to her mother, she pours forth an epic of excitement, hand-wringing, indecision, and philosophy as she grapples with her immediate future. Rachel begins, "Dearest Ma," then shares general news of school before getting to the meat of her letter. In a tumult of script, growing in size and irregularity, she writes out a list of pros and cons:

	For Going		For Staying *(leaving inclinations out!)*
1.	*Money!*	1.	*Ought I to stop if Prof. B. thinks now is the time to finish up the technique part?*
2.	*If I am ever going to start in publishing work, I must take any opening when and wherever I can, as they are so difficult to get.*	2.	*Prof. B. may not give it year after next, and he is delicate, he may drop out any time, take him when you can get him.*
3.	*If I am ever going to write or be any good at it, I will do it on the side and work at it myself.*	3.	*Wouldn't it be easier to take the year now before I get started, and be sure of having had it—*
4.	*I will get more ideas to write about.*	4.	*Next year there will be so many men out of the workshop there will be more chance to do acting and work in producing the plays done by girls, and also the girls will get more individual help from Prof. B.*
5.	*Next year and probably until the end of the war will probably be very bad theatrically, so I'd better begin earning something.*	5.	*If I am on the spot Prof. B may give, not only the "Pills", but my long play (that is a very doubt-ful, but if I revise it, he might possibly) Anyway he probably won't give the "Pills" unless I'm here to keep him at it, and to get the benefit of seeing it given.*
6.	*A year is only putting off the job-getting several months, it will mean starting in all over again.*	6.	*Also I have been so interested in Mr. Weber's class in making stage models, & I should so like to work more under him next year.*
7.	*I would get more out of 47A by waiting and taking it when I have had more experience.*		

8. *It would be different if I were getting a degree, but isn't it foolish and self-indulgent to take another whole year without working—just to fool around at what I enjoy, but what won't assist me to get a job later. (that is it won't get one for me)*	
9. *Do me good to get out of academic atmosphere and do real work.*	

"You see how it goes," Rachel goes on, "I am dreadfully torn between the two—<u>Reason</u> is all (very nearly) on one side, and <u>Inclination</u> on the other—and what is one to do!" She carries on for several pages more, enumerating jobs in publishing and the unlikelihood of acquiring them, worrying about what to do. Then, in characteristic fashion, she turns from fretfulness to a philosophical acceptance of whatever fate may have in store: "Well, things always happen,—they have to, no matter what kind they are and that's a comfort."

In conclusion, Rachel jumps among apology, uncertainty, self-deprecation, optimism, and reassurance. She is still a young woman on the cusp of maturity, but one with a clearly evolving sense of responsibility:

I didn't mean to rave on like this, only it's dreadfully inefficient sitting round not getting a job here, but I don't know who to go to, one can't bob in and demand a job where one isn't known. And anyway, I'm afraid I'm not very "up and coming"! Anyway, we've got Sutton ahead, and that's the best thing in the world! . . . This is a dreadful letter, and you mustn't mind it, also, please do not take what Prof. B. said as meaning that I have any unusual powers, for he knows I haven't . . . and you mustn't plan to help me come back, for I won't use money from the savings bank—it's too risky just now, and things are so uncertain; if I get something to do I'll come, if not, I won't—Good night, I must hurry to mail this, ever so much love and please excuse this mess,

Rachel

In the end, Rachel did return to Radcliffe, though she quailed at the thought of broaching the subject of her departure with her boss at *Publishers Weekly*, R. R. Bowker (who had been a member of the audience at nine-year-old Rachel's performance as Rebecca of Sunnybrook Farm). She wrote of the encounter to her new friend Ruth Stanley-Brown (later Feis), whom she met at her summer workplace: "I, too, miss you dreadfully, especially to-day when I longed for your support in going in and informing Mr. Bowker of my intention of going back to college. . . . Well, I was scared to break it to Mr. Bowker, but I got my courage up, dashed in, and informed him all in one breath. I never stopped till I had got the tale all out, though I could tell he thought I was a fool."

YEAR BOOK BOARD

Rachel Field at Radcliffe, 1918.
Rachel is in the top row, the third person in from the left.

Though Rachel cowered under the stern eye of her summer boss, she also made a lifetime friend in Ruth Stanley-Brown, granddaughter of President Garfield. Ruth too was an aspiring writer, two years older than Rachel, and Rachel held her in very high esteem. The two young women commiserated over their toils at work and began a playful correspondence which included references to imaginary elfin friends, the occasional sketched elf decorating the margins of Rachel's letters. The friendship lasted throughout Rachel's lifetime, and Ruth preserved all of the cards and letters that Rachel sent her, a treasure of insight not only into Rachel's delightful devotions as a friend but also into some of Rachel's more intimate concerns and trials.

Belying stereotypes of the reclusive writer, Rachel spent a great deal of time socializing with friends and family, new and old, throughout her life. She especially loved Christmas and birthdays, and even during her busiest times, she sent lively letters and greetings throughout the year to the many people she cared about. "Wasn't she the most alive and enthusiastic friend?" wrote Ruth. In a letter to mutual friend Louise Seaman Bechtel, Ruth describes a scene from the first summer that she met Rachel. Ruth's birthday came around in August, and she invited Rachel to visit without mentioning her birthday. Ruth writes about her first experience of Rachel's birthday "enthusiasms":

"When the cake came in, shining with candles, her eyes were like stars, and she said, 'Oh Ruth! why didn't you tell me it was your birthday? I adore candles and cakes!'"

Ruth saved the next twenty-five years' worth of homemade birthday greetings, which arrived without fail from Rachel, no matter where in the world Ruth was living.

Rachel's writing did indeed progress extensively during her fourth year at Radcliffe. Her letters to Ruth express both triumphs and the familiar insecurities that hovered at the back of her mind. In August 1917, she writes to Ruth: "I just received an unexpected $5 royalty for a performance of "Three Pills" at a girl's camp in NH, and when you come back will you go with me on a nice respectable little bat to celebrate my first royalty?" Then there is this in October: "As for you—well it's a continual marvel to me how I ever came to know such an efficient, skilled lady—the reviewer of books, the receiver of $15. . . . They say people make friends by contrast—it seemed so with us—for I'm certainly shiftless enough —how you ever stood me, I don't know, but I'm so grateful you did." In November, Rachel was busy in rehearsals for *Three Pills in a Bottle* when she sent this note to Ruth: "I've written nothing since I came back, except some revising—you can't do a thing when your mind is on rehearsals. Anyway, I think my young 'genius' has had its growth and is now turning a sickly green and withering on its stalk. Farewell, I'll inflict you with no more of this."

As Rachel's last year of college progressed, her search for employment of some kind intensified. In June, still uncertain of her future, she took a civil service exam with a friend. Not knowing where life might lead her, she signed a form indicating her willingness to go anywhere in the world. What she most hoped for was a job that would offer her a living wage as well as flexible hours to allow her to work on her writing. That summer, in spite of joblessness, she immersed herself in the balm of Sutton Island's spell, and marveled at her renewed self on the island. In a chatty letter to Ruth, Rachel extols the therapeutic medicine of Sutton:

I think so much of last summer and it seems incredible that it can be the same R.L.F. skipping free along springy trails with sea and hills and little firs, even the same person who took her toilsome and sweltering way to Barbour House. I can remember almost to the day when I first got to know you and all the little zests and excitements of our own that made those days possible (for me, at least!). Oh Ruth, you will let me keep along with the things you're doing, won't you? You're so clever and efficient, and I feel so absolutely no-good and as if I'd begun to peter out already, but you'll not erase me from your list of friends, will you, not after we've stood the fire of Maori together!

She goes on in her letter to offer news of her job prospects.

> I may get a call to New York about the middle or last of
> August, a friend of mine who makes synopses of books
> for Famous-Players Moving pictures scenario dept. is go-
> ing to France, and she thinks maybe she can get me into
> her place. The reason I want it is because you can arrange
> time to suit yourself, don't have to be at the office all the
> time, and you make from $20 to $30 a week. That would
> give me a chance to do some writing on the side, and
> that's the kind of job I'm after, so I hope this won't fall
> through.

RACHEL DID GET that job at Famous Players, so she left her island haven in Maine for the island of Manhattan. New York City
became Rachel's primary home for the next twenty years, a home
that would nourish Rachel's youthful energy with its dynamism,
leading her to blossom both personally and professionally. Every
summer she returned to Sutton Island with undiminished bliss,
but she embraced the contrasting islands of her life with equivalent ardor.

Dear Rachel,

The path that my life took after marrying Jonathan wouldn't seem at all strange to women born in your day. Jonathan taught with me for a couple of years, then he started medical school. First his education and then his professional life carried us around the northeast—New Hampshire, Rhode Island, New York, Massachusetts. I didn't love teaching, I had no burning drive toward any other profession, and I was more enthralled by motherhood than I'd expected to be, so I became a full-time wife and mother. In your day that was the norm. I, on the other hand, grew up through the early years of the feminist movement, which taught us that women should fight for the right to work side by side with men rather than suffer the default drudgery of housekeeping. Between that rallying cry and my Ivy League education, I often felt diminished by my choice to stay home with my four children. Many women I went to school with had furthered their education and cultivated professional careers, so what was wrong with me? I felt like a throwback to an earlier century, falling into women's secondary role in society.

One saving grace for me was the fact that I had a supportive husband who was prepared to work with me as a team, no matter what I chose to do. Jonathan told me that if our arrangement ever became untenable for me, if I wasn't content to be home full-time while he worked the demanding schedule of a medical professional, he would quit. He'd find something that worked for both of us. I can't imagine what could have arisen to make me ask him to quit, but having him say so changed my whole outlook. That is a luxury many women have lacked, in your time and in mine.

Yes, I did some writing, sporadically. I published my second newspaper article after my four children were born. I took writing classes and seminars here and there. With Jonathan's encouragement, I even went back to school to get a master's degree in English while he stayed home with our children for a year, working part-time in the emergency room to pay the bills. I managed to sustain a fine thread of my childhood attachment to writing across many years, but I couldn't seem to weave it into whole cloth. A scolding interior voice told me that I lacked conviction, which is one of the reasons why I found such admiration for yours. The more I read your writing and read about your life, the more I aspired to emulate your work ethic.

There you were, alongside the bold and courageous women of your time, pursuing a professional life without depending on a husband and family to define you. You gave free rein to your aspirations and worked ceaselessly to reach them. As I studied the life you chose, the life you worked for, my admiration for you grew in a brand-new way. Rachel, it was more than your literary skill that captured my attention; it was your brave independence, your drive, your dogged persistence even in the face of personal sacrifices. It became clear to me as I delved ever deeper into your story that your writing success was only part of your story. There was turmoil in your family life and in your love life. Having a family of your own was something you longed for, ached for across a span of decades without success. Nevertheless, you gave wings to your passion for writing. Part of your obstacle was probably the societal standards of your time. During the 1930s, when you were gaining renown as a writer, it was not considered feasible for women to have both a family and a career. Is that what got in your way? How strange that you and I struggled with the same two callings in such different ways and times.

As ever,
Robin

s i x

~~~

Taxis and Toadstools

For young Rachel Field, New York City was a world of wonders. Since Rachel allowed her characters greater expression of intimate personal reflection than herself, I will turn again to one of her fictive protagonists here. Like Rachel, at least two of her characters arrive in the city of New York filled with flutters of anticipation, and we can imagine that they express an echo of Rachel's own thrill upon moving to the city. Here are the thoughts of "Jane" as she gazes through a taxi window for the first time at the crowds of New York: "Soon she too would be hurrying along with these people who thronged the sidewalks. She would be rubbing against an author maybe, or a salesman, or a chorus girl! She sat back with a little jounce of pleasure and let the taxi carry her." That first night in her new room, Jane's sense of awe continues: "She felt stirred and swept by varying moods:—wonder, fear and secret joy, delicious secret joy at being alone there in a room of her own, with lights beyond her windows and the sound of voices somewhere across the hall."

The sight of tier after tier of light-flecked skyscrapers in the night city always reminded Rachel of a Christmas tree, and in her world of ecstasies, nothing surpassed Christmas. For her heroines too a Christmas tree was one of life's dazzling treasures, filled with the promise of wonders to come. That is the analogy she summons in order to illustrate Jane's sentiments as she gazes out the window of her first city home: "It IS like a Christmas tree! . . . when you first look through the doors and the lights are so bright you can't even see the presents, but you know they're there!"

When Rachel moved to New York, it was not her first visit to the city, but it was her first time embracing the place as her own, living and working as an independent adult. The glow of anticipation was strong in her imaginative mind. As an adult, Rachel was once described as "a big, sunny child bringing in fresh flowers from the country." Somehow, she carried that wide-eyed, outdoorsy vivacity with her even as a city dweller. As she began her new work, tedious though it often was, Rachel held fast to her joyful, hand-clasping enthusiasms. She loved the "hurdy-gurdies" (organ-grinder musicians) in the streets, the antique shops, the throbbing of dynamic activity in full swing. For twenty years, the island of Manhattan was an essential hub of Rachel's identity. It offered her a wealth of connections and growth, both personal and professional, and an exciting world of human energies from which to draw literary inspiration.

When Rachel wasn't doing editorial work at Famous Players–Lasky, she was writing and submitting creative work at every opportunity. Alongside the romantic emotionalism of her poetry and fiction, Rachel's humility and pragmatism were ever present, especially in the public sphere. Rachel once said to an interviewer, of her decision to write, "I saw that writing was the thing that came easiest to me. It was in my family to write. We have all known how to express ourselves, and I think the thing which you do most easily is the thing from which you are likely to make the most money."

It was a long time before she made significant money, but in her first years out of Radcliffe Rachel continued to work on plays that she had begun in Professor Baker's playwriting workshop. She wrote new plays as well. *Three Pills in a Bottle*, published in 1917, had long-lasting popularity. *Rise Up, Jennie Smith*, published in 1918, won Rachel the Drama League of America's patriotic play competition.

In the five-year period during which Rachel juggled her regular job and her writing, the majority of her publications were one-act plays (she also illustrated a book in 1923—*Punch and Robinetta*, by Ethel May Gate), but plays were by no means Rachel's only endeavor. She was constantly at work on poems and longer manuscripts, battling to break into print and collecting rejection slips. Her persistence never flagged; her congenial spirit caught people's attention. There was also a bit of good fortune in the timing of Rachel's entry into the literary profession.

The world of publishing in the United States was largely a man's realm until the early decades of the twentieth century, when women and children began to play a role. Historian Jacalyn Eddy wrote an insightful history of a twenty-year period during which the output of children's books nearly tripled and women emerged as a powerful presence in some of the nation's top publishing houses. *Bookwomen: Creating an Empire in Children's Book Publishing, 1919–1939* traces the dynamic emergence of children's literature as a recognized genre. In her book, Eddy examines the lives and influence of six women who were instrumental in expanding the literary prominence of women authors and illustrators. The beginning of that twenty-year period coincides exactly with the time that young Rachel Field arrived on the scene in New York City, filled with youthful ambition. It was into this world of powerful "bookwomen" that Rachel Field made her debut as a writer.

Eddy points out important societal forces at play during this period, forces that contributed to Rachel's experience. Women, in general, were seen as unfit for most jobs in the business world. Their entry into publishing came largely out of the notion that women were particularly attuned to a child's world; therefore, they were acceptable candidates for publishing jobs in a child-centered branch of literature. The complicating factor was that there was a stigma around the "working woman" that separated her from domesticity. A woman commonly had to choose between a career and a family. Of the six women highlighted in Eddy's book, several married quite late in life, and none had children. This common fate for career women was a reality that Rachel Field faced with an increasing ache as the years passed. It is evident in both her letters and her fiction that this romantic young authoress yearned for romance, marriage, and a child, but no such family materialized. Still, the powerful network of mutual support amongst the bright, ambitious women in the world of books and publishing contributed enormously to Rachel's career and to her growing confidence.

At least four of the six women highlighted in Eddy's book were closely connected to Rachel Field and her writing. Bertha Mahony, who created the country's first bookstore for children, was a founder of the *Horn Book Magazine* in 1924, a publication dedicated to literature for children and young adults that is still in print today. Anne Carroll Moore was a children's librarian and book reviewer, a pioneer in the field of library space and programming dedicated to children. Both women were enthusiastic supporters of Rachel Field's early writings for children, and their influence on the exposure and sale of children's books helped expand the reach of Rachel's renown.

May Massee and Louise Seaman, as heads of the newly created children's departments at Doubleday and Macmillan, respectively, were two of the first woman department heads in major New York publishing companies. Both became friends and promoters of Rachel Field and her work, and both published some of Rachel's early works. Louise Seaman in particular became an important mentor and lifelong friend to Rachel. Rachel extols the virtues of her editor and friend in this letter to George Brett, president of Macmillan:

> My connections have taken me to all the other juvenile book departments in New York and I speak from personal experience that I have never found such a combination of practical knowledge and creative inspiration. If I have been able to contribute in the smallest way to children's books in the last few years, it is entirely due to the understanding and guidance Miss Seaman gave so freely.

In both publications and personal letters, Louise Seaman's respect and admiration for Rachel are clear. She recognized Rachel's unusual astuteness in envisioning books beyond the mere writing of them, and she gave Rachel more leeway in determining things like illustration and graphic detail than she did for most authors. She recalled in a tribute published after Rachel's death:

She was one of my very first authors, when I was a new young publisher, and soon I found out that she had much more of a "publishing sense" than I had. Her wide range of friendships lay mostly among people who wrote or drew or acted or sold books. Ideas of what they might do with their talents, and suggestions about their work, both to them and to publishers, were quite as much a part of her talk as her own work. She enjoyed all the aspects of bookmaking and bookselling, and had hundreds of friends in both fields.

As to her writing, I think other writers should know how hard she worked at it. She liked both pen and pencil, but thought best at the typewriter, and rewrote and corrected at the same battered old machine. She wore out work chairs and tables and bit off all her fingernails.

Rachel worked at her writing, collecting rejection slips and persevering. But that is not the only thing she was collecting. Somehow, even as she poured her efforts into her career aspirations, Rachel's personal life was a rich one.

Unlike the stereotypical artist in the garret, Rachel Field was extremely people oriented and gathered friends in profusion. She regularly made arrangements to meet at cafés or attend performances with friends and acquaintances. She liked to entertain and loved to cook. Even in her hardest-working periods, she dedicated enormous efforts to cultivating and maintaining relationships with those she cared for. Through the eyes of some of those fortunate recipients of Rachel's hospitality, we get a window into her home life.

When she wasn't at her writing desk or out in the world,

Rachel kept busy with myriad creative hobbies. That constant drive to keep her hands busy that began in childhood never left her. She was always working on something—hooked rugs, drawings and illustrations, handmade cards and books. More often than not, those creations ended up as gifts to friends and family.

Rachel also loved to collect dolls, music boxes, and old quilts, largely inspired by the notion of where they had been and the histories behind them. Over the years Rachel filled a large display shelf in her New York apartment with antique dolls, doll furnishings, and music boxes. One of her most treasured dolls was the Empress Eugenie, a doll of 1870 vintage given to Rachel by an American family who had lived in Paris. Doll enthusiasts will enjoy these details, written up in a 1931 article about Rachel's New York apartment:

> The grand lady is living in comfortable if somewhat reduced circumstances in Miss Field's bookcase with a beautifully carved bureau about large enough to keep cigarettes in and a friendly white china poodle. On the bureau is a tiny lamp of carved ivory and blue glass which came to Miss Field with the Empress and is quite as elegant in its way as she herself.

Then there is a description of "Emily Roxanna," a doll from around 1820, who is

> tall and very stately, with head and Victorian sloping shoulders of papier-mâché and wooden legs discreetly hidden by long pantalets. Emily Roxanna can admire her well-preserved beauty in the mirror of a rosewood dress-

ing table that came from New Orleans. Actually, the dressing table used to stand on a fine gentleman's bureau, where he could hang his watch on a hook over the little mirror and tuck his seal ring safely away in the tiny drawer when he retired at night.

The article's author also notes that Wilbur Macy Stone, a friend of Rachel's who gathered an enviable collection of bookplates, children's books, dolls, and toys, had fashioned a new arm for Emily Roxanna since she had lost her original somewhere along the way. Incidentally, Ruth Feis's correspondence reveals that Mr. Stone was the inspiration behind an important character in the children's book that first launched Rachel to fame, *Hitty, Her First Hundred Years*. He was just one among the legions of professional acquaintances who was happy to go from colleague to friend in Rachel's world.

Laura Benét, editor and poet, wrote about her friend Rachel Field:

Few, if any, of the women of her generation, conveyed the impression of such abundant and overflowing vitality. There was a warmth about her personality, her quick walk, the tones of her voice, the wave of her hair, and those intense honest eyes of hers.

Rachel's keen interest was in life—in every little homely, everyday item of it—her friends, their joys and sorrows, the books she was writing for children and illustrating with her own pictures, dolls of various kinds, mottoes, favorite poems, old furniture, herbs, flowers, and special ways of doing cookery as well as the books and plays of the hour—especially "The Barretts of Wimpole Street." And was any author ever more generous with herself and her means, whether rich or straitened? Her apartment door stood open to her friends—that cosy (sic) apartment on St. Mark's Place, East 10th St. Here in her sitting room there hung on the walls two special great patchwork quilts made in chosen patterns for her. In a corner was a tall desk, once used by a Maine schoolmaster. A company of rare and ancient doll ladies kept house in an old walnut bookcase with glass doors, and there were several music boxes, one of which . . . had belonged to the English novelist and poet Mary Webb.

Even as she embraced her life in New York City, Rachel was always a woman of two worlds. Manhattan Island was her home and workplace for much of the year, but her treasured small island off the coast of Maine was never far from her thoughts, and she returned to spend time there every summer along with her mother, Aunt Kitty, and sister Elizabeth. Rachel lived two-thirds of the year in New York, and she occasionally traveled to distant parts of the world, but no matter where she was, Sutton Island bubbled up from her soul and effervesced in her heart.

A book reviewer once observed that one of Rachel Field's heroines, unable to attach herself to a person, attached herself instead to a place. The same was true of Rachel. Rachel's romantic nature was ever in search of that transformational experience of love. In the absence of an individual person to receive the ready depths of her devotion, Rachel turned to her beloved island of pointed firs and rugged shores.

In 1922, Rachel was by no means assured of success as a

writer. Though usually highly practical and financially cautious, she nevertheless used some of the royalties from her published plays and took a great leap of faith. From Sutton Island, she wrote this to a friend on July 14, 1922:

> As Elizabeth undoubtedly told you, I am being a most foolhardy creature this summer, not only buying this bungalow here where we have been so many summers, but also parting company with my movie job. All goes merrily for the present, but occasionally I do take thought for the morrow, or rather next winter, when I shall probably join the ranks of Hylan's bread line, or else take up my stand by the Public Library lions, with a tin cup in my hand. I wish I could have a hand organ and monkey, but you know that N.Y. ordinarily forbids the latter in city precincts....
>
> I feel like a proud landed proprietor, except once in awhile when there's a leak sprung in the roof on a stormy night or something goes wrong with the plumbing! However, I have been lucky so far, and we are having wonderful restful days after a N.Y. winter. I feel ready for them, which is, I suppose, a sign of age. I'm trying to get some writing done, but it is hard to when everything is so tantalizingly beautiful and there's so much to do to the house.

With the added commitment of ownership, the roots that Rachel had extended into the rocky soil of Sutton Island grew even deeper. There, off the wild coast of Maine, was her heaven on earth, the muse that informed and sustained her, whether it was under her feet in the summertime or in her mind's eye throughout the winter. "People become welded to places," Rachel was quoted to say. "As Willa Cather is welded to her prairie towns, I am fused with the coast of Maine. It doesn't matter whether I write Maine books in Maine or New York. The feeling of Maine is always with me."

The other thing that became a delight both to Rachel and to her dearest friends was that Rachel was now free to invite friends to join her on Sutton as often as she wished, and they came in profusion. Marion Severn, a socialist, lawyer, and lifetime friend fondly known as "Swish," spent her summer vacation on Sutton for several years beginning in 1922. Louise Seaman, Lyle Saxon, Ruth Feis, a slew of cousins, and many others were routinely enveloped by Rachel and her island hospitality.

"I am truly most myself here," Rachel wrote to Ruth in 1925, "—the self I was intended to be. This is especially true when I'm berry-picking, for I am happiest then and most efficient, too. Louise Seaman came over and spent the day with me here and she admitted berry-picking should have been my chosen profession. What a pity it pays so little!"

Inspired by both of her homes—the home of her heart and the home of her burgeoning career—Rachel carried on her work, submitting plays, poems, articles, and illustrations in increasing profusion and with increasing success. In 1924, Rachel published two books of poetry with her own illustrations. The first was *The Pointed People*, whose dedication reads, "For Mothers—And One in Particular." This earliest book of Rachel's work, accompanied by Rachel's exquisite silhouette cutout illustrations, reflects both of her island homes—the sea and the city—and her delight in each one. Even though it is ostensibly children's verse, it displays the depth and breadth of feeling that Rachel had shown in the pages of her personal notebooks for years. Magic and dreams, sensitivities and feelings, delight and quiet reflection—her verse has an appeal for all ages.

SOME PEOPLE

Isn't it strange some people make
You feel so tired inside,
Your thoughts begin to shrivel up
Like leaves all brown and dried!

But when you're with some other ones,
It's stranger still to find
Your thoughts as thick as fireflies
All shiny in your mind!

And Rachel's anticipation-laced enchantment in both city and island life is ever present:

CITY LIGHTS

Into the endless dark
The lights of the buildings shine,
Row upon twinkling row,
Line upon glistening line.
Up and up they mount
Till the tallest seems to be
The topmost taper set
On a towering Christmas tree.

RAIN IN THE CITY

All the streets are a-shine with rain
The other side of my window pane.
Each motor car unrolls a track
Of red or green on the asphalt's black.
Beneath umbrellas people ply
Like giant toadstools stalking by.

A SUMMER MORNING

I saw dawn creep across the sky,
and all the gulls go flying by.
I saw the sea put on its dress
Of blue mid-summer loveliness,
And heard the trees begin to stir
Green arms of pine and juniper.
I heard the wind call out and say:
"Get up, my dear, it is to-day!"

Several of the poems in *The Pointed People* illustrate a conflicted spirit, simultaneously tantalized by adventure and drawn toward the serenity of settledness in one place. The spirit in Rachel that poured forth in her verse was dynamic, but the responsibilities of the well-bred woman and working writer often kept her passionate inclinations in check. "My Inside-Self," published in *The Pointed People* for the first time, is a perfect example. The following two poems about home and the open road are more of the same:

ROADS

A road might lead to anywhere—
To harbor towns and quays,
Or to a witch's pointed house
Hidden by bristly trees.
It might lead past the tailor's door,
Where he sews with needle and thread,
Or by Miss Pim the milliner's
With her hats for every head.
It might be a road to a great, dark cave
With treasure and gold piled high,
Or a road with a mountain tied to its end,
Blue-humped against the sky.
Oh, a road might lead you anywhere—
To Mexico or Maine.
But then, it might just fool you, and—
Lead you back home again!

BURNING LEAVES

Whenever leaves are burning
And the blue and bitter smoke
Steals up from gardens and roadsides
On evenings in October,
Something in me stirs
And wants to go away.

I may be setting the table,
Or baking a little cake
With edges brown and scalloped.
I may be under the covers

Of the tall four-poster bed
When that scent lays hold on me.

And I would be leaving the fireside,
The willow plates on the dresser,
The quilt with its crazy patches,

For almost any road,
Rain-black or brown and rutty;
For almost any village,
So long as it's not home.

It is interesting to note that the early days of fall were Rachel's favorite time of year. That period of transition at the end of summer evoked a stirring in Rachel's heart. The shifting tides of change showed in the sea, in the slanting sunlight, in the movements of migratory birds. Rachel cherished that driving sense of urgency to move forward, away, and elsewhere, even while it caused a kind of ache of loss and longing. She expressed these sentiments with poignant simplicity in "Something Told the Wild Geese," a haunting seasonal poem about the waning year that begins, "Something told the wild geese / It was time to go. / Though the fields lay golden / Something whispered,—'snow.'" The popular poem has been anthologized numerous times and put to music.

In the latter part of 1924, Rachel published her second book of verse for children, *Taxis and Toadstools*, with her own "decorations" drawn with a reed pen. (For friends, Rachel was known to add color by hand when she gave books as gifts.) Her pattern of issuing collections of poetry inspired by both of her divergent worlds continued: the taxis of New York City, the toadstools of

Sutton Island. Part of the appeal in Rachel's verse lay in her keen observations of reality, even while juxtaposed with a childlike playfulness and contemplations of a magical world. Depths of introspection came alongside a celebratory delight in response to beauty everywhere. Her later poetry grew in depth and poignancy, as the hopeful sunshine of youth gave way to the more sober climate of life's long, uncertain journey.

Dear Rachel,

Fourteen years after my first summer in your house, I began to get serious about getting to know you. It helped that I had become a year-round resident of the state of Maine. If you were working on getting my attention all that time, I apologize for taking so long to get around to the job.

I have grown attached to the state of Maine just as you did. It is a place that loves its artists and writers, and I slowly —painstakingly slowly—found a place of belonging here as a writer. It was largely because of you that I finally broke into writing with conviction in the spring of 2008, when I bravely pitched an idea for a magazine feature to an editor at a writers' workshop in southern Maine. I told her about sharing a house with a famous Maine writer from long ago, and she was intrigued. That summer I got the assignment to write the story for Port City Life magazine. I began researching in earnest for the article that would come out the following summer.

I feel strange talking to you about what I read in your letters and journals. There are times when I wonder if I might know you better now than anyone ever knew you in life, because I read your childhood journals, your college letters, and all the stories of your evolving adult womanhood all at once. I got to spread the entire timeline of your life before me and study it. I unearthed secret chapters and put them together with the unexplained nonsecret parts and tried to figure out how everything fit. But I won't go into all of that just now.

I went through all the books on the shelves of the Field House (that's what everyone calls it now—see what a long-lasting presence you've been?) to see if I could tell which were

yours and which had been left by the interim residents, of
which there were very few. It wasn't hard. Some books still had
your name in them. One held a cardboard cutout of an elfin
figure that you must have used for one of your silhouette
illustrations. I found stacks of magazines in the attic, envelopes
with your name on them, and galley proofs of one of your books
of poetry.

I spoke with two women who met you as children. Becky
Nussdorfer is the daughter of your dear friend Honor Ganoe.
Becky's the one who told me which room you slept in, and how
you always spent mornings working in the studio room at the
back of the house, and spent afternoons with friends, picking
mushrooms or berries, picnicking, or just visiting. She told me
you went on a trip with Honor to Nova Scotia one summer,
and showed me some of the letters you sent her. I thought you'd
be happy to know that Honor's daughter remembered you and
was still coming to the island in the twenty-first century.

I thought you'd also enjoy knowing that Jonathan and I
added our family's layer of history to the Sutton Island house,
in the form of a new set of penciled growth lines. On the back
of the same doorframe that has the growth lines of the
Worcester children from a hundred years earlier, we have left a
record of Anna, Sam, Nellie, and Tessa's sprouting ever higher
on the wall. Sometimes when I mooned over my nonexistent
writing life, I was comforted not just by the company, joy, and
wonder that my children offered me but also by the notion that
maybe their presence in your home offered your restless spirit
satisfaction. Between us, we nurtured that magical home with
both timeless literary creations and the presence of children
discovering and becoming.

At first, searching the house, reading your poetry, and scanning through the brief biographies about you were all delight. I got little thrills of satisfaction at our shared experience, our shared space in our island home. I read about "flower-sprigged cups" and "the playhouse key" and knew exactly the items you meant, even held them in my hands. I found a map of Paris from 1920 and knew it was yours, since I had read your letters about your trip to Paris that year. So I hung it on the wall of your bedroom. I read about your love for Scottish Terriers and knew at once some items in our house that had been left there by you: the Scottie-shaped candle snuffer, the ashtray with its pointy-eared adornment, the ancient Scottie-printed cocktail napkins shoved in the back of a drawer, and the hooked rug of a girl holding a Scottie on a leash—they were all part of your Sutton world, and now they are here with me.

There was a friendly rivalry amongst Cranberry Isles residents because of some inhabitants of the other isles who claimed that your most famous poem, "If Once You Have Slept on an Island," was about their island and not Sutton. I felt inordinate joy (and maybe, I confess, a bit of smug satisfaction) in confirming from your archived notes that the island in question could be only one island—our own Sutton.

Each step of my research for the 2009 article drew me further on, because each new discovery only generated more questions. I read about your sister quite a lot, but then she largely disappeared from your letters. I also came upon a line written in your mother's hand in the August 1928 pages of an old Wanamaker's diary on a bookshelf in the living room. It referred to someone named Lyle, saying that you and Lyle were "all devotion." Who was this Lyle? I wondered. Was he a love interest? I didn't find out for the longest time.

In your later poetry, I found such magnified depth of emotional complexity—pain in love, heartbreak, a shattered self. What, or who, was the source of your sorrow? I began to learn about some of the more difficult chapters of your life.

Your devoted admirer,
Robin

seven

The Lonely and Difficult Years

R achel Field once referred to the 1920s as her "lonely and difficult years." Self-doubt continued to hover in the back of her
mind, and other forces threatened to squelch her motivation. She
faced health problems that slowed her down. There was an increasing weight of responsibility on Rachel's shoulders to care for
her family, both emotionally and financially. Somehow, in the
face of myriad stressors, or perhaps because of them, Rachel felt a
perpetual compulsion to stretch herself in her work—to produce,
to improve, and to expand her repertoire.

In 1924, Rachel submitted a novel called *Islanders All* to the
George H. Doran publishing company. She received a rejection
letter from Mr. E. F. Saxton, which was important enough to be
preserved in her permanent papers. Here is an excerpt:

> There are many things about the book which we like but
> there is a general feeling that the action of the story is too
> long delayed and that the interest is not sufficiently sus-
> tained to justify its present length.
>
> You will be wise enough to realize that these are the

impressions of only one group of readers and that there is nothing so fallible as a publisher's judgment. If you decide to revise the story, we should be glad to examine it again and also to see any other work of yours that you may contemplate publishing.

Rachel reported in several interviews that an early rejection letter was responsible for directing her down the path that led to her success. The rejection letter told her that the parts of her novel concerning the childhood of her heroine were very strong, and that she ought, perhaps, to pursue the genre of children's literature. This carefully preserved letter may well be the one that so directed her future, pursuant to subsequent interviews in person. The idea of writing a novel for adults continued to lure her, but in the following years Rachel turned wholeheartedly to children's literature and found the beginnings of her greatest success.

Rachel's humble apologies continued to appear in her work correspondence during this early part of her career. Typically, humility and enthusiasm came side by side, resulting in a sincerity and charm that flows off the page.

Dear Mr. Clark,

You were very reassuring about that question of the little one-act and as I said before I'm more than grateful. One is so apt not to trust to one's first impulse which is so often more nearly true than later ones. At least that is often the case with me. I get panicky at criticism when it comes as a surprise to me personally.

To do some plays with my own pictures has always been a wish of mine, but I don't consider that my drawing is quite up to that. I've always regarded it rather in the nature of a joke till lately, but it would be fascinating to try that sometime for some children's plays. They would have to be for very young actors, however, for I may as well confess what you can readily see at a glance, that I cannot draw anyone who looks older than eight.

Rachel's friend, the writer Josiah Titzell, once described Rachel's personality as a writer of poetry. "In verse she was most eager and least sure of herself," he wrote. She was aware of her shortcomings in technique, but she was often reluctant to change her poems from their original form as they burst forth from her mind.

She could say in a letter to a friend, "Do you think it gets over? I wrote most of it in my head as I drove back last week and stopped the car and dashed it down by the side of the road on an old envelope back. I could change the verses round, but I'd rather not." . . . Her honesty in her verse is as touching as her own fear that she perhaps hadn't done it quite right.

Rachel's physical health and family responsibilities threw challenges her way through the 1920s. At the same time, she began to hit her stride as a writer. Part of it was due to her nature and inclinations, but there is no doubt that she also felt pressured to earn as much as she could, for both herself and her family. During this decade, Rachel published more than a dozen plays, including two books of collections of her plays. She produced eight children's books and two books of verse, and saw several poems and articles published in magazines. She also worked as an illustrator and contributed editorial work for a collection of American folktales.

Behind the scenes Rachel often coped with health problems that obstructed her work, though she graciously belittled her trials. In a 1924 letter to a friend, Rachel writes of difficulties in the production of *The Pointed People*, partly due to the fact that she had been "in a hospital parting with my appendix and numerous gall-stones when the illustrations were first sent and the plates made."

In the late 1920s, at the age of thirty-three, Rachel sent a letter to Barrett H. Clark, author, editor, and executive director of the Dramatists Play Service in New York City. Her note concerns a collection of one-act plays to which Rachel hoped to contribute:

You'll think me a fraud if there ever was one, but really this time it isn't entirely laziness on my part. Just as I was half-way through one one-acter and with a second really getting in shape so that I had hopes of appearing with two under my arm at your door,—I came down with measles, of all things! It is humiliating at my age—but I suppose that's what comes of doing too many children's books.

Anyway, it's made it impossible to use my eyes much.

In another apologetic letter to Mr. Clark, she offers explanations of a delay: "Please pardon the messy shape this is in and the fact that it is my only copy. I'm usually a little less amateurish about both those things, but this seems to have been an off Spring with me all round."

One growing strain on Rachel's life came from her family. Rachel's devotion to her mother and Aunt Kitty was steadfast, and those two aging sisters were her most stalwart supporters. But the care and financial support of the two women fell more and more exclusively upon Rachel. Rachel purchased a house for them in Farmington, Connecticut, around this time. It was known as "Up-the-Lane" (years later, it became a part of Miss Porter's School). Rachel often left the city to visit her mother and aunt in Farmington on weekends. And, as ever, she found time to work there as well.

Rachel's sister Elizabeth seems to largely disappear from the record of her life around this time, and the explanation was, in Rachel's lifetime, a well-kept secret. Mental illness was a private matter and little understood at the time of Elizabeth's collapse. There are no official records of whatever events might have precipitated Elizabeth Field's crisis, but in June 1927 she suffered a nervous breakdown and had to be institutionalized. Eventually the family sent her to be cared for in a reputable residential sanatorium in Asheville, North Carolina, and Rachel paid the bills. The situation was kept painstakingly quiet. Even in the few letters where Rachel mentions her sister's condition to her closest confidantes, such references are veiled and quickly abandoned, but Elizabeth's condition was a source of perpetual worry and occasional acute stress for Rachel and her mother and aunt for years.

In letters to her friend Ruth in the fall of 1927, Rachel indulges in unusual outpourings of discouragement. In September, Rachel writes that it has been a gray summer, with hard times for a mutual friend who was ill, and also in her own home. "My mother also, has been depressed and unlike herself all summer (over my sister who is having a long pull after her nervous breakdown, only don't talk of it please, you know how things get handed about) so in many ways it's been a hard time for me to put through." In November, she begins another letter to Ruth, who has been working to make it as a writer as well, with further thoughts:

> You are bound to break in sooner or later if you keep at it. Of that I am sure, though it is sometimes rather cold comfort with rejection slips coming in—Well, I know all about it and I'm very low in my own mind about writing, so I can be specially sympathetic. You see, I feel it's time for me to tackle something bigger than I am and show I can do mature, adult work and, Oh Lord, it seems impossible to get started or to have a theme that stirs me enough. Oh, well, it's a lot to keep going at all in this Old World, I think.
>
> My sister's condition makes me realize that as I never did before. Not that I mean to go into details that are too depressing to recount. Only things are not progressing and the future looks about as dark as can be. These mental cases are so stubborn and difficult and really compared to what is known of physical organs we know so little of the complexities of the mind and nervous system.

In the midst of her trials, however, Rachel persevered in her work with that nail-bitten determination so aptly described by Louise Seaman, churning out little children's books, illustrations, plays, reviews, books of poetry, and one magically inspired book of prose and verse called *Eliza and the Elves*.

Eliza and the Elves, dedicated "to the island" where it was written, is a testament to Rachel's continued appreciation for Sutton Island. Whether she was writing realism or fantasy, however, the appeal of Rachel's work is in the straightforward sincerity of her voice. Her introduction to the whimsical *Eliza and the Elves* is a wonderful example of both her charm and her humility.

FOR ANYBODY WHO CARES TO READ IT
Please don't expect this book to tell you anything useful because it won't. It isn't that kind. Eliza says the Elves can't stand that sort of thing and she knows more about them than anyone I know. In fact, she told me about most of the sayings and happenings in this book, though several of the conversations I had myself. I have set these down exactly as I heard them and the rest word for word as well as I could remember. So the kindest thing to be said is that this is just a scrapbook of Elfin odds and ends, and anybody that doesn't like scrapbooks had better close it right away!

What follows is a hodgepodge of prose and verse, all elf-related and frequently evoking island scenery. Two of the prose stories share an oft-repeated theme—a high-spirited protagonist weighed down by the stodgy world of human society. Rachel's characters are unable to access that tantalizing place of dancing lightness that they know exists nearby. In the title story, Eliza and her wild, unruly hair are subdued and contained by her human caregivers, to prevent her escape to Elfland where she knows she truly belongs. In the case of "The Elfin Pup," one taste of human food turns his featherlight body into that of an enormous, clumsy beast. Through her characters, Rachel repeatedly plays out scenarios of misfortune for those who are overlarge, awkward, unbecoming, or unacceptable in civilized society. Those scenarios were familiar territory to Rachel.

The contrast between Rachel's spirit and her physique did not go unrecognized by those who met her. The following journalist's description of Rachel may have intended to be complimentary, but it likely evinced a resigned sigh from its subject:

> If perchance you should . . . look around for her, do not hunt for a small, elfin person such as you would expect would be the author of fantasies like Eliza and the Elves or The Magic Pawnshop. She is tall and strongly built, with a vast store of energy. . . . Of her outside appearance, only her hair betrays the poet. It is red gold with coppery waves and it crinkles when she comes anywhere near a steaming tea kettle.

Rachel responded to life's difficulties with stubborn perseverance and the best stiff-upper-lip public face she could muster. Yet in private, she never shook her regret over her square and sturdy Field-family physique. Perhaps she blamed it for her unluckiness in love. Like her elfin pup, Rachel felt herself to be weighed down by an ungainly exterior that belied her spritely spirit. Nevertheless, she held tight to the fairy tune dancing in her heart and continued to allow herself a hopeful openness to joy.

Dear Rachel,

I'm not sure how you would feel about the fact that your longest-lasting literary legacy was not your wonderful adult novels or your poetry but your Newbery-winning book about the doll Hitty. I know how much she meant to you when you wrote her story, however, and I think you'd be amused to know how many doll enthusiasts continue to be inspired by that tiny wooden doll that you and Dorothy found in a little shop in New York City. Without the Hitty hoopla, in fact, much of the world might have lost touch with the life of Rachel Field, including me. It was Hitty that brought many people to the Cranberry Isles for their summers and led to the founding of a special Rachel Field collection in the Great Cranberry Island Historical Society museum. It was Hitty that got several people immersed in snooping around for more details of your history, and those people helped me find my way further along the trail of clues about your life.

It was also Hitty that brought me to Stockbridge for the first time. The local librarian invited me to be a guest speaker at a national conference about Hitty, you, and dolls in general. As the up-and-coming "Rachel Field expert," I became a part of that world, and that world, in turn, offered me more leads and nudges to push my curiosity along. Your original Hitty doll now lives there, in the Stockbridge library, where there are many more bits of archival gems that illuminate your life.

Hitty is a particular joy to me too, because I know that she sat on the mantelpiece in our house during one inspired week on Sutton Island. Under Hitty's gaze, you and two friends began brainstorming her illustrious history. From there, her story took on a life of its own—and changed the direction of yours.

You should also know that your legacy of dogs in the Field House lives on. Sutton Island remains a dog paradise. Jonathan and I have introduced six furry companions to that magic, mossy place so far, and their boundings and splashings add to the life of each visit.

All the best,
Robin

Spriggin, the Whippet, and the Birth of Hitty

Rachel's openness to joy led her to welcome three particular additions into her life toward the end of the 1920s: a winsome little dog with pointed ears, a bright blue Whippet roadster, and a tiny wooden doll named Hitty. All three infused Rachel with delight; all three were featured in her writing. One of them transformed Rachel's professional life and evolved into her longest-lasting legacy.

In May 1927, Rachel's friend Priscilla Crane presented her with a little black Scottish Terrier. From that day forward Rachel was rarely without her canine companion. "Spriggin" accompanied Rachel to meetings with publishers and regularly chimed in with contributions in Rachel's letters:

> [Spriggin] is more enchanting than ever in spite of some fleas acquired on her trip down from Maine. She sends you many Scotch wags and wishes you could see her bright new green leash.
>
> ⚬⚬
>
> Spriggin is very much ashamed at having taken so long

about the cards, but she agrees with me that January is the most dreadful month of the year. It isn't just the old Christmas trees in ashcans along the curbs and the bills and the general post-holiday depression, but it's also the time when next year's Fall books have to be hustled through and you see she and I didn't have any ideas till just lately and now we are working at top speed.

Spriggin became a part of Rachel's persona, appearing in publicity photos sitting on Rachel's desk beside her typewriter. As an iconic representative of Rachel's "inside-self," the spritely Spriggin was perfect. In one essay, Rachel tells the story of her name:

About Spriggin's name—I really ought to explain how she came by it. It is rather amusing that I should have had the name a whole year before I had the dog! You see, it was like this—I was reading some odd folk tales in the British Museum in London back in 1926, and I came across the word Spriggin. It meant an Elf or Sprite who was supposed to come out of Cornwall. The word had such a gay sound, it caught my fancy and I said to myself that it would be a good name for a dog, if I ever had one. So I wrote it down in a notebook along with a lot of other things and forgot all about it until the day I heard that I was to have a black Scottie. I wasn't sure whether it would do till I saw her, but when I did and she stood up on her two hind legs and waved her short, stubby front paws at me, I felt she was quaint and humorous enough to match the name. So Spriggin she has been from that day to this,—Sprig for short.

The nickname also is very suitable, especially in summer when she goes with me to an island in the state of Maine, where there are hundreds of spike-y little Christmas trees all about. Spriggin's ears and tail are as pointed and her hair sticks out in every direction just like the trees—and so Sprig seems quite in keeping with the place.

Spriggin's life with Rachel was all too brief—only about three years—but the little dog achieved a permanent place in Rachel's heart, and also in some of her most charming poetry. After Spriggin's burial, Rachel wrote a long letter to Prentiss Taylor, describing her little friend's final days.

I was so glad to take her to a quiet spot, and not have to let her be carted off with a lot of "just dogs." I mean she was so much more than that always, and to so many people. . . . She was patient and good as only dogs know how to be—I feel as if somehow I must have been to blame for her getting this way, but there was no warning. . . .

Some people would say, "this is what comes of caring too much" for a dog, but I would not have had it otherwise and they do give us so much more of themselves than we can ever pay back.

It was not long before Rachel adopted another black Scottie to keep her company. "Trotty" lived with Rachel for ten years and solidified the perpetual image of Rachel with a pointy-eared sidekick. Scottie-dog paraphernalia appeared all over her shelves and tabletops; their figures showed up in her illustrations, and they provide the inspiration for some of her most charming poetry, as in these lines from "Epitaph for a Scotch Terrier": "Here four blunt paws now quiet lie / That once went gaily padding by. / Here rests a tail that never grew / Too limp for making glad to-do." In "For a Dog Chasing Fireflies," she wonders at our tendency to place ourselves above the wonder and excitement of dogs at simple pleasures, a sentiment Rachel well understood: "By what sure power do we place / Ourselves above such futile chase, / Who seek more fleeting lights than these / That glitter under darkening trees?"

In the spring of 1928, Rachel indulged herself in a purchase that greatly facilitated her travels to and from Sutton Island. In June, she wrote a letter to Prentiss from "the Sandpiper," the cottage of a friend in Narragansett, Rhode Island, and one of Rachel's regular stops en route to her island home.

> I finally bought a darling second-hand Whippet Sedan, with a prancing nickel-plated Mimi on the hood and a gay blue body—Altogether it's perfect and almost new, and it takes hills on high and behaves altogether more than satisfactorily so I don't care if I do more or less mortgage my existence for the next six months paying for it.

She waxes poetic in her subsequent description of the trip to Sutton, which she shared with friends both dog and human:

> It was a day of shifting sun and wild greenlit moments and it got lovelier and more familiar with each mile. At Saybrook we ate superlative food at the counter of the

station, lilacs were still in bloom and gold and blue iris all round the little "Sandpiper" here as we drove in round seven—and by ten thirty the dogs and us had dined and turned in, . . . All three dogs are splendid motorists—of course Sprig is best, but she has no legs to speak of to grow cramped.

That blue roadster was another exterior expression of Rachel's unbridled spirit, which she kept so well contained within the boundaries of societal acceptance. To be freed from those boundaries was a perpetual longing for Rachel, and she released those feelings most pointedly in print. Still, with the speed and freedom of the roadster, and her ability to use it to transport her friends hither and yon, she found great excitement, which she expresses in poems such as her "Song for a Blue Roadster," excerpted here:

> Fly, Roadster, fly!
> Leave time behind;
> Out of sight
> Shall be out of mind,
> Shine and shadow,
> Blue sea, green bough,
> Nothing is real
> But Here and Now.

The third and most significant addition to Rachel's life in this period almost eluded her—a jointed wooden doll of very tiny proportions. The story of that doll's serendipitous entry into Rachel's world was well known for decades but bears repeating now after so much time gone by. After dining together one winter evening in New York City, Rachel and Dorothy Lathrop, an illustrator friend, were walking along West Eighth Street. Here is a paraphrased version of Rachel's playful account of what happened next.

"Let us stop and say good evening to Hitty," Dorothy suggested.

"And who is Hitty?" Rachel asked.

Hitty was a very old doll, only six inches tall, which had been in the window of a nearby antique shop for some time. They were surprised to learn that each of them separately had taken great interest in the tiny doll wearing a brown-sprigged calico dress and a wise, weather-worn expression....

She did not look in the least like a doll. She had far too much character in her little brown face with its turned-up nose and long, wide apart eyes and her inscrutable smile. Dorothy had learned the doll's name from a scrap of paper pinned to her dress. She also learned that the price was an exorbitant $25 which neither of them felt able to afford.

Dorothy returned to her home in Albany, but Hitty was not forgotten. Since Rachel passed by the shop window often, she sent regular reports about Hitty when she wrote to Dorothy, filled with playful speculations about Hitty's history. One day Rachel passed the shop window and was distraught to see that Hitty was no longer there, which she reported in her next letter. In Dorothy's reply she made the belated suggestion that they might have pooled their money to purchase Hitty together, and that they could have done a book together about her. She asked Rachel to check, just to be sure that Hitty was really gone. To Rachel's relief, Hitty had only been shown to an interested customer but not sold. The store owner pulled her out of a desk drawer.

Right then and there it came to her how Hitty had lost her complexion on a whaling voyage that she had gone on long ago with a family from Maine named Preble. And it almost seemed as if Hitty must be telling her about those days on the Island where they all took refuge after the ship went down and where they would all doubtless have perished at the hands of the savages if she, Hitty, had not saved them.

Rachel had Hitty packed up and sent to Dorothy from the shop.

Through continuing correspondence, the two women exchanged ideas about Hitty's past. No one in the Antique Shop knew a thing about her, so there was no one to dispute them and Hitty sat on in the studio (Dorothy's) looking very pleased in her shy, early American way, but altogether approving of her book. Since she was well over a hundred years old, she must have had many more adventures by both land and sea and river boat. . . . It made one almost afraid of Hitty to think of all she had experienced since her features had been fashioned and her legs so neatly pegged!

The following summer Dorothy came to visit Rachel on Sutton Island, along with their friend Abbie Evans. Rachel wrote this to her friend Prentiss: "Dorothy Lathrop, Abbie Evans and I had a grand week together, mapping out the adventures of Hitty, the wooden doll. That is to be a real book, if it ever gets on paper and it must."

After her week on Sutton, Rachel's excitement about her Hitty book grew daily. "It was a real snowball of a book," she told one reporter, recounting how a great deal of her historical research and family recollections found their way into Hitty's story, the narrative account of the adventures of a one-hundred-year-old doll.

In a whaling museum of old Nantucket I pored over the log books of ancient whaling vessels. My best notes for the book came from a log kept by a first mate on one of the ships. I used that because it was racy and it was legible.

One day I came upon an entry recording the prevalence of scurvy on board ship and stating that one of the sailors had just been buried and also that he had been brought back to the ship. It appeared that burying a scurvy victim in the earth was considered an effective treatment. Mutiny, fire and rescue from savages were culled from the logs and before I left Nantucket, the whaling period was ready for writing.

The episode of hearing Adelina Patti sing in New York I got from my grandmother and Hitty's New Year adventure from my mother.

Rachel worked on the book throughout the ensuing winter of 1928–1929. Some letters she sent in June 1929 reveal a new kind of excitement and momentum in Rachel's writing as she worked through chapters at the home of a cousin (Lucy Talcott) in Farmington, Connecticut. Lucy left her alone in a "lovely back room," Rachel writes,

> and there Hitty and Sprig and I hold forth. Really, I have been working harder than anytime all the year,—more intensively and uninterruptedly, I mean, and I've usually managed to get a daily stint of 1800 words done. I've now got Hitty safely past the Civil War period—she's heard Patti sing, met Mr. Whittier and Mr. Dickens, and now is about to appear at the Cotton Exposition in New Orleans, dressed as a bride. Only five more chapters after I finish this one. I almost begin to see daylight ahead. . . .

> Only got back last night, but Hitty is done!!! I typed the last page yesterday noon after working 8 hours a day on it uninterrupted for two weeks. It was a new experience for me. I wrote 90 of her one hundred and eight pages there. Now the mss. is at the printer's.

When Rachel turned in the manuscript for *Hitty, Her First Hundred Years* to her friend Louise Seaman Bechtel, children's editor at Macmillan, Rachel pronounced with conviction, "This will win the Newbery Medal!" In her optimism, Rachel even considered requesting sealed bids from multiple publishers, but Louise told Rachel "that would not do." Rachel also received an offer from May Massee at Doubleday, but ultimately she accepted Macmillan's bid and signed a contract with them.

Rachel's confidence in the book was well-placed. She did, in fact, win the prestigious Newbery Medal in 1930, awarded each year for the most distinguished contribution to American literature for children published in the previous year. Rachel was the first woman to receive the award, and *Hitty* was the first Newbery winner with an American-history theme. The hoopla began, however, long before the award was given. In March 1929, Rachel was already receiving invitations to speak publicly about children's literature. Still afflicted by childhood insecurities, Rachel was appalled at the idea of public speaking.

> I was invited to make a speech before the Library Association Convention in Washington in May on any phase of Children's Books I wanted. I was certainly startled to be asked, really overcome by the honor, but I turned it right down. I couldn't talk for fifty minutes if I were to swing for it and I always get as self-conscious as in the days in Springfield High School when I had to go up the aisle before everyone. I always feel like a giantess of three hundred stone weight and my feet stretch before me like Charlie Chaplin's, and I fidget and squirm and speak in a high falsetto. No, Ma'am, no more such sufferings for me. As I say, Life is hard enough without adding things like that to it.

Nevertheless, speaking engagements grew to be a significant part of Rachel's life, like it or not. Throughout the fall of 1929, she promoted her book along with Spriggin, Hitty, and Louise. For Rachel, public speeches were a labor of duty and a professional necessity. Her preference was for intimate gatherings and written communications. However, thanks to her acting experience and her strength of character, audiences were delighted by her presentations. Rachel's effervescence and natural storytelling ability shone through, and she found deep gratitude for and satisfaction in *Hitty*'s warm reception. Notwithstanding her confident predictions, even Rachel was surprised by the book's explosive popularity.

Publicity photo of Rachel Field and Spriggin, circa 1929

In December 1929, Rachel wrote to Wilbur Macy Stone, her friend and fellow antiques collector who served as the model of the man who purchased Hitty toward the end of her hundred-year

adventure. Rachel and Wilbur shared an interest in old dolls and
their various accouterments. She wrote him a letter while she was
still on the road at Christmastime.

> I didn't have a chance to thank you . . . before I left for a
> hectic week in Boston where I made 5 speeches in 3 days
> and did many other equally foolish things in connection
> with "Hitty" . . . .
>   "Hitty" is in her 4th printing, I hear, which seems
> nothing short of a miracle to me. They were very kind to
> us both in Boston and many copies were sold. But I fear I
> have sent the old doll stock up too high for our own
> good. I saw an old naked wooden doll of much charm
> and character in a shop on Charles Street, and upon in-
> quiring was told she cost $55. Now was it a coincidence
> that that should have been the auction price I had you
> pay in Hitty's memoirs? Of course they did point out that
> this doll had pewter hands and feet. Have you any of that
> variety?
>   I enclose one of the lady's publicity pictures to put in
> your copy. Much love to Mrs. Stone and to you always,
>   Rachel

After Christmas, she wrote to Wilbur Stone again in regard to
his gift to Hitty.

> The exquisite little rosary would, I am sure, make any doll
> (New England Fundamentalist or otherwise) turn Church
> of Rome for the chance to wear it. Certainly I shall allow
> her to say her prayers upon it if she ever returns to the

comparative peace of New York or Albany! At any rate I shall keep it most carefully for her and shall for my own part enjoy the antics of the little Jack-O'Lantern Jumping Jack. Thank you so very much for both of us.

Thank you, too, for your letter which came just before Christmas. Yes, it is nice to have people like what you write, but I really don't like making speeches over the Radio or anywhere else, and I've made a vow to do no more in 1930.

It was a vow Rachel would be unable to keep. In 1930, though she still found time to publish *Points East: Narratives of New England*, a book of poetry, and several plays, Rachel made many more public speeches, including one delivered to the American Library Association in Los Angeles upon receiving the Newbery Medal. Rachel and Hitty were launched on an extended shared adventure, which included a historic plane flight—a first for both Rachel and Hitty—that transported the two celebrities on part of their cross-country trek to California for the Newbery award ceremony. Hitty the wooden doll became an actual character in Rachel's life, which was less odd at the time, perhaps, than it might seem today. The practice of anthropomorphizing a doll or a pet in letters, essays, or personal exchanges was not uncommon then, and Hitty had been a personality even before Rachel and Dorothy Lathrop purchased her from the old pawnshop in New York City. She was the star protagonist of her own book, and she became an important companion in Rachel's social circle. Rachel's friend Joe Titzell wrote this account of Hitty as companion:

Hitty came alive, became a person as Rachel wrote and Dorothy Lathrop drew. If you weren't there it may sound silly but the tiny figure had a dinner-party given for her on Fifth Avenue and later a theater-party to see and hear Evelyn Laye in *Bittersweet*. It wasn't silly. I stand champion for Hitty. I have to, because she rode to the theater in, and watched the performance from, my breast handkerchief pocket. Her publisher and her publisher's husband glanced anxiously from time to time, her author and her illustrator were unperturbed. They knew Hitty by now. Hitty took it bravely and with interest.

Amid all the excitement around Hitty, in the background of Rachel's life there was a great deal more going on—events and circumstances of even greater import, to her, than writing her first award-winning book. As very few people then knew, Rachel's increasing prominence and success in the public sphere coincided with an emotional upheaval that would change her interior life dramatically.

My dear Rachel,

You know, it took me nine years to finish writing your story. I often thought I'd lost the thread completely, that my life had simply moved on in new directions. I was wrapped up in the lives of my children and my parents, and all the other things that tugged at my attention. However, something seemed to keep setting you and your history squarely in front of me.

That first year, when I was researching for the article in Port City Life magazine, I became like a woman obsessed; maybe a bit like you when you were in the research phase of one of your writing projects. It also felt a bit uncanny, time and again, how conveniently my research dovetailed with the rest of my life.

In the spring of 2009, right when I was researching for the article, I flew to California to watch my daughter compete with her college softball team, so I had the perfect opportunity to visit the landmarks of your California years and the archive collections in Hollywood that taught me a great deal about your career. I even had a niece who lived in Los Angeles for that one year, so I had a place to stay. Your friend Louise Seaman (Bechtel) left her archives to Vassar, which also happens to be my mother's alma mater, so I got to spend a day at Vassar with my mom—something I had never done before. Mom happily read through your letters with me as my research assistant, and she became a part of my project, and one of my biggest cheerleaders. I think you know how important that is. Another central collection of your letters and writings is at Yale University. Two of my children went to Yale, so I combined research, once again, with family visits. *The mother lode of Rachel Field archival materials, of course, is at the Schlesinger Library at Radcliffe, your own alma mater. Another of my daughters lived in Boston when I went for a day of research at Schlesinger, and she too became a family research assistant, wrapped into my story and yours. You and your story always seemed to connect me to my family.*

By the time I'd finished that first year of research, I had gathered enough material for at least a dozen articles. I casually decided that I'd carry on and write your full biography, since no one else had done so. How naïve I was! I thought I'd spend another year or so on it, then send off a completed book to an eager publisher.

So many times I lost momentum. After that first year of research, I got pulled out of my feverish obsession and allowed life to distract me. But there was always something that drew me back in to your sphere of influence. A fellow Sutton Islander invited me to be a guest speaker on writing biographies at a literature festival in Florida. A librarian at Schlesinger connected me with a man who had called her about selling his private Rachel Field collection. That man turned out to be the godson of your dear friend Swish Severn, and I spent a day at his home in Vermont, learning more about you and looking through his Rachel Field collection before he sent it off to California, where it now resides. A gentleman in Maine invited me to take part in a "dead poets" day to be celebrated all across Maine. He asked me to read your poems on top of Cadillac Mountain. There was a woman who called me to ask about permissions and copyrights when she wanted to put your poem to music. On the one hundredth anniversary of Acadia National Park in

2016, the Southwest Harbor Library asked me to give a talk about you and Hortense Flexner, who lived in the Field House in between your time and mine. After that talk, the Great Cranberry Island Historical Society called me to ask if I'd give a repeat performance of my Rachel Field talk in their meeting hall. Every time a few months or half a year went by and I started feeling apathetic about this seemingly endless task, another exciting lead would come from nowhere and reignite my determination.

Was it you?

By 2013 I knew much more about you, and I had written a great deal of the book about your life. But I always felt that I was missing something essential. I knew about Arthur, that you married, that you moved to California, that Hannah came along, and much more. Still, there were your intense poems of heartbreak that I could never explain. I wondered if it could have been Arthur who broke your heart, but that relationship simply did not fit the impassioned voice I found in some of your work. What was I missing?

In July 2013, I had about three weeks before I'd be taking a long road trip with my youngest daughter, Tessa, who was transferring as a junior to Tulane University. We'd soon be making our way by car from Maine to New Orleans. I would drive her down and get her settled into her new life, then drive back home with Jonathan, who planned to fly down and meet us. I had no particular pull on my time for those few weeks, so I decided to drag out my notes about your story once again.

I stumbled upon those mysterious quotations about "Lyle" in your mother's writing once again. "Rachel and Lyle all devotion." "She has an almost maternal care of him." I hadn't thought about it for a couple of years. I did remember, though, coming across the name Lyle Saxon in some of my research. Could Lyle Saxon, I wondered, be the guy her mother wrote about in that 1928 Wanamaker's diary? Thanks to the wonders of computerized communications, I was in touch with two Lyle Saxon biographers in a matter of days. The second wrote me a response that took my breath away. Here's how she began:

"This is an astounding coincidence! Just yesterday I was reading online all about Cranberry Island and thinking how I would love to visit and eat at Hitty's Cafe! Not to mention that I have always wanted to see Sutton Island. I can't believe you live in Rachel's house!"

As it turned out, not only had Chance Harvey written a book about Lyle Saxon, she was also utterly captivated by you. In fact, she told me, there is a Lyle Saxon archive full of extensive letters—thirty long letters from you to Lyle—and those letters were a significant reason why she chose to write Saxon's biography.

Can you guess where that extensive collection of letters is housed? Tulane University, in New Orleans. Yes, I was dumbstruck, and got another one of those chills up my spine. Three weeks later I was in Tulane's archive library reading the most overwhelming collection of your letters that I'd seen anywhere. Would you be upset to know that these letters would be made public, or is this exactly what you and the hand of fate had been working toward all these years? I wish I knew.

In friendship,
Robin

nine

Mr. Mississippi

T he contrast between Rachel's private and professional lives during the late 1920s and early '30s, the period when she brought Hitty to life, brings to mind her poem about her "inside-self" and "outside-self." The burst of focused creativity and productivity that produced *Hitty* coincided with a tumultuous emotional period, when Rachel was assailed simultaneously by previously unknown heights of elation and chasms of despair. For the first time in her life, at the age of thirty-four, Rachel fell deeply, desperately in love. The poetry that begins to appear in her private journals bears witness:

> Love came late to me—
> As Spring to northern Maine
> Suddenly rearing its vehement green
> Where snows have lately lain.

Although her pragmatic Yankee exterior disallowed outward expressions of weakness or drama, inside she was aflame with a distracting passion for an achingly uncertain man. Only in her writing did Rachel allow her emotions a longer leash—and this time, it was not just in private notebooks. The letters she wrote to the object of her desire, though they retain a degree of restraint and apology, also reveal the most unfiltered Rachel Field of any other preserved collection of her personal writings. At an age when she was beginning to feel the urgency of time's inevitable passage, she threw caution to the wind in a grasp for love and companionship in letters like this one:

> Oh, Lyle, it is wonderful to feel the way I do about your work,—to know you couldn't do anything cheap or second rate if you tried to, and then to like you yourself just as much and more. Don't scold me, please, for saying that. You wouldn't if you knew how hard it was for me not to put two different middle letters in l-i-k-e.

Lyle Saxon was a well-known writer and journalist from Louisiana, highly respected and sought out by other authors throughout his lifetime. "Wherever Lyle Saxon lived," Saxon's biographer, Chance Harvey, has said, "that's where people hung out." Saxon's stint living in New York City was no exception. In November 1926, he established himself in a fourth-floor attic apartment in Greenwich Village whose address was soon synonymous with good times: "Number Three Christopher Street." Number Three Christopher became the place where people hung out—artists, actors, and writers who gossiped, laughed, drank lots of coffee, gaily defied Prohibition with absinthe and liquor, and discussed the big questions of art and life. Among those who embraced the genteel yet bold society of Lyle Saxon's salon gatherings were Sherwood Anderson and William Faulkner. Another regular guest was Rachel Field.

Lyle and Rachel had each seen enough success in print to be

embraced by the literati of New York City. They attended parties hosted by esteemed literary couples like Elinor Wylie and William Rose Benét, where they hobnobbed with the likes of Theodore Dreiser and Ford Madox Ford. Rachel and Lyle met at one of these parties in the spring of 1927, after which she began to spend a great deal of time at Number Three Christopher.

It wasn't only professional interest that drew so many to hover around Lyle Saxon. Chance Harvey's *The Life and Selected Letters of Lyle Saxon* describes his universal appeal.

> His was a clean, elegant figure, shaped not so much by expensive finery, for he had little money, as by careful dress and classic good looks. He habitually wore a black linen suit and black tie, and his grandfather's gold watch chain hung from a vest pocket. Big framed yet slender, he stood an inch or two over six feet. He had black hair and eyes "not just blue," as Elizabeth Kell recalls, "but pale blue, the kind you don't forget."

Saxon's dark, brooding beauty and Southern charm caught the fancy of a great many women. It was their misfortune, and sadly Saxon's, that he was most likely a gay man in a period in history when homosexuality was neither accepted nor understood in "polite society," not even among most of the progressive bohemians of Greenwich Village.

Christopher Street became a well-known hub for homosexuals during the twentieth century and would one day be referred to as "the Great Gay Way." Even in the 1920s it was beginning to attract both gay men and "gawkers" to a scattering of gay-friendly establishments. Nevertheless, between Lyle Saxon's desired persona of refined Southern gentleman and the societal conditions of the day, it is highly possible that Saxon fought his own nature, though to what degree he resisted is unknown. He had very close relationships with men, but none that indicate with certainty that they were more than platonic.

It is clear from one of Rachel's letters that Saxon was rather disdainful of their mutual friend, Prentiss Taylor, a lithographer associated with the Harlem Renaissance with whom Rachel did several artistic collaborations and exchanged scores of letters. Taylor, too, was a gay man who was, at least later in life, open about his sexuality. Possibly he was more open than most in the 1920s as well. Rachel once conceded in a letter to Saxon that Prentiss Taylor was "a pocket edition of a person," but she tried gently to defend him as well. Did Saxon disdain Taylor because he was effeminate? Did he eschew the society of men with overtly homosexual tendencies? And might that disdain have been directed internally as well, at himself, causing his life of chronic depression?

Saxon's letters indicate that he became quite close to many women, one of the most effusive being Rachel Field. He even seemed to court Rachel's affections in small ways—sending flowers, bringing gifts, and sharing intimate conversations. She was a highly animated, nurturing person, and Saxon liked to be cared for. Saxon's biographer asserts that he suffered a life-altering heartbreak during his New York years—1926 to 1932—but she was never able to identify the person who broke his heart. It was also during his New York years that Lyle Saxon became the beating heart of Rachel's life.

In 1928, Rachel's sister Elizabeth Field was in the throes of mental illness, still unresolved since her breakdown of the previous summer. Elizabeth must have been either unable or disinclined to travel to Sutton Island that summer, so it was only Rachel and "the Atwater girls," her mother and Aunt Kitty, who headed to the island to settle in for the summer season. They had their usual parade of guests throughout the summer; that was the same July when Rachel hosted Dorothy Lathrop and Abbie Evans and they shared the genesis of the Hitty story. After their departure Rachel began her work on the book in her back studio. August meant more work and more visitors to the island, including Lyle Saxon.

Lyle was respected, well liked, and admired, and he achieved great renown for his writing, especially in the South, yet he never seemed to be a happy man. He was chronically dissatisfied with his writing and suffered from low spirits often in need of buoying up. Rachel's sunny nature and nurturing inclinations would have been an ideal balm to Lyle's discontented soul. In August 1928, he made the long journey to Sutton Island to relax and recover from a recent stretch of intense writing to finish a book of his own (*Fabulous New Orleans*). This was the visit recorded in Lucy Field's diary when Rachel and Lyle were "all devotion." A few days after Lyle left, Rachel wrote to Prentiss Taylor.

> Lyle Saxon was here for 10 days. . . . I drove him down to Portland and fetched back another friend. Such a marvelous ride and Lyle was fascinated by this part of New England, especially the funny square box-like houses of this part of the world—so different from Louisiana. He is a grand person and we had a perfectly delightful time— He actually got the family broken in to daily cocktails— can you picture it?

As the fall stretched ahead, back in New York City, Rachel and Lyle began to spend a great deal of time together. One November invitation to Saxon from Laura Benét seems to suggest that Lyle and Rachel were considered a couple: "Will you come to dinner . . . you and Rachel Field?"

Late in December 1928 Saxon left for New Orleans and did not return to New York for several months. Completely smitten and aching with loneliness for Lyle after his departure, Rachel wrote the following poem in her private journal. It is dated "from December 31st to January 8th" and given the title "This Thing Called Love."

> Now I am all alone
> In this room that is blue and shabby
> And so completely full
> Of you that the very chairs
> And tables and cups and saucers,
> Can set my memory singing
> With:—it was so you sat
> On such and such an evening.
> That was the book you fingered,
> You turned those pages idly.
> Here is the music box
> With the moonlight scene on the cover,
> And the key you wound so often.
> There's the china coffee pot
> With its plump, incredible roses,
> Older than you and I
> By twenty or thirty years.
> I remember the night you brought it

Wrapped in the flowered paper
That I have yet somewhere.
Only a minute now
And the cuckoo-clock's brown door
Will open wide with a click,
The bird will bob and bow
And call,—twelve times precisely.
Whether I look or not
I shall know it's painted green
With red where the beak flies open,—
And I shall know you brought it,
That you hung it there by the highboy,
Hung it and set it ticking,
As if you had given me Time
To keep forever and ever.

*   *   *

The room is spinning about me.
The sofa and chairs and tables
And even the squat blue hassock
Seem part of a merry-go-round,—
The painted animals turning
To a tune that says,—"I love you",
Over and over and over.
All merry-go-rounds, hand-organs
And Street-pianos say that,—
It's why we give them pennies,
Or nickels and dimes in Spring.

*   *   *

Oh, God!—But why do I say that?
I haven't believed in God,
Not really, for years and years.
It's hard to nowadays,
Especially if you're young
And busy and impatient
Of sentimental clap-trap,—
And yet, it worries me,
Suppose He <u>was</u> somewhere, and watching,
And real,—there's always a chance.
Suppose He had really planned it:—
That a man that was you should go
One night to a party, and meet
A girl that was me? Oh, well,
I know it's foolish. He couldn't,
Not out of a world of people.

*   *   *

Of course I'm in love or I'd be
Ashamed to go on this way.
I don't give a damn who knows it.
I thought it could never happen
Like this,—to me. I thought
It was only people in novels.
But I know better now
And whatever happens to us:—
Whether you'll want me and need me;
Whether I'll ever feel
Your lips on mine again,
The way they felt last night;

Whether I'll just go on
The same as I'm going now,
Remembering things you've touched,
The sofas and chairs you've sat in,
And tunes we liked to hear,—
Still,—I'll always know I felt it,
And I needn't go down to death
With a spinster heart, like an apple
Shriveling on some bough,—

*   *   *

That's why I'd like to say:—
"Thank you, God." just once,
In case He should be somewhere.
I'd rather sound like a fool
Saying thank you to nothing
Than seem to be ungrateful.

*   *   *

There now, the clock is striking,
The bird's at his own front door,
I'm all alone in this room,—
Shabby and full of you.

RACHEL'S PROLIFIC LETTERS to Lyle during the next several
months are never quite as unleashed as "This Thing Called Love,"
but they do betray both the depths of her affection and Lyle's reluctance to receive it. They also offer a picture of a mature woman full
of complexity: self-possessed yet needy, confident yet vulnerable.

Always a brilliant letter writer, Rachel poured forth her usual humorous anecdotes and self-deprecating charm in her letters to Lyle, but there is more to them. She opens to Lyle not just her heart but all of her unbuttoned inside-self, openly despairing over the condition of her sister's mental health, her financial strains, and the occasional burden of her ever-present mother and aunt. She is also Lyle's champion, constantly offering him concern and support, asking after his well-being, praising and encouraging him in his work with both enthusiasm and professional expertise.

Rachel and Lyle had a great deal in common. They felt similarly about the pitfalls and thrills of the writing life as they bemoaned the trials of deadlines, strapped finances, self-doubt, and the burden of public appearances. Rachel's keener assessment of literature is evident in her discussions of various literary works she is reading—Hemingway, the letters of Dorothy Wordsworth and Katherine Mansfield, and the poetry of Emily Dickinson.

Another unusual aspect of Rachel's letters to Lyle is the disturbing bluntness she occasionally unleashes. Some of her gossip about mutual friends and acquaintances verges on pettiness:

Saw Sarah night before last and she held forth on the tale of Moo-Moo and Stokes and the poor, jilted girl who loved S. in the beautiful spiritual way. I snickered inwardly remembering your account of a like discussion, but was surprised as could be on the surface. Only I couldn't resist putting in a question as to whether S. and the girl had been anything less than spiritual to one another. (Don't worry, I was most discreet) Sarah hastened to assure me there had been "nothing wrong" between them. Well, I said, I wasn't one for knowing myself the right and wrong of such things. She seemed pained that I was so callous. Anyway I gather that Moo-Moo and Richard are still a-going of it. Moo-Moo was at the Century tea-dance, did I tell you? She was going round the floor with Joe when I saw her and the sight was almost too much for my face. However, I composed my features and was polite when Joe brought her over to speak to me.

Such outbursts are far from the norm, though. Given her fervent hope to connect with Lyle in any way possible, I am inclined to forgive these adolescent indulgences as unfiltered passion more than meanness.

The most poignant aspect of Rachel's letters to Lyle is the love she tries so hard to rein in, and Lyle's obvious rebuffs to her for expressing it. As time passes, she never loses her touch of humor and her writer's sensibilities, but she becomes less able to contain her amorous longings. One letter opens playfully with the heading, "first day of 1929 and ten by the cuckoo clock," but goes on to reveal a thinly concealed ardor.

Your wire came at breakfast this morning and gave me a happy New Year—almost one, at least. I rather hated to let 1928 go; it's been a pretty good old year, as years go, especially from last June on. Well there's just nothing one can do about years and I suppose it's as well.

It was terribly nice of you to send me the message, for you know just how I am missing you. I've been thinking of you along the various stages all the way and I could imagine the welcome you had at 257 [Saint Napoleon Street, his destination in Baton Rouge]. Do be sure and write me all about it.

It's been a muzzling sort of a day here, out of respect to your memory and to show it's rather put out to have you desert this town. Priscilla says it was snowing in Farmington this morning when she left, so it's as well I didn't try the motoring, but can you think how the General Cowles' house must have looked in it? . . .

I saw Dottie a few minutes late this afternoon on my way up to the Youngs—dropped in to wish her happy new year though I must say it was hard climbing the stairs to the top floor of number three.

In another early-January letter Rachel quotes the first few stanzas from an Emily Dickinson love poem, "I envy Seas, whereon He rides." Then she goes on.

Oh, well, you know the rest of it, and I'm only sorry that Emily Dickinson got ahead of me in saying it. Only I suppose, being me, and a practical and second-rate rhymer, I should have said I envied erasers and carbon-paper and typewriter keys!

Don't be annoyed because I must say things like this now and then, Lyle, for I promise not to bother you or make you wadgetty with too much affection. And please don't think I was ever like this before, I never was,—really, but then of course I never knew there could be anyone like you in the world. Don't be angry with me for saying that,—you seem to have routed all my most carefully hoarded New England pride, or perhaps I just mislaid it somewhere on one of those roads round Wiscasset, Maine.

Anyway, if I have said anything you'd rather not remember, why just forget it, please, and let me know if there's anything I can do between now and June . . . and for God's sake write to me once in a while.

So—we being about to cry, salute you,

Rachel

Dear Lyle,

You have no idea the effort I am making to keep myself from writing to you every day! But I haven't the influence over myself that I once had. It rather frightens me in fact to find how I can get around my own scruples! I said firmly last week that I should try and keep it to once a week, but just see how bad I've been and you only gone nine days so far. It is disgraceful and I shall not be surprised if you scold me. . . .

I am having a chowder party Friday night. Carl Carmer and his Bride; John and Liggy Cox; Chard Smith; Bill Spratling; perhaps Joe, perhaps Priscilla Crane and perhaps Louise Seaman. I dread it and of course it won't seem at all like a party to me without you. My idea of one as you know is coffee on Christopher Street with nobody dropping in. So much for that. Think of me on Friday.

The following letter, of January 12, echoes the sentiments and the imagery ("here I am in my cluttered up room . . . missing you") of the impassioned poem she'd written a week before. The attempt at lightheartedness at the end does little to mask her fervor.

My dear,

They have all gone to their respective cubbyholes—the Carl Carmer's [sic], Chard and Bill, Joe and Priscilla, and I have stacked up the dishes, the chowder bowls and the coffee cups and the cocktail glasses (that aren't really, but that I'm getting rather fond of for associations sake) for Bertha Bance to wash in the morning, and here I am in my cluttered up room clicking away to you for no reason except that I am missing you just a little more than usual. It wasn't a bad supper party, the chowder was quite masterly and Bill christened it sea-going gumbo. . . . I felt virtuous for having done my duty by Betty Carmer and I'd got just enough make-up on to satisfy my inferiority complex and yet not to cause P. Crane to lecture me in the kitchenette. But, oh dear me, how I did want you to be here! Nothing is right, Lyle, without you. I am just somebody playing round with some rather pleasant people and wishing I were somewhere else. And nothing seems real at all to me somehow.

But I won't go on like this or you will be cross with me. I will try and be sprightly and entertaining,—about what? God knows. Maybe he will give me an idea, more likely He won't. He's a pig for them himself. . . .

High-ho, a third page! Perfectly disgraceful and when I have nothing to say except what you know already that nothing is at all right since you went away or will be till you come back. Well, that's that. To whom it may concern. E Pluribus Unum. Tempus fugut [sic] and all the rest.

Yours especially, Rachel

March 13th, 1929

Dear Lyle,

Another thirteenth of the month letter and I hope you don't mind. I'll promise you that it shall be mostly business will you be charitable, please? Of course it isn't all,— you really couldn't expect that. Anyway this is how things are,—it's the 13th of March and very sunny and Springish on East Tenth Street and I feel like hanging my very diminutive harp on the first willow tree I meet between here and Forty Second Street and helping myself to the nearest truck. Why, I say to myself, should I clutter this already overstocked earth. Oh, dear me, the "empty bed blues" have nothing on R. L. F. today.

Bessie Smith popularized J. C. Johnson's "Empty Bed Blues" in 1927, a sultry blues number full of sexually charged double entendres. Given Rachel's frank reference, one can't help but wonder if she and Lyle had shared a sexual encounter, or at least shared a bed. At age thirty-five, all too conscious of her ticking biological clock, might Rachel have cast aside the rules of propriety in the name of love? Her passionate letters to Lyle suggest the possibility, not to mention the circles in which she spent her time. Rachel lived in the heart of Greenwich Village during the Jazz Age and Prohibition. Because of her family pedigree and her professional connections, she would never entirely shed the influences of the elite society in which she was raised. However, a part of her mounted vehement resistance against her own inclinations toward conformity with the caste of her birth. She took part at the fringes of societal rebellion. Some of her closest friends, like the lawyer Marion "Swish" Severn, were avowed socialists. Rachel enjoyed the dash of disobedience in clandestine parties with liquor. She rebelled against traditions of classist segregation not only in her fiction but, later on, in her eventual choice of a husband, a choice she felt obliged to defend to friends and family. Most women in Rachel's circles during that time period did not, in fact, exercise sexual freedom; the repercussions and societal judgment were still too powerful.

Wherever Rachel's conflicted heart led her—to honor the traditionalist in her or indulge the romantic poet—history has left her decision unclear. Perhaps she let love bloom in full, in spite of the pain that followed; perhaps not. Rachel's poetic heart thrived on the tension between love and grief, beauty and loss, time and change. To be fully alive was to feel fully, and the writing that came of that time in her life—when she felt so fully—carried some of the greatest weight of any of her work.

March 17th

Dear Lyle

I must write you today, but I will not mail it till tomorrow. It is like a sort of game I have with my own conscience, and the fact that it doesn't really matter in the least makes me play it with all the more vehemence. My conscience is usually so puny and such a nonentity that it surprises me to have it perform ever or in any way whatsoever.

Such a grand March day it is, too. I do love March for its queer, wild light. Emily Dickinson taught me to notice that, I suppose, but I always liked it without knowing exactly why. Do you remember her poem beginning, —"We like March his shoes are purple"? I am very fond of that one. I am sure his shoes would be purple anywhere else today, where there were hills, or pastures or orchards. Still, even on New York brick he is rather nice. In fact he's rekindled a sort of ancient fiery rose one had forgotten was there. What, by the way, do you think of the Emily Dickinson find? I can scarcely wait for the complete new group. The fragmentary ones I have read are thrilling, especially the love ones. I don't believe there can be any-one more glad to think they are coming into print than I. If I could only have one book of poems to take to the proverbial desert island I shouldn't hesitate an instant in choosing her's [*sic*]. And one of the new reasons why I'd like to believe in a Heaven is because she would be sure to be there and I could tell her that the Amherst church spire looks as white and peaked as it used to when she knew it and that there's still mountain laurel round about and incidentally that New England girls still feel as she felt about so many things.

Alas, there are no preserved copies of Lyle's responses to Rachel's letters, but it seems clear that they were not as overtly adoring, and it is equally evident that he openly disapproved of her more amorous outpourings. However, his letters must have held enough encouragement to keep her own coming. He sent her roses at Eastertime, news clippings, passages of literature, and photographs along with his letters, keeping her determined hopefulness alive. She made no secret of the joy his letters gave her.

Your letter came in the last mail Saturday, just in time to save my life like a last minute Governor's reprieve, for it was one of those days when the rope seems dangling very near—you know the kind.

Needless to say I picked your letter clean, as sparrows do a bit of suet by the window. Not that I resemble a sparrow or your letter suet, but I seem possessed with the spirit of simile this morning.

I was so glad to see the Baton Rouge postmark on your letter yesterday that I could have cried, but I didn't. I sat down and devoured every morsel of it. Do you remember the Emily Dickinson poem about reading a letter,—how she shuts the door and takes it off into a corner before she "picks its little lock?" Well, I am just like that with yours.

Your letter was meat and drink and peanuts and caviar to me. I can't tell you what it meant to see it there in our box when I came in late Saturday evening. I couldn't believe it was real till I'd read it all through twice and was half-way through the 3rd time . . . I was that joyful over it when I saw it among a batch of "just letters" this morning I wanted to sing Hallelujah and dance on the Woolworth Tower, only it was raining and I am not thin and graceful enough. It seems to me no one was ever more glad of a letter since letters were first invented. It has been one of the days when I am glad I did not hold out against learning to read as I very nearly did, or really did in fact up to the mature age of ten and a half.

Along with thinly veiled expressions of love, Rachel's letters include some of her most charming writing. In one letter of March 1929 she talks about an awful man she met in New York who narrated a woman's suicide with undue relish, then paints a charming street scene:

> Really a horrid little man, I thought, one of those clever dry looking little atoms with pearl-gray spats and little claw-like hands and a clever patter. Looks at you and tells you things about yourself. Said he could tell I had not "lived." I wish I had said "Well, not with the likes of you anyway." Oh, how I hate people like that. New York is full of them. I suppose every city is. Oh, Lord, Lyle I have such a longing to be out of it for a spell. I envy you more than you know. I'd have been so much more of a success as a tree somewhere. . . .
>
> One day last week I saw an old man on Third Avenue with a funny old barrow cart on two wheels and great chunks of charcoal and wood burning in the middle, and he had big sweet potatoes roasting over it under a sort of hokey-pokey man's ice-cream umbrella. I felt I must have made him up in a dream. The pretzel men with their beards and their baby-carriages full of pretzels still flourish round Union Square, and I gave the organ-man in the blue coat that has turned such a strange purple a nickel, in memory of the night he played under Number three. Why am I telling you all this nonsense? But after all what else is there that matters very much?

Rachel made several references during those spring months

to her desire to drop everything and head for Louisiana to visit Lyle, but personal and professional demands got in the way. One of her primary preoccupations was with her sister Elizabeth. After Elizabeth's crisis of mental illness in 1927 and before her eventual transfer to a reputable sanatorium in North Carolina, Rachel and her mother and aunt were at a loss for a period of time about what to do and how to care for Elizabeth. The severity of her condition had increased to a point where Rachel and her family feared she might do herself or someone else harm. The three women spent weeks trying to place Elizabeth in a care facility where she could be both comfortable and safe from herself.

Oh, how I have been trying not to think of Louisiana today. So warm and springlike and if only I were setting out or on my way there. I feel as if I must just chance it but then in my more sober moments I realize tis but a vain hope, and that pretty well diminished. Things are still terribly gloomy and unsettled here. I couldn't possibly leave till some arrangement was made. Mother and Aunt Kitty went up to the State Hospital while I was away and their accounts of it really are enough to make one shudder, even for a so-called modern place. We couldn't have that on our minds and hearts all the time. And so something in between has got to be found. We have heard of one or two possibilities and are investigating them, one is in the Berkshires, and it sounds like a possibility but it is not a regularly organized place and I fear the responsibility involved without that. You see, I was the only one around that time two years ago when the lid blew off and I know better than the others do how suddenly and apparently without cause these upsets can come up, also one never knows at the beginning whether it is going to be a serious or more or less mild affair. Well, no more of this, we are just back at the same old cross-roads we were at two years ago and running round in the same old circles. But I do feel something will turn up to point the way. Lord knows what. It's a comfort to write you of this. I'd rather not talk much if I can help it, it just wears one out; Mother is really being wonderful, but of course, she thinks of little else. I think Aunt Kitty is a little less miserable than she has been. I am going to try and get her away to the country somewhere for a week away from us and the apartment and all the problems. I know how much good it did me.

The following month, Rachel reveals a bit about some of the sources of Elizabeth's trouble. Jealousy of Rachel was a chronic issue, and it was a sorrow and frustration to Rachel.

We're still more or less on the old volcano, but there is a rather vague chance that the doctors will let us send E. to that farm in Berkshire Mother visited. . . . I am not even trying to go up to the hospital much anymore, as there seems to be a return of much of the old jealousy of me. God knows, why anyone should think I have anything I want out of this damned old world, but there you are.

Rachel mentions her sister's trials in letters to at least two other friends, but she offers no one else the full disclosure and degree of trust that she gave to Lyle. She may have been chided by Lyle for her loving outbursts, but it appears that he had no objections to hearing her other kinds of confession—about her family, friends, and work. Perhaps there were obstacles to physical intimacy between Rachel and Lyle, but there was a profound intimacy of trust and friendship.

Once it became clear that a trip to Louisiana was out of the question, Rachel began to hang her hopes on another visit from Lyle to Sutton Island during the summer of 1929. Elizabeth was finally settled in a secure place, allowing Rachel and her family to make their usual trip to Maine. Rachel knew that Lyle planned a return to New York sometime around June, after completing the manuscript for his current book project. She sent several encouraging letters from the Playhouse. There was more than a touch of personal motive behind her supportive cheerleading that Lyle should finish his job as quickly as possible.

> Lyle, a year ago this minute, do you know what we were doing? We were all over at number three Christopher Street having coffee plus absinthe cocktails with you. It makes me very low in my mind to think of it and wish that it were happening all over again. Well, we must have it later in Maine instead. You really do mean to come, don't you? I don't dare own to you or myself how much I am counting on that. Everything I think of about the summer turns in my mind into a single phrase,—"when Lyle comes—."

> Spriggin would certainly send you messages innumerable, but I regret to report that she is a bad girl, and has gone off on a squirrel chasing expedition of her own. She is a

lovely girl except for this weakness. But perhaps when you come to visit us in August or early September you can have a little talk with her. Now since you are not here, I suppose I must start out and do a little hallooing through the woods on my own account.

On one trip to the mainland, Rachel picked up a copy of a magazine in which Lyle had an article. Lyle also happened to be on the cover of that particular issue of the *Century Illustrated*, a monthly magazine. She sends this amusing account:

I can't tell you how exciting it was to see you on the cover of the August *Century* sitting out in the sun on Ellsworth's Maine Street yesterday, just after I'd started a friend off on the Portland train. You remember that very cluttered little shop where you got camels and coca-cola? Well, you and the Dangerfields were right next door almost, so I've no doubt all the naked ladies in the pictures over the soda-fountain, not to mention all the dusty, stuffed birds have been taking a peek at you before I carried the magazine off to Sutton.

Our new "Playhouse" note paper has arrived, as you see, a last year's birthday present to me, and I wanted to write you one of the first letters on it. I need little excuse, though, as you already know, Sir! I suppose it would be more fitting if I took to green ink to match, but I never could quite achieve a perfect whole in my own get-ups or any what-not. If my shoes are spick and span, then my hat is ancient or unbecoming, or my costume inadequate somewhere or other. . . .

This is the bluest of blue days and so hot and still there's scarcely a stir of pebbles on our little shingle beach, though the tide's been coming in for several hours. Do you remember your first Sunday here last August, how blue it was and how you and I lay out in the sun by the shore path and looked in on that small green and dappled world of moss and root and twig and grass-blade under the lower branches of the spruces? Well, it's just another such Sunday and I suppose that little secret community is busy going about its same root-y business as before, only I have not looked to see. I am waiting for you to come and peer with me. I never enjoyed spying quite so much as that time. Do come before frost catches the inhabitants of it unaware. . . .

Some friends from Cranberry are coming over for supper. . . . I've just finished making up a whole cauldron of fish chowder for us to eat from the big yellow bowls. If only setting out an extra one would fetch you how quickly would I run to get it down from the shelf!

An unpublished manuscript, called *Plenty of Time*, expresses a less lighthearted version of Rachel's impatient waiting for an uncertain suitor. The story's protagonist, "Cally," is a thirty-five-year-old artist (a painter, not a writer) who lives in New York City, the same as Rachel was in September 1929. Other autobiographical parallels abound: Cally spends summers on an island in Maine with her mother, who was widowed early and raised her two daughters by herself. Cally is in love with a writer named "Hugh" whom she knows from New York. Hugh lives on the top floor of a building in the West Village of lower Manhattan. His

letters lack the frequency or fervor she longs for, and she is waiting anxiously to hear that he will come to visit.

In the fictional story of thirty-five-year-old Cally, we witness
the true story of thirty-five-year-old Rachel, her fears and her
despairing impatience. The story opens with Cally awakening on
the island, thinking rather enviously about her sister's children (a
non-parallel) who are sleeping nearby.

"If I have any children I'll certainly try to make the most
of their good points." Cally struggled to sit up without the
usual racket from the bed springs. "If," she caught herself
up sharply, blinking against the blue between the spruce
tops. Once it had been "When I have children." Now it
was "If", and she avoided even that most of the time. Of
course there wasn't any real need for her to, thirty five
wasn't so old. Elizabeth Barrett Browning had been thirty
nine, and that was comforting to think about. But one
wanted more than vague comfort on a morning like this.
If she could only be sure there'd be a letter from Hugh in
the mail. Over two weeks now and just that one note
scrawled off ten minutes before he took the train for that
weekend. . . .

"P. J. Lorimer seems to think you're the Emily Dickinson of water colors" he had written in those fifteen hur-
riedly scribbled lines she knew by heart, "but he can't tell
me anything about you." Oh, if that only meant what she
wanted it to mean! If he'd added "my dear", or ended
with anything but that dull "Yours as usual". If he'd just
said "Cash and contract can go to blazes I'll be on the
express next Friday and don't you dare not be on the plat-

form wearing a red bandana with yellow toadstools on it so I'll be able to recognize you!" Well, he hadn't said positively he wouldn't come. That was something.

Later Cally muses over Hugh's letters again:

Once he had signed it "positively yours". That had been a year ago when he was out on the coast giving those lectures. He never had again. But it couldn't have been an accident his doing it that once.

Hugh's professional and financial difficulties echo those of Lyle, and we get a sense of the nature of his relationship with Rachel.

If Hugh got that advance from Lowe and Fowler on the first three chapters of his novel then he wouldn't have to worry for awhile either. But maybe if he did he wouldn't need her to buck him up anymore. If he got to be a successful novelist would he still like to come over to the studio and play her music-box while she cooked supper because they were too broke to go to Tony's Chop House? Would he ever want more than just that of her? Time will tell. What an idiotic phrase. That was the trouble with time, it never did tell. It just went on and on, and you wore little ticking images of it on your wrist or kept one on your mantelpiece because you mustn't ever forget how terribly you were in its power.

There is a great deal of insight into Rachel's life and relationships in *Plenty of Time*. Her narrative shifts its point of view so that we see into the minds of other characters as well, such as Cally's mother, who ponders the challenges in the lives of both Cally and her sister, Ada. She is aware of Cally's lovesick preoccupation and frets over the changes in her artist daughter.

> She had been the most eager, open sort of child. Always running home from school to show her mother the little pictures she'd painted, nearly bursting to tell her about the silver badge she'd won in St. Nicholas League for the illustrated poem when she was eleven. They'd had ice cream for supper that night to celebrate. . . . Ada had acted a little sulky about the prize, but Cally had been too happy to notice.

After rising from sleep one morning, Cally joins her mother in the kitchen, wishing she could open her heart to her mother.

> Why couldn't she just say:—"Oh, mother, you think I'm hard and independent and a success. But I'm not. I'm a failure and I'm miserable. I love Hugh Burton so and he won't even bother to answer my last two letters. I know he's weak and selfish and lazy, but it doesn't make any difference. It's awful to want someone who doesn't want you. I'm not getting any younger. I'm nearly middle-aged, and when I see Ada and other people married and,—I can't go on much longer the way things are. I can't."
>
> But you couldn't tell your family what really mattered. They cared too much, so you just had to keep to

coffee and dish towels and what could have happened to day-before-yesterday's paper.

Similar sentiments appear in poems that Rachel wrote during this same impassioned period. Even when they reach for the cheerful effervescence that is Rachel's usual nature, it is a faintly desperate reaching that thinly masks an underlying melancholy and the bitter necessity of hiding one's interior sorrows.

THE BUSY BODY

Now fields are striped in green and brown,
And every dooryard's sweet,
So I will take the road to town
And nod to all I meet.
I'll smile and say—"A pleasant day."
I'll praise the sky's far blue,
And none will guess I'll be so gay,
My heart is set on you.

I'll pile my wicker basket high
With parcels at the store,
Green peas and buns and eggs I'll buy
Citron and nuts galore.
Each one I'll choose with such a care
As if we two should dine
From bowl and plate of willow-ware
By fire and candle-shine.

But when the plates and cups are dried
And set upon the shelf,—

I will put off this foolish pride,
This sprightly, hard-earned self.
I'll miss you to my heart's content
And not be dubbed a fool,—
For who pretends to ticking clocks,
Or wooden chair and stool?

IN DEFENSE OF LAVISHNESS

If I'm too lavish of my love,
As skies are of their blue,—
Remember, 'tis the way with hearts,
And skies, when suns pass through.

In one letter of May 1929 it is clear how hard Rachel tries to release her more spritely inside-self for Lyle on paper. She wants him to see that she is not strictly practical all the time. The combination of the letter with its companion poem, however, gives her attempts at frivolity an air of desperation rather than delight.

I went on a wild tear the other day—just to show you how practical I sometimes can<u>not</u> be. I went to Altman's to buy a pair of good sensible shoes and ended by getting the most intricate and really fascinating ones of reptile (kind rather vague) skin, and also a dress of ice-berg green linen because it was a color I could not resist when I really needed a neat and dark crepe. Such is Spring in the City!

In a vein of similar whimsy tinged with despair, Rachel's poem "Because I Know" begins with these lines: "Because I know that clocks must tick / Our lives to dust someday, / I will wind up the music box / And listen to it play." The poem was abbreviated for publication, but these last two stanzas appear in her private papers.

> Because fear dogs the lightest foot,
> And envy and despair,
> I will put on my leaf-green dress,
> And pause to curl my hair.
>
> So I will smile and cherish toys
> And knick-knacks till I die,—
> Since sadness comes so cheap to all
> And anyone can cry!

Echoes of the raw emotion in "This Thing Called Love," the intimate poem Rachel wrote after Lyle's departure in December 1928, also reverberate in Cally's story. Cally experiences not only the pain that now seems to her to go hand in hand with beauty but the existential ache of even bigger ideas—life, death, and the existence of God. All the accompanying angst plays and replays in Cally's mind as she rides over the sea with family and friends to go picnicking on a neighboring island. The glorious scenes around her expand her heart's ache to bursting. She sees seagulls swooping over a fishing dory, "whiter than snowflakes in the strong sea sunshine," and gets a close-up view of a single gull taking wing, its bright orange feet "flattened to a shining underbelly," and she is overcome.

Beauty caught her; stabbed sharp and fine as a needle point. She'd never be able to get through the day if it kept up like this,—never.

"Beauty crowds me till I die,

Beauty mercy have on me,"

That was Emily Dickinson, in a poem she'd found day before yesterday. Ever since Hugh had sent the clipping she had been reading those poems. Well, Emily Dickinson had known all about it years and years ago. Those little words were hot and alive with what she had felt on just such a morning, but she was dead. Oh, God, I don't want to die without something more than this. Let me have what Ada's got; what mother's had; even what fat, talkative Elsie has, and I won't ask for anything more. Good heavens, she was praying; actually trying to bargain with a God she hadn't believed in for years, not really. But if Hugh should wire he was coming tomorrow; if he even wrote a fraction of all those things she wanted him to say, she'd believe in God, in Providence, in anything.

Love had transformed Rachel, and her poet's sensibilities wondered at her own transformation.

STARS USED TO BE ENOUGH

Stars used to be enough,
And windy blue,
Gnarled apple trees in bloom,
Moons old and new;
Fir-cone, green bough and scarlet berry,
Woodsmoke and dew,—

These were once enough, my dear,
Now I need you.

For you have stretched my heart too wide
For any Spring-green rain,
For sun or moon or bough to fill
Quite to the brim again,
And it may be love and it may not be,—
But only this is clear,
Stars used to be enough,—
Not now, my dear.

SUBTRACTION (FROM A LADY'S ARITHMETIC)

Three things there be
I love and need
When all is said and done,—
Only these three:—
You and the sea,
And grasses in the sun.
But lest I seem demanding
As I've no wish to be
I will give up the grass, my dear,
And do without the sea.

A NURSERY RHYME

I wanted a house and I wanted a house
And I wanted it by the sea;
I wanted a car all painted blue
And a dog for company.

And I've got my car and I've got my house
With the sea at its own front door,
And I've got my dog with a wagging tail
And still I'm wanting more.
For though my house is snug and green
And my car as blue as blue,
And my dog the waggingest ever seen—
I seem to want you too!

Rachel's work of this period also allows us a glimpse of anger —an emotion Rachel rarely courts, even in fiction. But it is there in these lines from "To a Certain Gentleman": "I can feel my blood turn chill / And thin before your pride, until, / Cowered, I shrink before your stare / As any hard-pressed fox or hare / That, desperate, turns upon its track / To meet the hounds' relentless pack."

The climactic moment in *Plenty of Time* occurs when Cally stumbles upon two young people in the woods, in the throes of lovemaking. It is too much for Cally to bear: "She trembled with horror and envy." Her reaction betrays Rachel's conflicted heart, bound both by convention and the longing to defy it.

Now that her heart was quieting down the old resentment flooded her. Those two,—together in the wood, helping themselves to what she had never known: to what she might never know. It wasn't enough that they were young; they must have this, too. Well, they'd had sense enough to seize love and each other. Why hadn't she known enough to? If Hugh were different—. But perhaps it was she who ought to be different. Perhaps she was too old to make him want her that way. She had let Time cheat her out of this. Time was making her middle-aged and bitter. She felt powerless before it, like a fly in the everlasting spider's web.

Time. Time. Time.

Everything about her seemed to be repeating the word. Unseen insects chirped it from the grass; the sea pounded it on the rocks, and the little watch ticked it on her wrist.

Cally felt all her love for Hugh pressing down upon her in a nagging weight. Even when she struggled against it, it piled up, and he wouldn't take any. Or at best such a little bit of it.

The manuscript amounted to only sixty-eight pages and was never published, but the themes of time and unrequited love appear throughout Rachel's subsequent work—most prominently in her first novel for adults, *Time Out of Mind*, a National Book Award winner published in 1935.

Lyle never made it to Sutton Island in the summer of 1929, but he and Rachel were both back in New York that fall, where they continued to spend a great deal of time together. Those exquisite days with Lyle, filled with both ecstasy and wistfulness, mingled together in Rachel's poet's heart to produce some of her most poignant expressions of human longing. "The Pawnshop Window" begins "I meant to put you from my mind / And do my work today, / But by the pawnshop I forgot / To look the other way." Alone at the pawnshop window, the poet goes on to say that in her mind she sees her absent love, "standing there / Beside me in the rain." It ends with this stanza:

Queer odds and ends out of people's lives
In helpless litter spread
And now my mind is full of all
You ever did—or said.

OCTOBER 14TH

It was too much to ask
I know it now;
That slantwise light of afternoon
On the swamp maple bough;
That hump-backed, russet hill
And far white spire;
That smell of apples in the grass
And dry-leaf fire—
These should have been enough,
But, oh, my dear,—
If you had touched my hand or drawn
One step more near.

THOSE YEARS OF longing took their toll, but Rachel, ever the pragmatic optimist, sought alternative shores on which to land the unrequited passions of her heart—and in time, she reached them.

Dear Rachel, my friend,

It's hard to describe to you the emotional upheaval I experienced as I read your letters to Lyle in Tulane's archives. I was euphoric on the one hand, because I could finally identify the source of overwhelming intensity and heartache I'd read in so much of your writing. My journey through your letters was a revelation, the culmination of a long, unfulfilled quest for understanding; it completed the unfinished portrait I'd painted of you in my mind. On the other hand, I also felt the exquisite depth of your sorrow, and I ached for you. I even detected a simmering fury in my stomach toward Lyle for the pain you suffered. I felt tearful—whether from sorrow or anger, I'm not certain.

How you were able to keep grinding out such excellent work, even as your heart was breaking and your sister was suffering nervous breakdowns, I'll never know. It almost seems that hardship pushed you harder and gave your writing the power of passion and urgency. But maybe I'm wrong to be surprised. Sometimes I wonder if suffering is the very thing that gives us access to the core of our deepest emotional artistry. Perhaps the laggardly nature of my writing career is due to a life of minimal suffering. But how can I complain about having a good life?

Positively yours,
Robin

ten

The Newbery Medal

Perhaps it is no coincidence that at the height of Rachel's intense infatuation with Lyle Saxon she wrote the book that would become her first big breakthrough into widespread fame. *Hitty, Her First Hundred Years* also became Rachel's longest-lasting literary legacy. It is evident in her letters that Rachel herself felt a strong association between Lyle and the writing of *Hitty*. It was Lyle, she told him, whose inspiration pushed her through the final stretch to get the book finished. She even confessed that she would have liked to dedicate the book to him. Instead she dedicated to Lyle a small book called *Polly Patchwork*, one of several that she was writing during that feverishly busy period. "To Mr. Mississippi," the dedication reads, "who gave me my first patchwork quilt." We get a sense of the progression of her work and her personal life through her warm letters to Lyle through the spring of 1929.

Dear Lyle,
It is one of the days when if you were here you would surely hear two rings at your door about four o'clock

maybe even earlier, and one of them would be for me and the other for Spriggin. Yes it is one of those days and there's nothing one can do about them. I have no business to write you on one, but seem to find myself doing so instead of returning to click away on "Hitty" after feeding Spriggin her dinner.

I am just about frantic with work these days, all my own fault for having left things till the last moment. . . . Having three books going all at once makes me feel like a nervous juggler. I get cross-eyed keeping track of the balls of literature as I toss one or another up into the air and I'm sure I shall drop one. All I really want to do is Hitty. Lyle, I swear, I believe that is good. I don't know why and I hardly dare say so to you, (I wouldn't naturally to anyone else) but I sit down and type it off first draft and I seem to do it without much effort, almost as if I were in a trance of some kind. I never had anything act just like that.

Tomorrow I return to Hitty, who is to have her daguerreotype done in Philadelphia in Civil War time. I really do like doing her now I'm started. She is really a doll of parts. I hope you are going to approve of her and I wish she were going to be dedicated to "Mr. Mississippi" too, instead of "The State of Maine and Abbie Evans," but there are times when one's own preferences must be waived.

I shouldn't be writing you in the middle of the morning, but I felt I must, so I'm leaving Hitty in camphor, literally, for these few extra minutes. She's very obliging and won't mind.

I shouldn't be writing you in the middle of the morning, but I felt I must, so I'm leaving Hitty in camphor, literally, for these few extra minutes. She's very obliging and won't mind.

By doing your little stunt of sticking to a typewriter for eight hours a day I managed to write "The End" on the mss. of "Hitty." Yesterday I turned it in to MacMillan and now I'll only have the pictures for a silly little Doubleday book to put through. This bout of work has made me realize as never before what a lazy critter I am and how rusty at really getting to work. You put the rest of us to shame.

It is not clear when Rachel finally gave up her romantic hopes regarding Lyle, or whether his sexuality was ever openly acknowledged between them. We do know that she finally got to Louisiana at least once, early in 1930. During one of her trips from New York to California, working on book promotions for *Hitty*, she spent a week with Lyle at a plantation in Melrose where Lyle and other artists worked in their cabins under the solicitous care of "Aunt Cammie" Henry. Cammie Garrett Henry, whose family owned the plantation, was a great supporter of the literary community. She opened her family homestead to a variety of authors and artists, turning it into an exclusive artists' retreat. It is highly likely that Cammie created the elaborate doll's bedroom used in Hitty's traveling box display, described in an article Rachel wrote for *Child Life* magazine:

In Hitty's room the most unusual piece is a four-poster bed with a canopy that was made on a plantation in Louisiana where she and I visited the year we went out to the coast to get the Newbery Medal. Our thoughtful hostess took Hitty's measurements and months after, the bed arrived all fitted out with sheets and pillows and two handmade patchwork quilts, a calico one for summer and a silk one for best with no less than a hundred and thirty tiny patches in it.

Rachel's attachment to Lyle and to her memories of that emotionally elevated chapter of her life lingered for years, but something must have ultimately come about that made the impossibility of the love affair clear to Rachel. Strangely, in Tulane University's archival collection of Lyle Saxon materials, Rachel's effusive and prolific letters to Lyle abruptly cease after the summer of 1929. Yet we know that Rachel visited Melrose Plantation early on in 1930, and she references that visit in a letter to Lyle years later. Were there intimacies expressed in subsequent letters that were too sensitive to save? Was it during that 1930 visit that Lyle and Rachel finally confronted their romantic conflict? Were they forced, at last, to face the truth of what they could not have? Though it's impossible to be certain of what did or did not transpire, we do know that some time in the early 1930s Rachel finally gave up on her hopes for Lyle and opened her broken heart to another man. The full-blown passion that she felt for Lyle retreated into the guarded depths of Rachel's memory. Instead, Rachel found a new kind of attachment—slow-growing, more careful, and ultimately one that would blossom into the full maturity of love she had sought for so long.

If Lyle came into Rachel's heart like one of Maine's raging nor'easter storms, Arthur came like the gradual turning of the tides. Arthur Pederson was a Broadway actor from Saint Paul, Minnesota, also one of the coterie of regular guests at Lyle Saxon's Christopher Street home during his stint in New York City. At some point Rachel and Arthur crossed paths in Lyle's apartment, perhaps discussing a recent performance or a recently released book, or just gossiping over cocktails. Knowing Rachel's lifetime love of the theater, it is easy to imagine her feeling a gravitational pull toward a man who knew life on stage.

Acting in plays had been a pinnacle experience of Rachel's childhood. In addition to the starry-eyed memory of sitting in the back of a theater with Kate Douglas Wiggin, one of her most treasured childhood memories was meeting the famous actress Maude Adams outside the stage door after a performance of *Peter Pan*. It is safe to say that her enchantment with theater never fully left her. This scene from one of her manuscripts gives a sense of her depth of emotional response to the world behind the footlights.

> The lights went out. For a second it was darker even than going down cellar for apples after supper, but a different kind of darkness, all warm and tingling. . . .
>
> It was always to remain the Never, Never, Land . . . that country across the footlights. . . . It lay in that great square of brightness and all the people moving across the magic spaces were tinged by it.

Playwriting had gotten Rachel into college and gotten her a job in New York after college. Her own original plays were the source of her first professional success. It was that success that enabled her to purchase the Playhouse on Sutton Island. It is also worth looking back here at a story from Rachel's trip to Europe in 1920. Two letters to her mother, sent from London and published decades later in the *Horn Book Magazine*, reveal Rachel's undiminished glow over all things theatrical. The first gushes over J. M. Barrie's most recent play, *Mary Rose*. "It is beyond my feeble powers of description," she begins, "like light on water; or a sudden thrush; and all the beautiful things that stir one strangely." In the second, Rachel has just come from a face-to-face visit with Barrie, the author of her beloved *Peter Pan*. "It's all over," the letter opens, "and you will know from experience that I'm rather low in my mind as a result, and grieving considerably that I didn't acquit myself better."

No record explains how she was able to arrange it, but there was twenty-five-year-old Rachel, on a July Friday in 1920, knocking on the door of 3 Adelphi Terrace at five o'clock in the evening, "with more palps than I've ever had in my life before."

> What happened next I don't quite remember, except that I felt him giving me a funny stiff little handshake like a very shy boy at a party, and I felt just as shy myself—indeed quite all tied up in knots.

Rachel's description of Mr. Barrie is worth reprinting here.

> He is like his pictures, only again he isn't. He looks younger than they make him, and his face is squarer and stronger—a strange combination of squareness and sensitiveness. He is hard to talk to, and yet easy. One rather

progresses in jerks; that is, once he starts on a subject, he seems to forget all about himself and he will tell you all sorts of fascinating things about it. Then, quite suddenly, he will come to the end of what he has to say, and a disconcerting silence will fall. I just began to get used to this about the time I had to rise up and drag myself away.

Barrie showed her the view, recounted some of the colorful history of Adelphi Terrace, and sat for tea with his young guest. They talked a great deal about *Mary Rose*, Maude Adams and *Peter Pan*, "the Irish question," and a lake in Scotland where Barrie planned to go soon for vacation. Immediately upon taking her leave, Rachel told her mother, she berated herself for all the things she wished she had asked and hadn't, for her shy awkwardness. "Oh he is wonderful," she said in closing, with the rapture of idol worship, "and wasn't it dear of him to bother with *me*?"

In October 1928, Arthur Pederson had a role in a Broadway play called *Gods of the Lightning*, a play that ran only twenty-nine performances and closed in November. It is possible that Rachel's first view of Arthur was onstage, which would have left an impression. Arthur was eight years younger than Rachel, slender, very tall, powerfully built, and extremely handsome. His *Gods of the Lightning* performance was Arthur's most prominent Broadway role—perhaps his only Broadway role. Whether he found steady work in less prominent theatrical settings is unclear. What is clear is that Arthur became a part of Lyle Saxon's Christopher Street circle, and by 1930 he was searching for other ways to make a living.

Rachel's earliest reference to Arthur is in a letter of referral that she wrote for him on March 20, 1930, to Barrett H. Clark of the Dramatists Play Service.

Dear Mr. Clark,

This is to introduce my friend Arthur Peterson and to hope that you will see and talk with him sometime. He has considerable stage experience and is interested in getting some more or less related work.

> always sincerely,
> Rachel Field

The fact that Rachel misspells Arthur's last name (using a "t" instead of a "d" in "Pederson") suggests that she did not yet know Arthur well in 1930. By February 1933 they were a couple, and Rachel wrote what may have been her first Valentine's Day poem to Arthur. It is handwritten in one of Rachel's many personal notebooks filled with poetry.

A VALENTINE (FOR ARTHUR)
A HEART TO HEART TALK

Said your heart, to my heart,
"What if our love should go,
To dwindle like an old moon,
To fade like the snow?"

Said my heart to your heart,
"We might as well be gay,
For if love's gone tomorrow
It must be here today!"

The sentiment of the poem expresses more than a lighthearted jest. Several years passed during Rachel and Arthur's slow-moving courtship, and Rachel's remarks in letters indicate that she had to struggle once again for patience while courting a confoundingly uncertain man. In the case of Arthur, though, the uncertainty was of a different nature. Not only was Rachel almost eight years older than Arthur, she also carried a social pedigree and professional prominence that normally would have rendered her inaccessible to a struggling young actor from Minnesota. The mixing of such divergent social castes was no small thing in 1933. However, Rachel had always chafed against the restrictive exclusivity of social hierarchies. The heroines of her books regularly defied social boundaries and faced the consequences—most pointedly in her first novel, *Time Out of Mind*. That novel, dedicated to Arthur, came out in 1935 and became a national bestseller. It also caught the interest of Hollywood; selling the film rights to *Time Out of Mind* gave Rachel and Arthur the financial security that led, finally, to their long-delayed marriage plans.

Arthur's reluctance to make a commitment could have grown from insecurity over his professional and social status, but it probably went beyond that. He suffered from bouts of insecurity and depression throughout his adult life and was prone to drinking to excess. A sensitive artist with a tortured soul is the primary love interest in *Time Out of Mind*, a characterization which could apply to both Lyle Saxon and Arthur Pederson in varying degrees. Arthur, however, lacked the presence and charisma of Lyle, who attracted so many aspiring artists to his soirees on Christopher Street. There is little doubt that Arthur was the primary model for Rachel's tragic hero in *Time Out of Mind*.

Arthur's insecurities were by no means the only complication in his relationship with Rachel. Once again, I turn to her fiction to speculate. Kate Fernald, the heroine of *Time Out of Mind*, is imbued with many characteristics possessed by Rachel herself: like

Rachel, Kate lives with her widowed mother and grows up with enormous responsibility to care for herself and others. In Kate's case, the care is for the wealthy Fortune family, who hire her mother as a housekeeper. Young Kate's insecurities about her physical appearance are likewise familiar. They echo the sentiments of "My Inside-Self" and "The Quiet Child," representing the same woes suffered by Rachel's main characters in "The Elfin Pup," "Eliza and the Elves," and the children's novel *Hepatica Hawks*. When ten-year-old Kate meets the great shipping magnate Mr. Fortune for the first time, the imposing man looks at her and says, "A square-rigged girl and no mistake!" For young Kate, his words cut "like a splinter of ice."

> In that fraction of time it took for him to say them and for his eyes to find me, I was suddenly aware of my stockiness under the new blue woolen dress that was too long at the hem and sleeves. To save time and trouble mother had had my mop of sandy hair cropped close only a few days before. I could feel my ears turning scarlet without so much as a wisp to cover them. My heart pounded in furious misery as I stood silent and flushed before him.

Like many of Rachel's fictional characters, Kate has a sturdiness of character to match her sturdy physique, and she often rues both attributes. Kate is admirable, responsible, makes sacrifices, and abides by the rules of decorum that run human society. And yet, like the "Quiet Child" by day who harbors fantasies of turning into a "wild bad witch" by night, she often envies others who dare to break the rules. On the other hand, those who break the rules in Rachel's books generally come to no good in the end, even if they enjoy temporary triumphs that elude the good girl entirely. It was a perpetual conflict for Rachel—abide by society's standards or follow one's heart—and that conflict likely illuminates the path of Rachel's real-world romantic life.

Surely there were suitors, in spite of Rachel's woes over her physical shape and size. Men who spent even a short time in her presence immediately referred to her with phrases like "the delightful Rachel Field." She was great company, a sparkling light, a fount of warm sincerity accompanied by a twinkle in the eye. There was something pure and childlike in her spirit that she never lost, even at her peak of adult toughness and New England practicality. Some of Rachel's friends speculate in their letters that one of the men who sought Rachel's affections was the poet Josiah Titzell. In Rachel's exchanged letters there are references to "old beaux" from Radcliffe, and hints that men of high standing certainly did seek her out. It seems that in love, however, Rachel's rebel child held sway, and perhaps Joe Titzell was one of the disappointed suitors who failed to win Rachel's romantic heart.

Joe spent time as a guest on Sutton Island more than once. He was a poet and writer, another Lyle Saxon connection, part of Rachel's circle of literary friends in New York City. Rachel's letters, though, indicate that she viewed him more sympathetically than romantically. She wrote her concerns to a friend that Joe's employer overworked him, "which isn't a good idea for one of his constitution, but I don't think it's anything serious, though of course I always rather worry over Joe's health. I don't want him to get used up before he has a chance to do the gorgeous beautiful stuff that's in him." She also tried to cultivate connections for Joe with other women—perhaps seeking someone other than herself to take on the role of caring for him.

In a rare example of criticism, Joe hints at an aspect of Rachel's personality that might reveal the character of their relationship. In a written tribute to Rachel filled mostly with praise for her undeniable warmth, Joe also points out Rachel's temper:

> Not that Rachel couldn't be difficult, with that impatient upshrug of her shoulders that was a brick wall; it was irritating when you were on the other side of the wall but it defined a characteristic of her personality. It said, We'll never be able to agree on this subject, ever, so there's no point in wasting any more time on it. We might as well go on to another one.

It does not surprise me that a man of sickly constitution, perhaps overly fretful and officious, might ignite Rachel's impatience. Joe's remarks call to mind another character type that appears often in Rachel's fiction—the solid, upstanding man who loves the heroine yet excites no love in her heart in return. "I do like him," says her protagonist in one unpublished manuscript, "but whenever I think of John Nelson I think of a brown serge suit I had once—I knew it was a splendid piece of goods, all wool and warm and strong enough to wear forever, and yet somehow I could never make myself like to put it on."

You can almost hear Rachel's stubborn resistance, the brick wall of her shrugged shoulders. When it came to love, she found no appeal in the brown-serge-suit men, the solid, upstanding, successful, boring men. The suits that Rachel wanted were impractical and daring, exuding a dash of rebellion and risk. In love, Rachel's bolder side won out, and both Lyle Saxon and Arthur Pederson, each in their own way, fit Rachel's specifications.

One parallel between Rachel's relationships with Lyle and with Arthur was the "almost maternal care" Rachel gave each of the two men. Lucy Field wrote about her daughter's solicitous treatment of Lyle in the Sutton Island journal, and Rachel's behavior toward Arthur was similar. She cheered him, defended him, and encouraged him with her rosy nature and her untiring ambition on his behalf. She may have been a physically robust woman, but Rachel's greatest strength was in her spirit. It is not surprising that Arthur, whose sense of worth descended regularly into darkness, was drawn to Rachel's light. She was sustenance for a starved sense of self-esteem. Conversely, Rachel was the kind of person who found nourishment in giving herself to those in need, in fueling belabored spirits with her own spritely optimism. She had energy to spare, which she poured into people as well as into her writing.

Nevertheless, her resources weren't bottomless. During the stretch of years between 1930 and 1934, as she approached the age of forty, Rachel worried about the passage of time, her ability to bear children, and the uncertainty of her future. She indulged her worries mostly through the characters in her books, and she remained patient and philosophical on the outside, writing with greater diligence than ever. In letters to Louise Seaman Bechtel written from Sutton in 1933 and '34, Rachel reports on both Arthur and her writing.

> I really feel in grand productive form. I think all the thy-roid I've been consuming is taking effect. Then too, I feel a bit more settled emotionally. I don't know why I do because nothing new has happened, but I somehow feel that A. is more sure of himself and me and I don't feel as

if I were so frantically straining at the reins. Of course it may just be the heavenly anodine of this Island.

Arthur never did get here and I'm sorry. He could only have managed to be off that one week when I couldn't have him, so fate was against us, but he'll have a week in Oct. and he can come to Conn. And maybe to Clare Kummer's in Narragansett with me if she stays late and that will be something. I think maybe it was a good thing I made the long summer away. His letters are more eager—and, but Lord knows how it will all come out and I begin to believe only some great catastrophe might settle it once and for all.

These letters do not burn with the same impatient ardor that consumed Rachel during her romance with Lyle, but the love she nurtured for Arthur had the capacity for long-term growth that her infatuation with Lyle lacked. She was sincere in her love of Arthur, but she was complacent enough to wait and see what came about. And while she waited, she immersed herself in one of the most prolific periods of her career.

Lest we forget that Rachel Field was always a woman of many dimensions, it is important here to remember that her life as a dedicated writer, sister, daughter, niece, and friend never faltered, even in the fullness of her infatuations. Appreciation for all those who touched her life was as essential to Rachel as eating and sleeping, and her friends and family felt it. After she was awarded the Newbery Medal, she wrote to Louise.

Dear Louise,

I don't want to go off to Rhode Island tomorrow without putting a thing or two on paper that I couldn't quite manage to say to you. One never is able to somehow, but I hope you realize that I know just exactly how much you are responsible for my getting the Newbery Medal. You know perfectly well how much of your own enthusiasm and spirit, not to mention hard work, went into getting "Hitty" over as D. P. L. and I wanted. No one but you could have given us so much cheer and confidence along the way and we have both talked of that part often. You know without my saying so, what having you behind us has meant.

But aside from "Hitty" herself, I want to say here and now that you were one of the first to make me feel I was any good at this sort of thing. You really were, whether you remember what you said or not, and so I want you to remember that I remember it very well indeed. You always made me feel that I was worth taking a chance on, whether the actual piece of work I brought in was any good or not. That's why I'm so glad "Hitty" has brought us luck and a little bit justified your belief in her biographer.

Now please do believe every word I say, for I don't feel so about anyone else in the whole game. Incidentally I think you are a grand person as well as a publisher and you might share this last bit with Ned who comes in for a hand himself, even though it's at the small end of this sheet of paper.

Lots of affection and very special thanks—
Rachel

Hand-drawn and colored note from Rachel Field to Louise Seaman
Bechtel, 1932. The handwritten notation below the image is from
Louise, who kept the note in her private papers.

In 1930, the year that her love affair with Lyle ceased, Rachel won the Newbery Medal for *Hitty*, began speaking tours around the country, lost her dear Spriggin, and adopted Trotty. It was the start of an extraordinary stretch of productivity, which included the publication of many poems, reviews, and essays in various national newspapers and magazines every year between 1930 and 1935. During this same period she came out with *Points East*, a collection of plays titled *Patchwork Plays*, and another play called *The Sentimental Scarecrow*. In 1931, she published *Calico Bush*, a young adult novel set on an island off the coast of Maine in 1743. The heroine, thirteen-year-old Marguerite Ledoux, travels to the rugged coast of Maine as an indentured servant for a family of settlers. Although it did not win the Newbery Medal for 1932, it was a Newbery Honor book, and many people consider it her best work for children.

Two more pocket-sized children's books, *The Bird Began to Sing* and *The Yellow Shop*, went to print in 1932. She published poems in magazines and another full-length children's book called *Hepatica Hawks*. Although she regretted her procrastination that led to a rush job of sending it in for publication, Rachel once said that *Hepatica Hawks*, the story of a young giantess who travels as one of the cast of "freaks" in a circus caravan, was the most autobiographical of all of her books. It portrayed many of the experiences she contended with in her own childhood related to her ungainly size. In the next two years Rachel published several more of the pocket-sized books for children, which she called "juveniles," but she came out with two more significant books in 1934: her third book of poetry, *Branches Green*, and her first prose work for adult readers, *God's Pocket*, the story of Captain Samuel Hadlock, Jr. of the Cranberry Isles. *God's Pocket* was a particularly important step along Rachel's path toward breaking out of children's literature. She had no idea at the time just how far her skill in writing for adults would eventually carry her.

Rachel, my dear,

I wish I knew how overtly you and Lyle communicated the unfortunate truths that divided you, but maybe no one will ever know. He was your first true love, and perhaps he would always be the source of poignant regret, but how glad I am that you and Arthur found each other. It may have been a long and roundabout romance, but he became your heaven on Earth at last.

In my research I found two songs that have become small treasures to me in my quest to know the sensory experience of your emotional world. Nothing summons the depth of our hearts as music can. You knew this; music was the focal point of your first adult novel. I have often wished I could know what music you imagined or listened to as you wrote the story of Nat Fortune, tortured pianist and sensitive soul. What I do know is that "Empty Bed Blues" was a song you knew and liked well enough to mention it in a letter to Lyle. I listened to Bessie Smith sing it on my computer. Between the music's soul-stirring power and my awareness that you sat and heard this very rendition in Bessie Smith's voice, I felt transported into your world and your heart as never before.

I found a copy of the other song unexpectedly in an archive library. That was your song for Arthur—more on that in my next letter.

Fondly,
Robin

eleven

Love and Pain, Bound Up in Time

The release of *God's Pocket* in 1934 was a landmark event for Rachel, who had been struggling to expand her reach beyond children's literature for years without success. It was also a project intimately intertwined with her beloved Sutton Island and her passion for history and artifact. In a 1933 letter to Louise, Rachel recounts the story of her encounter with Captain Hadlock's grandson on neighboring Great Cranberry Island.

> Since I wrote you last the perfect, authentic piece of Maine lore has fallen into my hands. Do you remember my telling you about the old man on Cranberry whose Grandfather Hadlock took Indians and showed them all over Europe in the 1820's? He brought back a Prussian lady for wife and he later was lost tragically sealing in Greenland. It's a tale that has haunted me for years, but I never had enough fact to go on and since the old man, Sammy Sanford was still alive I dared not go ahead and fictionalize. Well, in late July I went over to see him with an Island friend [Rosamund Lamb]. We had a marvelous

time with him and he was so touchingly glad to see us that it quite broke me up. He got out the Journal his Grandfather kept on his travels showing the Indians and put it in my hands "to keep as long as you want to". He had only let me look at it once before, so I was thrilled and got his permission to copy it. I was in the midst of doing this when I stopped to write a poem about my visit to him. I didn't want to stop and do it, but something forced me to, and I tried not to make the poem all about death for it seemed wrong so soon after seeing him. Well, the next day I heard that he had died over there all alone in his little house, so he must have been trying to get in touch with me. I can't but feel it was more than just a fleeting idea, for I fought so against doing it. I will show the verse to you when you get back and you will see why it seemed especially strange. But to go back to the Journal. I have just finished copying it and it took me four weeks of hard deciphering to do it. But it really is a treasure and I am going to tell it as a straight American novel-biography. It is more full of romance, adventure and human tragedy than anything I could ever have thought of. I really know I can do something with it, and though it isn't juvenile I feel sure you'll be glad I'm back at this type of thing. It's just in line with "Points East" and "Calico Bush" so it ought to help them, too. Anyway we'll hope so and I can hardly wait to show you and Ned the Journal. Wasn't it strange that we went over just two days before his death and that he put it in my hands. Almost as if he had known how soon he was going?

The poem Rachel wrote that night, and another that she wrote about Captain Hadlock's grandson, were surely inspired by the same day and were published on facing pages in her 1936 collection of poems, *Fear Is the Thorn*. These lines from "North of Time" read almost like one of Rachel's letters: "We sat together in the small square room, / Late sunshine fell across the kitchen floor / In yellow patches. I could hear the boom / Of turning tide along the island shore. / 'Why, yes,' the old man shifted in his chair, / 'That's Grandfather's own chart hung by the door.'" The second poem, "And the Place Thereof . . . ," describes Rachel's visit with Mr. Sanford in similar terms before ending with a clear premonition of what was to come so soon thereafter: "The peas he planted hang in long green pods / Ripe for his picking now, and here a score / Of yellow squashes fatten in the sun. / Others will bear them all away before / Frost comes. . . . O, ancient Psalmist, well you knew,— / *The place thereof shall know him now no more.*"

Rachel published *God's Pocket* in April 1934. Reviewers wrote, "Here's life masquerading as a story, a fragrant restoration of Old Maine. Miss Field has done a lovely thing" (the *New York Herald Tribune*); "A fascinating narrative" (the *Boston Post*); "Homely, genuine, inherently New England" (the *New York Times*). *God's Pocket* was especially treasured by the people of Maine's Cranberry Isles, as it still is to this day. With that book, at last Rachel fully crossed over into adult literature. During that summer of 1934 when Arthur never made it to Sutton, Rachel's old friend (from their working days under R. R. Bowker) Ruth Stanley-Brown (Feis) made her first ever visit to the island. Ruth's connections to Washington, DC extended beyond being President Garfield's granddaughter, since she had married Herbert Feis in 1922. Feis was a Pulitzer Prize–winning historian and economic advisor in the Department of State for two presidential administrations (Hoover and Franklin Roosevelt). The two friends had seen each other regularly, if not often, over the years. They overlapped in Europe during one of Rachel's trips overseas; Ruth hosted Rachel at her home in Washington, DC, on occasion, when Rachel traveled there to give talks or to do research in the Library of Congress; and during some of Ruth's visits to New York City, she made a point of meeting Rachel for lunch or tea. The weeklong visit on Sutton Island, however, was unusual. It rekindled the closeness between the two women. Ruth's journals are archived with her husband's papers in the Library of Congress, and through them we get an exquisitely detailed view of Rachel's Sutton Island life. Ruth's description of her visit begins with her departure from the pier in New York City and recounts her trip to Portland, Maine, then Bar Harbor, where Rachel picked her up.

Saturday, July 21

As we neared Mt. Desert the thick spicy fir trees sent their fragrance across the green water to me. I stood in line 55 minutes to get off by the first tender as Rachel had advised and took exciting peeps at the unbelievably pointed spruce and fir trees and grew very agitated inside. Finally 9 on each side of the staircase were allowed to descend and get aboard the little tender, and we flew across to Bar Harbor when I caught a glimpse of Rachel's green coat—and soon I was on the dock hugging Rachel and meeting Miss Tucker who is also a guest of the Fields. Rachel brought her car and in we piled, and started out for Seal Harbor where Rachel keeps her car. Beautiful cool clear air so packed with exhilaration and vigor. I've

never smelled such pine-y smells—blue water, golden
sunlight (a hot wave for Maine) and every possible beauty to soothe the eye. At Seal Harbor I took out from
Jumbo all that I'd need and we stowed it over the arm and
in R's Radcliff [sic] bag. Then began the ride in a small
launch over blue-green water, Rachel showing Schoodic
and every island, and as we approached the pier Ki
[Stimson] was waving and Mrs. Field's white signal flut-
tered. I was excited at seeing Ki—and when I heard that
Betty and Henry were coming for the weekend it was
simply too much!

The Bill Stimsons have a large lovely old house and
then Rachel's Playhouse lies up through pine woods to
the left—a low-roofed rambling place circled by wide
piazzas and furnished with simple worn furniture. My
room is way off by Rachel's work-room and 2 other guest
rooms—the old servants quarters.

Then follows a pencil sketch of Rachel's Sutton Island home, the
Playhouse, with Ruth's room and Rachel's workroom labeled at
the south (inland) end of the cluster of buildings. She goes on.

Betty and Henry Beston had arrived at the Stimsons.
[Betty Beston was the married name of the writer-poet
Elizabeth Coatsworth.] Just before supper I'd waved to
her excitedly from the point. So later on as twilight darkened Rachel suggested we go over a minute. Which we
did—found them all on their point—Betty warm, lovely—
alive. Her hair has grey streaks, but she is just the same.
Ki is father and peppered with grey. We sat in the big

lovely low-ceilinged living room with them and reacquainted ourselves. Talked of my adoption plans. Talked of Betty's new book <u>Away</u> <u>Goes</u> <u>Sally</u> to come out this spring. Of Rachel's new volume of verse, also for fall [*Branches Green*]. . . .

I mustn't forget the scarlet bunchberry or the harebells growing on the grey and yellow rocks, and it's juniper and fir and spruce. <u>not</u> <u>pine</u>!

Sunday, July 22

I awoke to the lovely silence, to sun coming through the skylight. Such a happy day. I put on mauve gingham and Rachel and I had breakfast out on the porch. Orange juice toast and coffee. The lovely blue water, the lively sun making sharp shadows and light etched so clearly after the Chesapeake's soft cloudiness. Rachel showed me the harebell growing out of rock crevices so jauntily, so gracefully. . . .

I wrote after breakfast in my diary and a letter to Mother. Aunt Kitty and Aunt Lucy and Miss Tucker went off in city cloes [*sic*] and Rachel and I breathed long breaths of sparkling air before going back to write. Rachel goes to her little room, a nice ratty disorderly room where she can hurl papers at her feet and not have to be distracted by order!

Ruth goes on to tell of visits with island neighbors, some of whom Ruth knows through other literary or society connections. She extols the perfection of their simple meals—toast and orange juice, clam soup and johnnycake, salad and tea and fruit—and recounts their evenings listening to Rachel and her mother read from Sarah Orne Jewett's *The Country of the Pointed Firs*. Ruth mentions taking some time to write, but more often she was drawn to outings like a walk around the island or a trip to watch the boat races. Rachel wanted to work, Ruth wrote, "so I said I would go." However, Ruth also records a vivid image of Rachel's spirited response to her Maine home, giving us a sense of her animation in the company of the wheeling gulls, rocky shores, and pointed firs that inspired so much of her work. On one daylong trip out to Gott's Island with a large group, Ruth meets "dear old" Captain Sprague, to whom Rachel dedicated *Calico Bush*, and sees firsthand one of Rachel's favorite places.

Rachel Field in a boat near Sutton Island, circa 1932

Monday, July 23

It was a blue blowing day and Rachel adores Gott's with
an intense and vehement joy. She simply bubbled over it
and told me of Miss Peterson who lived all alone in a tiny
house on the point, of her beautiful garden and the tall
delphinium that grew on either side the steps of her grey
house. She was a kind of hermit, a beneficent hermit—
and one night the house burnt to the ground, and she in
it—not a thing left, clearly burnt to the ground, and a
wind that swept off-shore so not even a tree was singed. It
was from this that Rachel took her setting for <u>Delphini-
um</u> in <u>Points East</u>.

They returned from their explorations around the rest of
Gott's Island to the rose-red rocks where they'd landed, where a
black iron pot of haddock chowder awaited them. "I've never
tasted such chowder, pork and onions and potato added the most
delightful flavor to the haddock. 15 quarts of milk went into it!"
After a period of "digestive repose," they continued their wander-
ings, visiting what remained of a small island village.

It was like a half-forsaken village, not quite deserted but
yet the era of prosperous bustle has passed it by. It lies on
its hilly slopes, lonely, drowsing in the sun and heavy
with aromatic scents of clover, juniper, wild roses and
underwood growth. The earth is good rest and such here.
I too was exalted with Rachel who seemed to have grown
little wings at her heels and shoulders, a sort of wild exs-
tasy [*sic*] possessed her on this island which she so adores.

It was at the end of that rare and soul-filling day that Ruth recorded her renewed attachment to Rachel, after a sleepy bedtime chat. "She has given me a picture of her life in NY, her friend Arthur Pederson and all the mixed emotions that have been patterning her life in the last 2 or 3 years. We have revived our intimacy and I feel for her an even deeper affection than ever." Before Ruth's departure, she and the Field family household were invited to a "fancy dress party" at a Sutton neighbor's home, something we'd call a "costume party" today. People came dressed as a woodland elf, a barmaid, or nonsensical creatures. Rachel decided to go dressed as Captain Samuel Hadlock, the adventuring protagonist of *God's Pocket*. Hadlock went seal hunting in arctic waters, then traveled around the world with an exhibition of arctic curiosities—including, disturbingly, an indigenous couple and their baby—that dazzled the aristocracy of Europe. Hadlock returned to Maine with a Prussian woman as his wife. Looking for a costume idea, Ruth was struck by the inspiration to dress as the "Proosian Lady." Ruth reported Rachel to be quite handsome, and the following day they redressed for photos. The photos of the two friends are startling. Rachel, dressed in black coat, waistcoat, and white stock around her neck, her hair swept back, looks very convincingly male. However, Ruth also expressed some relief after they had changed back into normal clothes. "Rachel made almost too good a man and I was glad to have her become Rachell (as Jim Sprague calls her) again."

Rachel Field on the porch of her Sutton Island home, in costume as Captain Samuel Hadlock (the protagonist of her first book for adults, God's Pocket), July 1934

The summer passed, and 1934 wound to a close. Rachel's professional life charged steadily forward, and she resignedly watched her personal life continue in an uncertain kind of limbo. Then, early in 1935, *Time Out of Mind* changed everything.

Time Out of Mind tells the story of Kate Fernald. The book begins when ten-year-old Kate and her widowed mother come to work for the Fortunes, a wealthy Maine shipbuilding family. The story is set in the 1870s, during the dying days of the great era of tall wooden ships. Kate, a hard worker of durable New England stock, grows up alongside the Fortune children, developing a lifelong love for Nathaniel, the sensitive and musically gifted son of her employer. Aware that their relative social status makes any relationship between them impossible, Kate keeps her feelings under wraps throughout most of her lifetime. The book overflows with stirring descriptions of coastal Maine and well-researched depictions of an era gone by, including one vivid scene of a boat launching. It also tells a poignant love story about a relationship which comes to fruition in a manner considered unseemly by many readers of the day. "The book is rich in passages of verbal beauty, and is notably skillful in design," wrote a reviewer in the magazine *The Catholic World*. "It is, however, wholly alien to our standards of morality."

After years have passed and Kate has resigned herself to living the remainder of her life alone, calamitous circumstances throw her together with the man she loves, alone at their old homestead. Kate has seen Nat turn away from his feelings for her. She watched him marry another woman and become miserable, while Kate rejected a highly suitable marriage offer in deference to her true love of Nat, even knowing it could never be. Now Nat has returned to her, defeated, devastated by self-hate, his marriage in ruins, his boyish face imprinted with suffering. Gradually, buoyed by Kate's solicitous care, he recovers some sense of worth and acknowledges his love for Kate at last. She welcomes him simply and unquestioningly. "Nat should have anything he wanted of me, or nothing if he wanted that more." Kate knows that there will be scandalous talk in their little town about Kate living alone in the old house with a married man, but she no longer cares about talk.

She brushes aside Nat's fears that he is no good for her, that he will only hurt her as he has hurt so many. "I know I wouldn't take all the rest of my life for what little we've had," she tells him. "I never thought you could want me like this. It seems like some kind of miracle."

He buried his face against me for a long time. I didn't dare say any more, but I could feel him trembling. His forehead was damp under his hair.

"Kate," he said at last, "are you sure?"

"Very sure, I think I've always been."

But it would have been the same if he had not asked and if I had not answered. I hardly felt the stairs under my feet, though I heard the familiar creak of loose boards as I followed him up.

It was my turn to tremble.

"You're not frightened, are you?" He spoke out of the darkness.

"Only that you may be disappointed in me, Nat. You see, I've never—and I wish I could be beautiful for you tonight instead of the way I am, clumsy and—"

He kissed me into silence.

"That's like you, Kate, to make it seem as if you're not giving me the most precious thing a woman can give."

"But it's not precious till someone you love needs it. Oh, Nat—"

I woke to darkness and the steady drip of rain. He was still there. I felt his chin pressing my shoulder; his arm flung across me, heavy with sleep, and I knew it had not been a dream. I was glad he could sleep like that beside me.

My body felt light and far removed from my mind and all
that it would carry to the grave. Whatever happened, this
had been. I told myself that, over and over. What must it
be like, I thought, to know it when you were young and
untroubled, without the busy, lonely years of waiting between? It couldn't be the same, for how could the careless
and happy have strength to bear this fierce necessity of the
flesh that was high and swift as a full-moon tide, and yet
simpler than the push of roots and mounting sap? I
couldn't reconcile it with happiness as I had known that
before; this was too secret and strange.

Given the state of Rachel's real-life relationships, one cannot
help imagining, in the passionate scene when Kate casts off social
mores to nurture and care for the tortured soul of the man she
adores, that there are elements of her love for Arthur behind the
writing, and perhaps elements of her love for Lyle as well. The
layered emotional complexity of discovering sex in the maturity
of adulthood is limned with such exquisite detail and poignancy
that one suspects Rachel knew what Kate felt and shared Kate's
bold decision to ignore the arbitrariness of society's rule book.

Shivering there in the dim chillness I got into my clothes
and crept downstairs. Maybe I ought to have felt guilty
and ashamed, but I couldn't somehow. It seemed right to
me then; it does now.

Like many of Rachel's books, this one was criticized by some
reviewers as too sentimental. Try as she did to avoid sentimentality,
Rachel's innate romanticism crept into most of her books, but her

gift for descriptive writing, her meticulous depictions of history, and her depth of insight into human nature always gave her books wide appeal, as this *New York Times* review proclaims:

> It is a romantic novel of sentiment, wistful with memories of past glamour, insistent upon loyalties and lifelong love which find small place in modern fiction. Ironic references to "escape literature" cannot, however, destroy the book's great charm, nor minimize in any way the perfection of mood and atmosphere which Miss Field achieves. Those who are sworn foes to romanticism may not like this novel, but they can scarcely deny that it is beautifully done.

Eleanor Roosevelt gave a nod to Rachel's book in one of her regular columns titled "My Day."

> I wonder how many people have read Rachel Field's "Time Out of Mind." The New England characters are good. The unforgiving young man wrapped up in his own ambitions, and the absolutely self-forgetful woman, who became one of those village characters everybody knows has a history, but whom nobody really remembers much about, are thoroughly typical. The description of the times when she tried to be just hands and feet, a mechanical automaton that moved and yet was numb, is very poignant. For one reason or another, many of us can remember times like that in our lives and therefore appreciate the understanding shown in the development of her character.

Time Out of Mind was the book that elicited one reviewer's remarks on the heroine's devotion to place rather than a person, since her love for a man went unreturned. It is a striking observation, since the same was true of Rachel Field. Sutton Island, Rachel's haven, her poetic muse, the place where she was "most herself," became the heart and soul of her existence during all the years that she remained unrequited in love. The island was a cherished and worthy alternative for Rachel's devotion, but in the end, it wasn't quite enough.

Rachel's first adult novel won wide acclaim, and Universal Studios promptly purchased the film rights. The sale gave Rachel a boost of financial security, allowing her and Arthur, whose relationship had remained circumspect up to that point, to plan their marriage openly at last. Rachel shared their plans with friends and family by mail. At age forty, Rachel continued to write diligently, but her diligence sprang more from financial responsibility than from some pure drive to produce. Given her druthers, she would have spent most of her time on less lucrative pursuits like poetry and hand-painting letters to friends. She often confessed her preference for things like berry picking or cooking a good pot of fish chowder over sitting down at her typewriter. But Rachel had her mother, aunt, and sister to consider, and her husband-to-be struggled to find a job with consistent income. In April 1935, Rachel writes to Ruth about her hopes of getting to Sutton Island that summer.

> Just now I always have the feeling that I'll never get there
> again and this year there are some rumors of California
> in the air. But say nothing please, as yet, for they are
> movie possibilities and you know how those can rise and

fall in a night. I don't particularly want to go and yet I do need to make as much as I can these years while the going is good. It would seem nice to pay off debts and start fresh and free, if one ever can.

Even in the month prior to their wedding, Rachel was no more specific in her letters to friends than to say that the wedding would likely take place some time in June. The exact date remained uncertain until quite close to the day, as the following three letters indicate. The first letter, to Louise Seaman on May 25, tosses out myriad plans and ideas, revealing the uncertainties in Rachel and Arthur's future, in spite of Rachel's recent success. In typical fashion, Rachel downplays Arthur's job insecurity, casts a hopeful spin on their future and Arthur's prospects, and then recounts recent personal events, including an "official" visit with Arthur to her family in Connecticut. She opens the letter with a thank-you to Louise for a gift of fancy silk stockings.

I'm saving a pair to wear at my wedding—if it ever comes off, which I cannot believe it will now that we're actually beginning to talk about it! Yes, my dear, we are planning to be married sometime between the 15th and 20th of June and of course we want you to come! I don't even feel "engaged" yet and certainly I shall <u>never</u> feel married and I am suffering (ridiculously but rather acutely) from the prenuptial qualms! Well, you know how it is and you certainly won't be surprised in one way, though in another I suppose you will be—even as I!

Arthur went up to Connecticut with me last weekend and the visit went off so well that I am almost frightened!

He was angelic with the family and they seem almost reconciled now the die is cast! There's no point in waiting any longer, we both feel, and he seems happy to have things settled—not that they are really as regards next year, for I may still go to California on short notice and I really only want to because his chances of work would be better there.

I've only told a few friends this much, but I wanted you to know right away, only don't tell anyone except Ned as yet—please. We think we'll be married in church (maybe St George's) here—no reception or fuss or such and then drive straight to Sutton for a couple of weeks and open the house. If Cal. doesn't develop A and I hope to go to England and Sweden for a month the cheapest way we can—It's extravagant, but we may never have a free summer once he gets work and I'm so tired and on edge I feel even Sutton won't iron me out and I don't want to plunge him into a lot of in-laws the first thing. I hope I can get the family to keep house on the Island while we're gone and then I'll go back in Aug. when we get back and have a couple of weeks with them while A. stays here and hunts work and I can fetch them back. Whether I can get them to stay at Sutton and have Trot with them, is still uncertain—as everything seems to be with me at present. I'm too upset with work and plans to feel as excited and happy as I should be. Also everyone I tell says "Are you <u>sure</u>" till I get worse stage-fright, for who is <u>sure</u> of anything in this world—or of oneself above all?

A letter of June 2 to Prentiss Taylor provides more information:

> I wanted to tell you then,—what may not surprise you
> very much—that I am planning to be married to Arthur
> Pederson this month. We have really been engaged for a
> good while, but things were too uncertain for us to talk of
> it before—they're still uncertain, but we are just going to
> go ahead and not wait till Fall.
>
> One reason is that the chance for me to get a 3
> months contract to work on motion picture writing in
> Hollywood looks as if it might come off later this summer
> and we want to be able to go out together on short no-
> tice—of course it may fall through—but anyway—
>
> We hope to be married quietly at some church in NY
> (no reception or fuss) and then go to Maine as long as we
> can have (maybe nearly all summer—more of this later)
> but I wanted you to know and I'll be back tomorrow and
> with my nose to the typewriter probably till an hour be-
> fore it's time to be married!

In this letter to Ruth a few days later, on June 7, it appears
that Rachel is still feeling uncertain of her wedding date, less than
two weeks before she and Arthur finally married on June 20.

> Your letter was a joy to have and I shared some of it with
> Arthur, who is eager to know you. Everything seems to
> have got simplified and smoothed out over night and we
> are happy and hopeful as we haven't been in three years. I
> hold my breath about it all and feel extraordinarily like

Andersen's Ugly Duckling finding suddenly that he is a quite different variety of bird than he thought himself to be. Well, you know—

The most poignant letter Rachel wrote in the weeks preceding her marriage went to Lyle Saxon, with whom she still shared a level of intimacy unmatched in her other letters. One thing the letter indicates is that she had still been in love with Lyle at the time of her 1930 visit to Louisiana, the one that might have signaled Lyle and Rachel's final acknowledgment that theirs was a doomed relationship. Clearly, that loss still reverberated in Rachel's heart five years later. She wrote in response to a letter from Lyle praising *Time Out of Mind*.

Dear Lyle,
Your letter broke me all up. I was quite unprepared for it, and what you said of "Time Out of Mind" was so wonderful that it didn't seem as if you could be writing of something that I had had a part in. It's queer with books, —one seems to lose them completely in the writing and it is only when people say real things about them, or mention some bit they have liked, that we get any sense of reality or are able to capture again the slightest feeling of life and vitality that was in us when we were getting the words on paper. I know you have the same feeling and you could have expressed better what I mean. So it was strange having you give me back my novel as you did; one of the strangest sensations I ever had,—marvellous in a way, and terribly moving to me in another. You gave me back more, almost than I was conscious of feeling in

connection with it. I suppose because you have always been able to make me feel things more than most people. Your words were so generous and splendid that I know you were kinder to me than I deserved, but still it is a letter to cherish always and I am sure you knew how it would hearten me. I can't believe it is as good as you say. I know it has a lot of faults and that it is old-fashioned and sometimes over-written, and yet it was somehow the essence of feelings and moods and so much that has been gathering in me all these last twelve years of my life, that I find it hard to have any sense about it, though I feel curiously detached from every word. I am happiest that you think it shows growth and maturity, for that is about all that matters when all is said and done. I mean, there's no point in going on at all otherwise. The thing that pleased me most of all in what you said was that you began by feeling me in it and that you lost that as the book went on. People are so apt to say—"It's autobiography of course," and of course it isn't, for all that one naturally makes use of what one has actually thought and felt. I'd rather you had lost me in it than anything else and I am so grateful to you for saying just that to me in so many words.

In the letter she also shared her plans to marry Arthur, their mutual friend. Evidently, Lyle had remarked on the book's dedication, "To A. S. P.," and asked about the initials. Was he fishing for a confession from Rachel about which man actually inspired the love interest in *Time Out of Mind*? Even though he couldn't love Rachel the way she wished he could, did he still take comfort and satisfaction in her love for him, and the fact that he was her first true love?

> I thought you would recognize the initials of the dedication. Arthur has been keenly interested in the book from the start to the finish and he was the one who thought of the title. At least he noticed that phrase in a poem of Edna St. Vincent Millay's and drew my attention to the beauty of a phrase that had seemed commonplace to me all my life. Arthur and I have come to be very fond of each other in the last couple of years, in fact, I guess we have really been engaged for almost that length of time, but we didn't trust ourselves to think we were or to say so. We've had spells of being miles apart, actually, and in ourselves, but we've always managed to get back to the old footing and I think that we will probably be married this June sometime, though our plans are still very uncertain and we're only telling a few very close friends as yet. But I wanted you to be one of the first to know because of course you are responsible for our meeting.

Arthur was a friend of Lyle's before he knew Rachel. The two men even exchanged letters occasionally, so it was not strange that Rachel felt compelled to share with Lyle the news about her relationship with Arthur and their plans for the future. Before getting to the news, however, Rachel reminisces about Lyle's Christopher Street apartment. She nostalgically recalls all the people who gathered there and the goings-on of that time. Even now, Rachel is more candid with Lyle than she is with almost anyone else.

I can see all of us so plainly, too, and I can't help feeling that I am quite another person from the one who sat there. If anyone could have told me this then, I shouldn't have believed it. I hardly do now, and I'm a little frightened because I want to make him happy and I want us to have something permanent and real in this shifting, inexplicable world, and perhaps I am not the one to give him what he needs. But he is very dear to me and we seem to need each other out of a city full of people and the very fact that we are so different may be the best part of it. I know you always liked him and he always did you. He's had hard luck with jobs and he's taken it so much better than I should have, and he is proud of my work and respects it as so many wouldn't. Time is so short and precarious at best, Lyle, I don't believe we are making any mistake in taking what we can now and not being afraid of love and what we feel. Doubting and thinking is the ruination of us all. I've given up trying to analyze what I feel or don't feel. Human need and love is so much and we have that, so I know you will wish us well. It seems funny to both of us to be engaged. We never used the word till a couple of weeks ago and we're still a little self-conscious about it. . . .

Our plans are very much in the air. There was some talk of my going out to California to work on the movie script [for *Time Out of Mind*] but I doubt if that is coming off now, and in some ways I am not sorry, though the money would have helped and I think undoubtedly Arthur could get something in one of the studios out there, for he had an executive job in the Long Island one till last February. He has given up the acting end of things but he would like to keep on in radio, the theatre or the motion picture line, and I know he will be able to find something. So unless something turns up for the west we'll probably get a little larger home here and stay on East Tenth St. next winter.

The interplay between the two loves of Rachel's life is complex. Arthur had a friendship with Lyle outside of his connection to Rachel, and he wrote to Lyle on occasion to ask about networking in the literary field, or possible collaborations. Lyle was a respected and successful writer to whom many turned for advice or support; the popularity of his Christopher Street apartment was testament to his inspirational charisma. Most people felt privileged to be counted as Lyle's friend, and Arthur was no exception. He wrote one letter to Lyle from Sutton Island shortly after arriving there with Rachel for their honeymoon, humbly observing, "I am not going to tell you about Sutton for you were the first to tell me about it." He continues:

Thanks so much for your telegram, Lyle. I read it in the car driving away from the church. Sorry you could not be at the wedding. There were many friends of yours there. We didn't have any music, but Priscilla Crane arranged to have a hand organ going full blast as we were standing in the vestibule of the church greeting our friends.

We went to Farmington the first night, and then the next morning we drove to Narragansett where we spent a few days with Clare Kummer. It was warm enough for a few dips in the surf, and we enjoyed walking on the beach and cliffs. Clare was in grand form as usual, and we thoroughly enjoyed ourselves. Marjorie was there too. Roland didn't get back from London where he is making a picture for Korda. On Monday we set off for the North. We stopped to say hello to Laura and Lizzie Hills in Newburyport, and in Wiscasset a Miss Sortwell loaned us a colonial house for a day and night.

Reports of Rachel's wedding day indicate a glowing bride. She and Arthur took out their wedding license on June 19, 1935, and were married the next day in the chapel of St. George's Church in New York City. In a published tribute to Rachel, years later, writer Sophie Goldsmith describes Rachel's wedding day in her memory:

Just as Rachel and her husband left the church, the sun shone extra hard—she said so afterward—and a friend who knew about a certain fancy of hers saw to it that the tinkle of a hurdy-gurdy on the street outside gave a touch which delighted her.

Priscilla Crane was the friend who hired the hurdy-gurdy, a typically whimsical fancy of Rachel's that went along with her love for music boxes, old dolls, and patchwork quilts. Priscilla also took some time before the wedding to punch holes in colored paper to use as confetti, another gesture sure to be appreciated by Rachel with her homespun tastes. Goldsmith goes on to describe how Rachel looked on that day:

Tall and strongly built, she had the white skin which is the envy of girls who do not have auburn hair. It's easy to imagine that hair glinting in the June sunshine, and her gray-blue eyes luminous with happiness. The skirt of her blue crepe gown gave an extra happy swing as she turned to smile at the hurdy-gurdy man, and to throw him one of her wedding roses. She had the sort of smile that goes deep back into the eyes and warms the person who shares it. Whatever was hers to share she shared in full measure. As she said in Time Out of Mind, "No matter how much of my love I spent, there was always more in me that could possibly be put to use."

Rachel and Arthur headed for Sutton Island shortly after they married, with their long-term plans uncertain. She wrote from Sutton Island that summer to an absent island friend, Rosamund Lamb, extending her thanks for Rosamund's praise for *Time Out of Mind*. Then she went on with characteristic animation with her news, plans, and descriptive anecdotes, offering an inside view of Rachel's early married state.

What a lovely letter from you! And how welcome it was in the old green Island mailbag that Kenneth Bunker brought over one day last week. You were one of the friends I had particularly wanted to write to about my marriage. . . .

I am happier than you can possibly guess at what you say of "Time Out of Mind." Yes, you know the state I was in about it last January and I can hardly yet believe that people feel the way they do about it. I didn't believe it had a chance after "Mary Peters" [a popular novel by Mary Ellen Chase] came first, but it just goes to show we must put what we have on paper and not worry about what will go or not go. But praise from an Island neighbor is sweet and means more to me than what any critic can say. I've been working on that book in my mind for nearly a dozen years and it was a year getting on paper in the present version. I feel "dreened dry," as Jim would say, but I am very happy about it and the sale to Universal Pictures was what really made our marriage possible. . . .

Now we're just taking the summer here quietly and happily on Sutton and we're not yet sure of next fall's plans. . . . I'm sure you will like [Arthur], for he is a dear and very social and interested in people. He comes of Swedish stock, though his family settled in Minn. and he was born and brought up in St. Paul. But he loves New England, especially Boston which quite took him by storm a few years ago. Also you'll approve of him when I tell you that on our first walk around Sutton he decided that he liked your point best, next to the view from our piazza. We came straight here in my Ford from our very simple little wedding in New York stopping with friends along the way at Narragansett and Wiscasset and the weather did its best and was blue and beautiful for us for ten whole days. We spent a good part of our honeymoon here, rather unromantically I'm afraid, for we cleaned this house from top to bottom and Arthur could hardly be parted from a mop he bought at Seal Harbor. My mother and aunt got here Saturday, just ahead of an Easterly blow which has been going it ever since. A and I hope to be here most of the summer except for several short motor trips to visit friends along the coast and in Nova Scotia.

In spite of their uncertain plans, Rachel's life with Arthur moved her toward a security and solidity that she had never yet known. Her well-considered love for Arthur is a stark contrast to the fiery passion she once effused over Lyle. For better or for worse, her love affair with Lyle was profoundly transformative, and its imprint upon her psyche was permanent. As she wrote to Lyle in spring 1935, before her wedding, "Growth is apt to be painful and discouraging, I guess, but it has to be." She had come to a point in her life where she could appreciate the growth that sprang from her pain.

Two years after their marriage, Rachel and Arthur coauthored a novel about a newly married couple, "Dora" and "Ham," who move to Hollywood to try their luck in the film industry. *To See Ourselves* did not achieve the popularity of Rachel's other novels, but it paints a picture that surely contains aspects of Rachel and Arthur's early life together. There is the cross-country drive to California, the homey, suburban flavor of Hollywood in the 1930s, the brushes with celebrity, and the transience of work. The newly married couple experiences the joys and the conflicts in discovering each other and learning to live together—the simple treasure of a shared meal, the secret wonder of a shared bed, Dora's hope for children, Ham's perpetual sense of his failure to be a provider. The book even reveals, perhaps, some lingering angst over Lyle Saxon.

The character Nick Ames is "authoritative, swift, and on the way to big places" in Hollywood. He is also Ham's friend, the promising connection that brought the couple to California. It is Nick who opens up opportunities for Ham to get his foot in the door of the writing world, then wishes him luck. Though the character of Nick is subtly handled, probably to keep the book from being rejected, it is clear to a modern reader that Nick is a homosexual.

Nick's Hollywood success is a source of perpetual envy for Dora and Ham, who struggle mightily to make ends meet and end up leaving Hollywood by the end of the book (just as Rachel and Arthur would leave Hollywood after their first year there). To Dora and Ham, Nick appears to have everything—renown, friends, money. Near the end of the book, Dora goes to visit Nick at his Hollywood studio to pour out her worries about her husband and is surprised to find Nick looking terrible. Nick's former roommate and close friend, a man named Stanley, has just moved away to New York, and Nick is looking harried and haunted. When I read the following intimate scene, I had to wonder if I was seeing shadows of a one-time interchange between Rachel Field and Lyle Saxon.

> "Nick!" Impulsively she touched his hand that lay on the desk between them. "You look tired and not too gay. What is it?"
>
> "Nothing very exceptional." He shrugged and looked away. "I don't seem to be getting along with myself very well these days. That's all. What about you?"

Dora goes on to confess that Ham has had difficulty finding work. Ham has become disappointed to the point of despair, sometimes drunkenness, and she fears he might do worse to himself. Nick assures Dora that Ham would never do such a thing, because of his love for Dora. Dora is startled to discover that the tables are turned—Nick is envious of the two of them.

"Two people together the way you two are—why, you've got everything."

"We do love each other but sometimes I think if he wasn't anchored to me—"

"Anchors don't pull you down. They keep you from drifting," he broke in. "A person alone can do things of course, but it's only half a life. Two together make something different again. You ought to know, m'dear." His voice thickened, but his eyes still held hers in a strained and anxious plea. "That's what it is to be married if it's the real thing."—

"Nick, if you feel this way, why don't you—There isn't any girl who wouldn't . . ."

But he cut her short. For a moment his hands were busy straightening a pile of papers before he spoke.

"That's the trouble, Buttercup," he said quietly; "there isn't any girl."

He turned back to her with a deprecating shrug. A smile moved his lips, but the pain in his eyes troubled her. Again she picked up those signals of personal distress. Cross currents of despair met and mingled between them. She could only guess at his, and he at hers. They could do nothing for each other, and yet there was comfort in sharing mutual misery.

Mutual misery may well have been the end result of Lyle and Rachel's relationship. The profound heartbreak that Lyle is reported to have suffered during his New York years may, in fact, have been over Rachel Field, albeit not in the traditional sense of heartbreak. I imagine Lyle and Rachel as soulmates. Rachel was deeply in love with Lyle Saxon. Lyle loved Rachel Field, but not in a reciprocal way that could offer them both fulfillment. His divided attentions are evident in a letter he received from Joe Titzell, a mutual friend of Lyle and Rachel's. In a letter that opens with thanks for Lyle's long letter, Joe interrupts his own train of thought with this:

> Interlude: Rachel just telephoned. I carefully asked her if she had heard from you before I mentioned my letter. When she sadly said she hadn't I said I'd had a tiny note in answer to an insistent demand that you inform me if you were sick. So don't mention having written me a long letter.

However, it is possible that Lyle might have tried to corral his feelings for Rachel in a direction they simply could not go. The realization of that impossibility, and of his own sexual identity that he couldn't wish away, might have been even more wrenching than Rachel's more traditional heartbreak. Rachel and Lyle were star-crossed lovers of a particular sort; the two loves they had for each other were incompatible, in the end. That would explain the warm friendship that carried forward in Rachel's letters. Her hurt was deep, but she recognized Lyle's pain as well—"There was comfort in sharing mutual misery."

Rachel's pre-wedding letter to Lyle in 1935 goes on at great length with outpourings of sincere wistfulness unique to Rachel's Lyle Saxon communications. The intimacy of her writing summons an image of Rachel at her typewriter, sitting quietly for long stretches of time between each paragraph, thinking hard about exactly how much to say and how to say it. It feels as though she is writing the conclusion, at last, to a long-unfinished story, mending fences after years of harboring a deep-rooted pain. Rachel reveals the lingering power of Lyle's chapter in her life, despite her attempt at denial, in "A Rhyme for Greenwich Village," published years later in *Fear Is the Thorn*: "At Christopher and Gay Streets / My knees began to shake, / And I gave the organ-man a dime / For old time's sake."

Over the ensuing years Lyle continued to receive scattered letters from both Rachel and Arthur. Arthur's were mostly business. Rachel's were warm, newsy, full of talk about Lyle's work and her own. None of them ever raised the specter of the past again, like the one she wrote to Lyle on the eve of her marriage to another man. It seems, in writing that letter, that before she locked the door forever on her heart's doomed effusions of love for Lyle, she desired one last free expression of an intensity of feeling she might never know again.

I loved your description of reading my book in your cabin and how the sun came up and you heard the coffee being made in the big house and the sounds of morning all over the plantation. I loved your description of the garden, and the white cat and kittens by the blue delphinium. You gave the whole place back to me in that sentence or two and I felt again so much that I felt all through that marvelous week of going about Louisiana with you. I don't suppose I shall ever feel just that way again in my whole life, because I shall never be the person I was that summer, and so much that is beautiful and so much that can still hurt me to the core is all bound up with that time.

My very dear Rachel,

Even knowing the pain that preceded your marriage, or maybe because of knowing it, I am, even today, so giddily happy for you, happy that you found in Arthur this elusive grail that you'd sought for so long—this solid, grounded love that was made to last. There is no question that your star was on the rise; your love life and your fame came to fruition all at once. Did it diminish your "edge" as a writer, as Ruth Feis once suggested? Perhaps, but who cares? Your goal was never to develop a hard edge anyway; that is not what drew in those who loved your voice on the page. What are we here for, after all, but to love and be loved?

In shared hopefulness,
Robin

t w e l v e

Newlyweds and Nomads

After their wedding in June 1935, Rachel and Arthur packed up Rachel's Ford (she had replaced the old Whippet), plunked Trotty in the back seat, and made the several days' trip to Sutton Island. Though Rachel's mother and Aunt Kitty usually made the annual Sutton trip with her, they delayed their arrival for two weeks that year, presumably in order to give the new couple some time on their own.

In Rachel's letters during that honeymoon period, she makes liberal use of the first-person-plural pronoun. In her "we" one hears her pleasure in being no longer one, but part of a couple.

I wish now that I'd made you and Dale come to our wedding—and even S. G. though at the time I felt I <u>couldn't</u> quite steel myself to that. It was a nice wedding and everyone seemed to approve and as far as I know nobody cried.

We've had a perfect trip and people have been wonderful
to us all along the way—loaning us houses all fixed up
with fires and flowers and food and drink—our only anxiety is that we can't possibly live up to what is expected of
a newly wedded pair! But we're doing our best. The Island is heavenly—I need say no more.

Rachel always had strong leanings toward domesticity that
stood in contrast to her disciplined professionalism as a writer.
She liked to tell interviewers that she was in her most natural element when she was hooking rugs by a fire, making a patchwork
quilt, hand-coloring pictures for a book, berry picking, or cooking
up a pot of New England fish chowder. As a newly married
woman, Rachel may well have relished the concept of being a wife
and homemaker. In practice, however, at age forty, Rachel would
not easily shed her long-cultivated drive toward professional productivity and success. She had carried the responsibility of supporting herself, her mother, her aunt, and her sister throughout
her adulthood and during the years of the Great Depression. Certainly Rachel's family and society connections provided her with
great privilege in contacts and opportunities, but not so much in
money. It was the combination of Rachel's talent, her dogged
tenacity, her work ethic, and her irresistible charm that won her
hearts and contracts. Perhaps it was only circumstance that put
Rachel in the caregiver role for so many, or perhaps it was in her
genetic makeup. Either way, by 1935, she was fully entrenched in
the role. It is no surprise that she ended up marrying a man who
needed support and encouragement.

Part of what Rachel offered Arthur was simply her love, respect, and admiration. Rachel's mother once wrote that her

daughter looked up to Arthur and depended greatly on his counsel and his opinions. There likely remained a lingering strain of
self-doubt in Rachel too. How could a man so young, dashing,
and desirable fall in love with the matronly, "square-rigged"
Rachel Field? Whatever the nature of the attraction between
Rachel and Arthur, it seemed to be mutual and genuine. Rachel's
life, at the onset of her fifth decade, was looking as sunny in its
prospects as it ever had, in spite of her husband's uncertain employment.

Rachel's honeymoon letters strike her usual balance between
the poetic and the practical, discussing several options that she and
Arthur were considering for their future. Some of her written descriptions of Arthur sound a bit overly convincing, as though she is
still trying to reassure her friends that her choice to marry this un-
employed, unpedigreed actor was sound. She mentions her own
Hollywood prospects in passing but gives more attention to
Arthur's career, such as it was. As much as both Rachel and Arthur
might have aspired to a traditional household arrangement where
Arthur provided the steady income, his work life stuttered on and
off throughout their marriage.

The summer is slipping away "like a knotless thread" as
an old fish woman who worked for us used to say. I can't
realize August is only a few days off. It's been a happy and
utterly relaxing time and A and I haven't a regret for not
rushing off on a longer trip. We needed this longer, less
intensive summer to get caught up and A. hasn't had a
real vacation in ages. To be sure he will clean and chop
and heft and haul, but I can't find it in my heart to discourage that and we get short jaunts and swims at the

Seal Harbor pool. Next week we go on a week's junket up to Vermont to visit Anne Parrish.

Rachel and Arthur's future plans would remain uncertain for the next three and a half years. Hollywood periodically expressed hints of interest in Rachel's work, and Arthur was open to working on either coast, so the couple kept one eye on California and the other on New York for a long stretch of nomadic living. Rachel wrote to Prentiss Taylor near the end of their honeymoon summer on Sutton Island.

As things look now we expect to be back on East Tenth Street in late Sept.—California hasn't materialized so far and I'm really ever so relieved (to be perfectly candid) though it would have been a good chance for Arthur to get West Coast studio experience. We've taken the old apartment at "111" that Mother, Aunt K and I used to have and we got it for only a little more than I was paying for my old one—It has a nice big living room on the garden; what used to be my back bedroom is now a real kitchen and there are two bedrooms in front,—The smaller of which I can use for a work-room (if I ever manage to do any work again which seems unlikely to me at present!) Doubtless we'll no sooner get ourselves and our things settled in it than the call to California will come and we'll have to sublet. But at least it will be an easy transfer of possession.

The call to California did come, but not for nearly a year. Rachel took the uncertainty in stride with her characteristic combination of optimism and practicality, determined to enjoy her new husband and the bliss of Sutton Island while she could. She talks at length in another late-summer letter to Prentiss about a Stockbridge-based novel (*For Life*, by Natalie Colby) she recently received from a publisher: "Well, it's terrible and I'm thankful I'm not reviewing it." She goes on to talk business, revealing more evidence of growth in her self-assuredness. Although she still expresses humility and playful self-deprecation, those qualities are countered with a clear sense that Rachel is taking herself more seriously as a professional, even beginning to exercise a shrewd business sense with regard to the future success of her career as a writer.

Not a lick of work have I done all summer, but now I must begin working on a lecture which I'm to give at Camden, Maine on Sept. 6th. It's a paid one and if I'm going to do others after January, I might as well get broken in here before a friendly audience. But I rather dread it—I've been terribly lucky to have "Time Out of Mind" keep on selling well all summer. It frightens me, rather, for the more it sells the more sure I am it was some lucky fluke and I can never hit the bull's eye again. But I suppose everyone feels so about things. It's all a mystery,— what goes and what doesn't. But thank heaven, this did. The picture production, I hear, has been held up because the principals are scheduled to do other pictures first. I'd just as soon it was delayed for that may re-stimulate interest later on when the sales drop. . . .

The Island has never been so lovely and there never was such a prolific year for blueberries, cranberries and apples. It's been warmer than I remember it in many seasons and we've been swimming a lot in a tide-water pool the other side of the Island. An idyllic place with trees wading in their own reflection at high tide and gulls overhead and the topsails of vessels going by outside the wall of small stones.

This is a stupid letter, though the thanks it takes you are none the less real and deep—as ever,

Rachel

One Friday in early September, Rachel and Arthur drove to Camden for her talk. A review of the event appeared later in the Rockland *Courier-Gazette.*

Rachel Field, a magical name to be added to my Hall of Fame; a jewel to be laid away in my treasure trove of priceless memories. Rachel Field, author of many children's stories, among them "Hitty," a winner of the Newbery medal, poems of rare loveliness, and in more recent years "God's Pocket" and "Time Out of Mind" which remains at the head of the best sellers after many months and has taken the young author far up on the ladder of success. . . .

It was from Sutton she motored up to Camden the other afternoon to address the Maine Library Association meeting and it was my great privilege to hear her. She came to Camden with her husband, a blond giant with so much distinctive personality that one cannot imagine speaking of him as "Rachel Field's husband." His name is Arthur Pedersen [*sic*].

Rachel Field is young and lovely. Dark auburn hair curling back from her face and caught in a soft knot at the nape of her neck. Vivid blue eyes, very white teeth. A warm glowing face. To me she conveyed a composite picture of Hedwig Benedict and Ethel Lee Hayden, interesting? She was wearing a blue knitted suit, one of those heavenly blues so popular this season; her hat was a darker blue felt.

The reviewer goes on in great detail, repeating Rachel's "delightful" anecdotes about how each of her books came to be and her comparison of writing to baking a cake or berry picking. Rave reviews like this one helped guarantee that Rachel, despite her domestic leanings, would be on the road a great deal in the coming years.

For the remainder of 1935 and early 1936, Rachel and Arthur sought work and settled into their new life as a married couple amongst their familiar circles, back in lower Manhattan. Rachel's time was largely taken up with book tours and talks. Despite her habitual dread of giving speeches, her aversion gradually abated, perhaps as she came to recognize her gift for winning a crowd— or, I should say, rediscovered her gift. The skill she had summoned up to play the roles of Shylock and Rebecca as a nine-year-old reemerged to serve her well as a professional public speaker. Not only did she have a pleasing, melodic voice and an engaging presence, she also spoke with natural candor, modesty, and a sense of humor that gave each member of her audience the sense of being her personal friend. "In talking of her auctorial adventures from a platform," wrote one journalist, "Rachel Field does not become the oracle, or even the priestess speaking the oracle's wisdom. She has the pleasant gift of diminishing the proportions of a recital hall so that it seems to be a small room, suitable for an intimate conversation between two people."

In Rachel's interviews, we begin to see a particular aspect of her growing appeal—she was an enthusiastic advocate for the role of "simple housewife," a role played by the vast majority of her female audience of the time. As a married woman, Rachel gained the credibility of being an everywoman, unspoiled by her stardom in the literary world. That ability to remain familiar, even amid her fame and success, was at the heart of Rachel's wide appeal. The fact that Rachel could cook became a significant talking point in many write-ups about the emerging authoress. Another charming circumstance brought to light in this particular story is Arthur's great pride in and admiration for his wife, which he shares enthusiastically (almost defensively) with Rachel's interviewer.

> Miss Field plays many roles. She is a writer of fiction and non-fiction, writes children's books and poetry; she does bookbinding; she is a splendid cook; she makes hooked rugs; sews, draws, illustrating some of her own books; paints; she is a dramatist; does silhouettes; raises flowers; runs a home—these are but a few of her accomplishments. . . .
>
> Asked about her culinary ability, Miss Field shrugged. "I'm just a plain cook," she said. "I don't care much about fancy dishes. Whenever I want to cook something I open a cookbook and find a suitable recipe. If I don't happen to have the required ingredients in the house I experiment, and employ substitute ingredients, just change the recipe to suit myself. Fish chowder, however, is my specialty."

This literary woman was reminded that as an author she was not supposed according to popular belief, to be a "homey" kind of woman pre-occupied with household tasks and cooking.

"That's all rubbish," Miss Field replied. "Why shouldn't a writer be a good cook, too? All the writers I know are. Inez Haynes Irwin, for example; and I have heard from one of her sons that Mary Roberts Rinehart is a particularly fine cook.

"Creative women bring imagination to the business of cookery: besides, they know the value of good food, and its importance in the scheme of things and they also know the value of time. So they work quickly and efficiently. They turn out unusual and appetizing dishes in no time at all, in more or less effortless fashion, and without undue waste."

"Rachel loves picnics," said Mr. Pederson as the conversation led from cooking to amusements. "And she also likes to go berry picking or on a mushroom-picking jaunt, or simply out in the garden to plant some new kind of flower or bulb. Between times she works with great speed on hooked rugs."

He urged her to show her latest rug, not quite completed. . . .

"She finds all these varied activities stimulating," continued Mr. Pederson. "They do not interfere with her main business of writing, nor does the writing interfere with her domestic tasks. She finds plenty of additional time, too, to travel, drive a car, and make collections of old music boxes and antique dolls and doll-house furnishings."

Mr. Pederson set all the old French, Dutch, and Spanish music boxes to playing and the tinkling medley was charming. Several of the boxes had scenes under glass: a baby in a cradle; a rustic setting with windmill whirling, cows grazing.

After we hear details about Rachel's doll collection, the article concludes:

"Change—stimulation—freedom from monotony, that's what the creative mind needs," says Mr. Pederson wisely. "It's all nonsense to say that a woman cannot bake and keep house because she can write books. My wife does both, and has a dozen other accomplishments, to say nothing of hobbies and diversions in addition."

So went Rachel and Arthur's first year of marriage. Rachel traveled extensively as a professional speaker, sometimes joined by her husband, and received prolific press coverage around the country. Perhaps she and Arthur were almost grateful to be knocked down in December by a terrible flu, which kept them home together in New York for a couple of weeks around the holidays. Early in 1936, however, Rachel was on the road again for a two-week lecture tour of the Midwest, in the midst of a frigid cold snap. She wrote to Prentiss about the event.

I've been far afield since I saw you and the cold wave began exactly as I pulled out of the Grand Central for my Middle Western tour—Two weeks of below zero weather and St. Paul treated me to 37 below. A. went out ahead and we met there and stayed at his father's—that is an experience I'd never be able to write—it needs telling— Then we re-met in Chicago where we had a very gay time between lectures—I'm back now for the Spring except for a few scattered dates and I hope to get some writing done at last.

In spite of the grueling speaking schedule, Rachel continued to produce some of her finest work. In March 1936, she published her richest and most deeply emotional collection of poetry. Although there is no direct acknowledgment of Lyle Saxon in the book, Rachel's journals, letters, and private notebooks hold the proof that many of the poems in *Fear Is the Thorn* were lifted from that period of intense passion and heartbreak over her unrequited love affair. It was during that same period that Rachel wrote about Cally and Hugh (in the unpublished manuscript *Plenty of Time*), the ache of growing old without a life partner, and an unrealized longing for motherhood. These poems, inspired by her reading of Emily Dickinson and the letters she poured forth to Lyle, express a terrible angst in response to time, beauty, and the poet's exclusion from the world's cruelly abundant fertility.

Because of the delay between composition and publication, a chronological layout of a writer's life can seem contradictory. Here, in the midst of her blooming happiness, it seems incongruous to see Rachel's most pain-filled, emotional work appear in print. Ruth Feis, some time after the publication of *Fear Is the Thorn*, wrote about the change in Rachel's writerly voice in her journal. In typically blunt fashion, she expresses regret that Rachel might have lost her incisive writer's edge, even knowing that edge came from unhappiness: "Rachel is a masterpiece. She adores Arthur so that some of her fire and poetry is dimmed, but anyway, she's happy, and Larry says that's worth more than poetry. Still, rereading some of <u>Fear is the Thorn</u>, I am unconvinced."

The material in *Fear Is the Thorn* was born of an earlier period in Rachel's life, and yet the awareness of pain and loss that grew from that time continued to inform her experience in the years that followed. She still had a husband prone to ennui and self-disdain, which he sometimes quelled with alcohol. She still felt the ache of desire for a seemingly inaccessible motherhood. The deepest chasms of Rachel's lonely heart, however, were filled with Arthur's love. Meanwhile, Rachel's consistent writing practice brought her steadily growing recognition.

In May 1936, *Time Out of Mind* won the National Book Award. That likely prompted the "call to California" which finally materialized for Rachel the following month. The film version of *Time Out of Mind* suddenly showed more promise, so the Pedersons packed up their car for the cross-country trek to Los Angeles. They did not know how far their Hollywood venture would take them—a few months? Longer? In any case, they left for the West Coast in June, resigning themselves to the capricious nature of Hollywood and the likelihood of a summer with no visit to Sutton Island.

In her early letters from California, Rachel recounts their westward journey, gushing over the beauty and fascination she felt particularly for the coast of Oregon and for San Francisco.

The coast was so like a higher, wilder, young Maine, with the same trees growing down the headlands to the lonely beaches of the Pacific, and miles and miles and miles of curving road with no sign of life except nibbling sheep.

The redwoods were unbelievable, like finding oneself in the set of an outdoor Wagner opera, and I loved San Francisco more than ever. That is my favorite American city, almost my favorite city anywhere. It has the stimulating cosmopolitan quality of NY with a feeling of the west and a queer mingling of the east and china and japan and italy and france (excuse lack of caps, but I am getting used to a new typewriter and the caps annoy me, so you won't mind).

Many of Rachel's sentiments about Oregon and San Francisco were reproduced in the book she and Arthur cowrote the following year, when they were back on the East Coast. Hollywood itself held less instant appeal, but it was also full of surprises for both her and Arthur during that first summer and fall. Rachel's agent, Rosalie Stewart, was representing Rachel's interests in Hollywood. She would later become Arthur's employer, but during this first California junket, in 1936, Arthur had hopes of entering the acting scene again. Jobs for both of them continued to hold only temporary promise. Rachel tells her story best in her correspondence. Here is a letter to Rosamund Lamb:

I can't tell you how touched and pleased Arthur and I were by your thought of us. Soon now, you will be leaving all that loveliness and another Sutton summer will be over. I have missed it so, but I suppose there must be gaps sometimes and this was the time for mine. We are being very social and having fun here but we don't know just yet exactly where we are or what we're supposed to be doing out here. I came out because the company that bought "Time Out of Mind" expected to do it with a certain producer part of this summer. But he stayed away in England till now and apparently doesn't want to do it now he is back, so whether I shall work on it or not is extremely doubtful. But I have several other irons in the fire and may sell one of my earlier juveniles, so if that should happen our being out here would have been well worth while. I hope to know in a short time and that will decide when we shall return. At the earliest it could not be until around early November because I took on some lectures here in October and several in the Middle West for late Oct. and early November so I shall lose another New England Fall.

It was so good to hear news of the Island, of you three and Jim and that the apples on the trees by the old garden are ripening. I can smell them this minute and I suppose the crickets have started in their fall chorus. They usually begin with punctuality the last day of August. They keep it up apparently all the time out here, and it's rather disconcerting to hear them and strange birds singing in the small hours of the morning or even around midnight. . . . We have a nice little kitchen and small dining alcove so I can cook if I want to and I have even made chowder. But it hasn't the flavor of the Maine coast kind or even the NY variety.

To Louise Seaman Bechtel, Rachel writes:

We've been here nearly six weeks, in Hollywood, I mean and I can't say I would choose it as a summer resort. Still, we're very comfortable in this apt. hotel and our living room looks out on a pleasant green patio with a fountain and dogs are made welcome which is more than can be said of some places. Trot has been a fine little traveler. . . .

So far we have nothing of financial importance to tell you. Rosalie Stewart takes us round to studio upon studio and we try to sell ourselves and our wares. No luck so far, but there is quite a bit of interest in a play that A and I wrote together last winter so we still have hopes of selling that. The situation as to material for juvenile stars is amusing. Here I am supposed to be the top in that line and I can't get anyone interested in ideas for originals for Shirley Temple, or Freddie Bartholomew or Anne Shirley or the rest. If you talk about redoing some juvenile classic that would be perfect (such as "Heidi") they tell you it would never do for this or that reason and if you explain that you could easily change that, they are just as doubting. . . .

I don't really care so much for myself, though of course, it would be fun to get a chance and make some money. But I do want so much to have Arthur tie up with some studio and it's so hard to break in unless you are related by marriage to Mr. Louis B. Mayer or Mr. Samuel Goldwyn. However, we really haven't given ourselves much time and I suppose as soon as we get all packed and ready to turn East again something will break.

It really is lots of fun going and seeing the different studios and directors in action and whether we go back or stay I am sure I've tucked away some ideas that will work into a book or something later on. It is a crazy place all right and I wouldn't stay here unless I were a success for anything. But at least it's being excellent for my driving. I used to be terrified of traffic but you should see me now plunging into perfect jungles of cars on Hollywood and Sunset Boulevards and then even braved the traffic and went in to Los Angeles to see the opening of the new George Kelly play with Tallulah Bankhead. . . .

If A. got a job and I could have a house of my own somewhere I think I might enjoy life here very much.

Rachel goes on to report to Louise of more personal concerns:

I loved what you wrote of the Stewart baby but it would finish me to see her. The only way I stand it is by shunning them because they make me pine so. I haven't entirely given up hope but I really almost have in my own mind and I suppose I might just as well get over hoping. Why should I, out of all the world, expect to have what I want most from life? I certainly shouldn't when I see nearly everyone wishing for the unattainable, only I suppose nature or something turns our surplus energy into wanting what we can't have. No more of that for the present. I guess I'd better just heave all the old gland pills overboard and try and think of something else.

She finishes with characteristic deference to Arthur.

As things look now we'll stay out here anyway till late October then if we come east I will do some lectures on the way back and we'll return to Tenth Street in early

November. I want to give this place every chance on A's account, it would be so grand if he could land anything at all.

By the end of September, Arthur had found some work, and the couple's prospects seemed to be shifting. The possibility of a longer stay in California was growing, as was Rachel's appreciation for the quirky personality of the town. Some of her observations betray a disturbingly racist outlook, especially to a twenty-first century reader. As progressive as Rachel may have been in some ways, she was the product of her era and her privilege. She writes to her friend Prentiss Taylor:

> The heart of Hollywood is rather, to be exact, like a southern suburban city where people go marketing with big paper bags and dogs and where they pile their cars full of household equipment and Philopino's [sic] make grotesque arrangements of their gardening paraphernalia on the runningboards and sides of their flimsy little second hand cars. All the intense heart throb of the place goes on, I guess, behind the studio walls and one seldom gets behind them. It is an unreal sort of place,—its reality is happening somewhere else, or rather perhaps it makes reality for other places to believe in. Anyway, it's not at all what I expected. Pleasanter and more simple in some ways, and more dull and childish in others. Of course there are obviously extra men and women in lemon yellow slacks and pea-green box coats and shorts and pajamas drifting about Hollywood Boulevard, but they are fewer and less objectionable than I expected and once

July got over and early August came the weather has been perfect. Cool nights and mornings, like Fall in Maine, and hot, sunny Septemberish days. They say it will be like this till Christmas.

Whether we'll be here that long I don't know yet, but we are happy that Arthur is working again. He started in last week in the story department of United Artists, one of the smaller studios here and he likes that part and the people he is with very much. It is somewhat in the nature of a trial for him and so we are not counting too much on its being permanent, especially here where things are less permanent than in any other place in the world probably, except perhaps in Spain at the present time. But A. is so glad to have this experience and in the end of the business that he wanted to be in, for he didn't feel strong enough to tackle the acting racket once more and have the breaking in and the long waits between. This job he has is small as pay goes, but as I say the experience is the important thing. . . . Arthur should be able to tell a little better how the job is working out by the end of October. I hope for his sake it will be for the winter, for though I shall miss my friends in NY if we stay out here for the winter, I could be very comfortable and really enjoy life out here for awhile. Apartments and bungalows are cheap and really very attractive. You can get furnished ones from thirty dollars up to around sixty five or more depending on the size and neighborhood, and one can take them from month to month which helps. Food is ridiculously cheap if you cook it yourself, though rather high and extremely poor in most restaurants. A car is essential, thank heaven we brought ours and I am getting to be pretty good in heavy traffic driving. So that is our history to date.

About her own work, Rachel reports to Prentiss that she is beginning to work on some new writing of her own for the first time in a while.

No one knows what is happening to "Time Out of Mind". When I left NY the office there expected that I would do some work on it when I got out, but I had no contract. However the Universal studio here took no notice of me save to say that they wanted no authors doing a thing on their own books. . . .

So I have just put the whole thing out of my mind and though my agent is trying to sell some of my other stuff, I am not taking the studios very seriously for myself, and am trying to get started once more on some other writing. Now that A. works from nine thirty in the morning till after six at night I can't complain that I have no time. I have hours and hours of uninterrupted time and I hope to get into harness again. I begin to feel a few ideas stirring in the dark of my mind once more.

By December, Rachel and Arthur have moved into a new place as their shifting fortunes continue.

We're in a little furnished house with a garden and fireplace and it's a vast improvement on cramped quarters at the Villa C. I really like being here now the weather is like October—cool nights and mornings when our woolens feel right and warm sunny days.

Arthur goes in and out of jobs as is the fashion here —at present he is "out" and we're planning to join friends in San Francisco for Xmas. Later he expects to be back in the story dept. again. I'm at work again on another book and find I can write as well here as anywhere now the start is made. Our Tenth Street place is sub-let by the month, so we've been very lucky all round. Hollywood is funny—very small town—or as Kaufman said—"Bridgeport with palms"—but we're enjoying it and NY really was no hardship to leave behind for me—only certain people in it and the theatres we miss.

Rachel and Arthur's first California sojourn ended in May 1937, just under a year from when they set out across the country. Since they had sublet their New York apartment, they moved in with Rachel's mother and Aunt Kitty in Farmington until it was time to head for Sutton Island. In her year's stay, Rachel's judgment of California shifted considerably. She began work on her next book, which would eventually become *All This and Heaven Too*, her most lucrative novel and a blockbuster entrée into the film industry. That breakthrough, however, was still over a year away. During these early years of Rachel and Arthur's marriage, the couple experienced their share of difficulties—financial, emotional, and relational.

Arthur's devotion to Rachel was profound and real. It was also fraught with a sense of inadequacy and self-hatred, the kind which can lead to self-destructive behavior. Several of Rachel's fictive male characters, beloved by her heroines, have character flaws that may have been shared by Arthur. Not only was Arthur known to drink to excess, but there are shadowy references to his having been a bit of a philanderer during the days preceding his relationship with Rachel, or even after they were a couple. In one of Ruth Feis's journal entries, Ruth tells of a visit from Elma Godchaux (nicknamed "Sprite") in 1934, about a year before Rachel and Arthur married but well into their "semi-engaged" period. "Sprite arrived. She was all agitated because Arthur, R's Arthur, had made a pass at her. I told her I thought she should not think much of it as she could not possibly be responsible." Though all evidence indicates that Arthur was staunchly faithful to Rachel after their marriage, it is plausible that Rachel could have had lingering worries over his behavior if he became depressed, inebriated, or both. Despite whatever growing pains the newly married couple faced, however, Rachel's optimistic practicality buoyed both Arthur and herself. Signs of her increasing enthusiasm for California and for the film industry begin to show in her correspondence, and every negative event is countered by a positive spin. Once again, she tells her own story best. "Letters have been almost impossible this winter," Rachel begins in a May 1937 letter to Prentiss, then explains why.

> First Arthur was laid up with a bad "flu" germ for most of January; then mother and aunt Kitty came for a month and the rainy season chose that period to come and then a solid month of one-night stands all over the middle west and Texas and since my return I've been trying to see all I can of California, keep house (which means all my own cooking etc.) and squeeze a little writing in. And then lately we've been sorting and packing for our East-

ward trek. We leave tomorrow in the new Ford:—Arthur, Trotty and me and two very nice friends from out here. . . .

We may be back here next Fall if a nibble that Arthur has should turn into a real bite with contract attached. We really have enjoyed it and having a house of our own and an all year round garden is exciting. Living is so cheap here and I'm constantly amazed and I should be happy to bring our things out and settle down for a bit. I've stayed clear of the studios, not from choice, but because they weren't interested and I find one can write as well here as anywhere except in mid-summer heat. One misses the theatre, newspapers and certain NY friends— otherwise we've felt no lack and don't believe any of the exaggerated things people tell you of Hollywood, it's a pleasant small town. I wish you could go marketing with me here—it's more exciting than any play!

We'll be in NY from about May 22 till the latter part of June when we expect to go to Maine for a couple of months at least. If A. gets the job then he'll have to return in August, but things are still uncertain. Arthur says the curse of the wandering Jew has been laid upon us, but we hope only temporarily.

Rachel's predictions came true through the summer of 1937, which she and Arthur spent on Sutton Island. While Rachel settled into her usual Sutton routine of working and enjoying the island, Arthur had editorial work for the Macmillan Company that he was able to do through the mail. Huge manuscript packets arrived and were dumped into the big green mailbag on the island's town dock. Arthur also made a trip of nearly three weeks back to New York City late that summer. Rachel's lighthearted references to Arthur's absence indicate a hint of loneliness, or even worry, over her husband. "Dear Charlotte," she writes to a New York friend on September 1, 1937, "Arthur will already have seen you and any news I might have would be old stuff by now." Rachel goes on to send her regards to Charlotte's husband, a colleague of Arthur's at Macmillan. In subsequent letters to Charlotte over the next three years, however, Rachel seems always to be expressing regrets over Charlotte's most recently ended marriage, offering congratulations on a new one, or both. Arthur sees Charlotte on trips to New York more often than Rachel does, but Rachel maintains a warmly friendly camaraderie with Charlotte on paper, full of support and hospitality, greetings to her cats, professional networking ideas, and offers to lend furniture from her New York apartment. If Rachel sees Charlotte as a threat, then she is using friendship as her weapon of defense.

If Arthur happens to be visiting with you when the mail brings this letter, you might remind him that he has an Island wife just in case he should forget her between now and September 16th!

Love from Trotty to you both—

Affectionately,
Rachel

To her friend Prentiss, Rachel reports from Sutton with more detail about her writing and their shifting plans.

This has not been a summer when letters flourished. Indeed it's been far too beautiful and far too busy a one for me to write much of anything and so I've neglected all my friends, my publishers and any public which may have once been mine! I make no apologies, simply say I've been far too busy seeing that there was food enough in the ice-box and storeroom and cooking it when meal times have come round. In between meals I've gone swimming and berrying, marketing and occasionally have got a page or two on paper. Arthur has been very busy all summer with the mss reading for MacMillan. Every week they expressed him huge tomes and he read and reported on over 30 manuscripts between July 1st and August 28th when he left the island to return to NY on business. He was very glad of the work and he enjoys it, but of course he had to keep right at it and only managed to snatch an hour here and there to himself in the days. But he was thankful to be out of town and it has been a rarely blue and perfect summer. We could swim almost every day and the Island has been its fairest. He hated to leave, but I shall be getting back to NY around September 16th as all the Islanders are leaving early this year and Mother cannot stay on after the piers get taken down. . . .

Arthur and I are still somewhat uncertain as to our abode this winter—We're continuing the 111 East 10th St. apartment, but as sure as we get it painted and are beginning to feel settled again, the summons will come to go West. Personally I'd like to go back to California. I love that State and the life, but I do want to know ahead and be able to plan my life and organize myself a little. A. and I must be under an uncertain star right now. We turned in the last chapters of our novel with the Hollywood background in early July and MacMillan plan to bring it out sometime in November. We aren't counting on much money from it or much critical notice generally, but it was good experience and I like certain bits of it quite well, though nothing I do has any reality for me once it's finished and on paper.

Rachel had spent much of that spring and early summer collaborating with Arthur on *To See Ourselves*, the story of the married couple Dora and Ham in Hollywood. Rachel's professional assessment of that project was lukewarm; even before the book was published, she mentioned it to friends almost apologetically. Her sense of what would be well received and what would not had become quite keen, and her letters suggest she knew that this collaboration was more a labor of love than a literary hit.

We have enjoyed collaborating and it's quite different from the usual Hollywood Cinderella success type. It's not at all the place one imagines, in fact it's an oddly staid and suburban small town dominated by a big industry.

Once this is off our minds I'll begin again on another novel I started last Fall, but that is one requiring considerable research and will take a long time to finish. This year was rather a broken one as far as writing was concerned because I had to be gone for 2 separate months of lecturing and I've crossed the continent <u>six</u> times in a year which doesn't make for long, uninterrupted spells of work. Still, I've enjoyed the change of scene and new places and people.

"To See Ourselves" is scheduled for early November and Arthur has got the pre-publication jitters badly. But I'm a hardened old war horse when it comes to that—I don't turn a hair when the gun-powder and smoke fill my nostrils. . . . Probably we'll take a bad beating if any critic notices our book, but no matter, it was a definite mood we tried to put over and the story is written sincerely and I'm not apologizing for it being in a different mood and manner from the things I've written before and alone. I'm tackling another long book of my own which is contracted to MacMillan for the Fall of 1938 if I can get it done in time. It needs much research, but I've made a fair start and it is beginning to carry me.

An interviewer from the *Christian Science Monitor* in Boston wrote about Rachel and Arthur's novel after its release, highlighting the fact that it contained a great many nonfictional elements. The review offers an interesting depiction of Rachel's character and the couple's process in collaboration.

The increasing disposition of people to read books which are both educational and entertaining is resulting in a surprising number of non-fiction books on the best-seller lists. It is a tendency which is pleasing even to writers of fiction like Rachel Field and Arthur Pederson, collaborators on "To See Ourselves" (Macmillan), in which they set out to prove that Hollywood is just another Main Street, more provincial than some Main Streets and as neighborly and simple at heart as any small town. There are not many stars in Mr. and Mrs. Pederson's book but there are a lot of soda clerks, grocery shop owners, and bungalow court dwellers.

Back in their own apartment, 'way east on Tenth street in New York City, they sat before an open fireplace the other day giving an excellent exhibition of collaboration in an interview.

They drove out to California, which accounts for some chapters in the book. They took their Scottie, which accounts for others. Miss Field had expected to work on the scenario of her "Time Out of Mind." But she didn't, which provided more material. And Mr. Pederson, who more or less went along for the ride, ended up as assistant story editor of one of the major film companies, which gave more grist for the writing mill.

No thrifty writer could possibly disregard all the incidents which practically dropped into their laps. The Pedersons started a notebook. Then they progressed to conversations, which developed into definite dialogue, and pretty soon they were outlining a new chapter each night. While Mr. Pederson was at the studio the next day, Miss Field wrote it all out in longhand. Then Mr. Pederson had a try at rewriting and typing. And so the book grew.

The Pedersons have a sense of humor, which was fortunate, for here was the name of the author of "God's Pocket" and "Time Out of Mind" meaning nothing to the butcher, the baker, or seemingly to the studio folk. What did happen, though, was that the shopkeepers liked the author for herself and their homely remarks went straight into the book.

The blunt reference to Arthur, "who more or less went along for the ride," belies the humility in Rachel's letters. She cites Arthur's prospects as their primary motive for moving to Hollywood, but it seems clear that it is Rachel's prospects that determine their path. On the other hand, there might well be truth in Rachel's claim; she is so devoted to her husband's happiness that, in her mind, it surely does take precedence over her own career to a great degree. The collaboration on a book that she knew would not be a hit is significant, but she is hopeful for the book's function to boost her husband and his career. One circumstance that becomes more evident in Rachel's letters in the summer of 1937 is Arthur's tendency toward anxiety and depression. In a rare moment of candor, she writes to a friend from Sutton Island about her concerns for Arthur's mental and emotional health. "Arthur has read six mss. in less than a week and got off reports on them this afternoon, so he feels a trifle exhausted. But I'm thankful the books have held up for it doesn't allow time for restlessness and depression to set in."

In addition to the nonfiction elements itemized in the above review of *To See Ourselves*, there were others that found their way into the novel. The book's insecure husband, Ham, despairs over his inability to make enough money to support his wife, Dora. He is jealous of her professional success and her social aptitude; he drinks to excess and causes uncomfortable and even upsetting scenes at home. Yet Ham and Dora also delight in each other, their dog, the stunning landscapes of the West, and the joyful wonder of discovering each other in their new roles as a couple. *To See Ourselves* is fiction, but there is no doubt that it presents a mood and memories that resonated in very personal ways with Rachel and Arthur Pederson. In fact, Rachel's ambivalence toward California was tilting increasingly toward attraction during

her summer back on the East Coast. The Pedersons were soon to
be back in their New York apartment, though for how long they
did not know.

> Arthur says I mustn't buy anything more for this place till
> we're a bit more cleared up (it's in a state of near collapse
> after our being away a year and a half and with three dif-
> ferent sets of tenants) and know what is on hand and per-
> haps by a miracle, settled into place again. . . . I envy you
> being in a <u>house</u> with a yard and garden these unbeliev-
> ably warm and beautiful fall days—I've come to hate N.Y.
> more than I care to admit. California made a complete
> Suburbanite out of me and I'm not ashamed to admit it.
> Also I miss the west. There seems infinitely more time to
> spare out there, though one seems to accomplish less in
> it. Also I miss being able to jump into my car and drive
> out to see the Pacific whenever I feel like it. Well, I realize
> I was a pretty provincial Easterner and the year out there
> widened my personal horizon tremendously wherever we
> eventually become anchored.

Rachel's rising career fortunes would soon grant her wish to
return to the Pacific coast, though other unmet yearnings lingered
with a haunting persistence.

Dear Rachel,

Hollywood has become a very different place from the one you knew. The whole world has become a different place, and I wish you could have seen a longer period of its evolution. You of all people knew the hurtful power of dismissiveness, yet still, you were guilty of that same cruelty. I like to believe that you would have evolved over time yourself. But you did not live long enough to have that opportunity, and I can only hope that I'm right.

I wanted to clear the air and tell you how I went through a stage of disillusionment about your character. I was so disappointed that I stopped working on your story for a while. After a time, though, I came to terms with it. Who is without flaws? Certainly not I. You were not perfect, but I believe your life and intentions all arced toward kindness.

Racist remarks aside, I loved learning about that slice of American history—1930s Hollywood—through your eyes. The first time I drove around Hollywood and Beverly Hills, in 2009, was all because of you. That was early on in my "Rachel Field treasure hunt," which is how I began to think of my research into your life. In that particular year my daughter's college softball team spent their spring break training in southern California. Most of the parents came along on these trips to cheer their daughters on, provide transportation, and feed the girls during those marathon multigame days. So I had the perfect reason for making the trip. My children opened up my life to many of the paths that led to my writing. That was a benefit of motherhood I never anticipated, but one that I cherish. Rachel, as much as I envy your writing successes, you also reinforced in my mind the treasure I had in my offspring.

Your longing for children helped me appreciate that we each must value the gifts that come our way.

The unfolding of circumstances that "just so happened" to fit perfectly with my research became almost commonplace. What unknowable forces kept leading me along this path? In any case, it also just so happened that my niece was living in Los Angeles for that one year as well, and she gave me a place to stay for two days while I haunted all of the places you lived and frequented during that stretch of time when you came and went from California, then finally settled down to stay.

I visited the houses and neighborhoods where you lived during all your comings and goings: the Villa Carlotta, at 5959 Franklin Avenue; 909 N. Orlando Avenue; 915 N. Orlando Avenue; 1544 N. Crescent Heights Boulevard; 714 N. Camden Drive. Your homes increased in beauty each time you moved, in Hollywood and then finally to Beverly Hills. I suppose it's a testament to your increasing success, as well as your growing attachment to this whole new world on the opposite coast. I took a walk down the quiet street from your last house on Camden Drive to the famous Rodeo Drive, with its luxury shops and famed extravagance. Then I walked by a lovely park to the Beverly Hills public library. Did you walk that same quiet neighborhood, breathing in the California sunshine with hopefulness? You still had so much to hope for.

Always,
Robin

t h i r t e e n

Not Every Bud May Bear

T ime played a central role in Rachel's work, and it's clear the pressures of time's relentless passage played increasingly upon her heart as the years ticked away. In her poem "Old Gardener Time," time wields a broom, "sweeping the gold and gay" from the world.

> Warm is my pillow and dreams beguile.
> I lie secure in a quiet room,—
> But Old Gardener Time is abroad to-night
> In the frosty dark with his tireless broom.

Rachel's life was intertwined with Ruth Feis's in several ways during that fall of 1937, both in person and in print. Ruth writes with relish about reading *To See Ourselves*, which she picked up at the Francis Scott Key Bookshop near her home in Washington, DC. "I read at a gallop all evening until late at night, quite carried away." This is impressive praise from Ruth, a highly judgmental critic of both personal and literary presentation. She admitted that it was "light . . . of course, but it appealed to me. And I saw R's and A's trip out there—their hopefulness, the small people, little people—of drugstore and delicatessen, done with the touching homespun way Rachel can do it."

Rachel was happy in love at last. However, there remained another unfulfilled love in her heart: the longing to have a child. No one was more intimately connected to Rachel in this particular wish than Ruth. In their exchanged letters over the course of many years, beginning long before Rachel's marriage, Ruth and Rachel expressed to each other a shared ache of longing. Both women yearned for children. Although Ruth had married Herbert Feis in 1922, twelve years later she still had no child, a fact which pained her. In shared misery, the two women simultaneously swooned and despaired over their encounters with other people's babies. In April 1933, Rachel writes to Ruth:

> I've just been over seeing Pamela Bianco's beautiful little red-haired baby—almost a year old, so you can guess the state I'm in as a result. Perhaps it's as well we haven't any. We couldn't take them as casually as they should be taken, could we, Ruth? Still I shouldn't mind trying.

Ruth and her husband finally adopted a baby girl in the fall of 1934, just after Ruth's long summer visit to Sutton Island. In her letters to Ruth, Rachel gushed with excitement over baby Felicia, thrilled on her friend's behalf. After the two women reignited their intimate friendship during their summer together, Ruth became a central part of Rachel's quest for motherhood—which might have begun, it appears, even before her wedding. In this June 1935 entry from one of Ruth's journals, Ruth writes about a visit from Rachel and Arthur at her summer place in Wiscasset,

Maine. The visit took place during the month following Rachel's wedding, when Ruth was meeting Arthur for the first time.

> Rachel's visit—She and Arthur arrived one afternoon about four—And we went swimming at Montsweep, it being too hot to breathe nearly. Rachel looks <u>lovely</u>. Arthur is natural outgoing and attractive. He listens a great deal, but when he speaks says something honest and perceptive. Poor Rachel begins to fear she won't have a child. And is miserable over it. I know her dismay only too well! She took some pictures of Felicia, which later proved the best yet.

If Rachel feared an inability to conceive a child during the first month after her wedding, it suggests the possibility that she had been hoping for a pregnancy since well before the marriage. At forty years old, Rachel's longing for motherhood was intensified by time's ticking clock. Her books and poetry constantly revisit the idea of time's relentlessness, the passing of opportunity, the ache of change and loss. Though we can only speculate, it seems plausible that this maturing, self-assured Rachel, accosted by a sense of limited time, might have secretly hoped for a pregnancy that would accelerate her wedding plans with Arthur. One might even say it indicates the strength of her convictions—both as regards Arthur as a husband and herself as a mother. Premarital sex would have been judged harshly by many echelons of her contemporary society, but Rachel's more progressive friends would likely have applauded her liberation from the social strictures against which she had chafed for so much of her life, just as her heroine Kate Fernald had done in *Time Out of Mind*. As an adult entering middle age, Rachel was a more assertive and confident woman, more likely to follow the rightness in her heart rather than the rightness of some elitist social code.

Rachel visited Ruth in Washington, DC, on several occasions during the early years of her marriage. Her visits to DC sometimes meant a speaking engagement and sometimes meant research for a novel at the Library of Congress. In October 1937, however, Ruth's journal indicates there was something more personal on Rachel's agenda. "Rachel arrived at 2:30 and we both napped, gossiping and talking til time for her to go to the doctor's. I waited til almost 6—then called up and she wasn't through and said not to wait."

Ten days earlier Rachel had written to Ruth about a subject near and dear to her heart—her persistent hopes to bear a child. Ruth told Rachel about a doctor in Washington who specialized in the field of infertility, and Rachel was ready to try anything. For the first time in about eight years, we also hear reference in these letters to Rachel's sister Elizabeth, who was still in Asheville. Because of her time in California with Arthur, Rachel had not seen her sister for over a year, which, she implies to Ruth, is an unprecedentedly long time between visits. This letter from Rachel tells us a great deal about her private life, which she otherwise kept guardedly under wraps. Arthur, she tells Ruth, will have to stay in New York to continue his work on manuscripts, but since she is going to Asheville to see her sister, she would love to come visit.

> You remember our talk about my seeing that Dr. Brown and getting him to look me over and see what he thinks. Well, I want very much to do it and this seems like a good

chance, so I'm wondering if you'd be willing to make an appointment for me.

Her plan was to see the doctor on her way south, then have a second visit "if necessary" on her way back from Asheville.

Arthur thinks it's all very crack-brained and foolish of me, but since I'm going to stop in Washington anyway I don't see the harm in getting his opinion of my reproductive powers, which God knows seem to be pretty feeble. Of course I'm not saying anything about this Dr business to my family or friends and I'm not very hopeful. I just feel one might as well leave no stone unturned.

In her journal, Ruth records some unfiltered impressions of what she has heard from Rachel about her sister. After an afternoon with Rachel, swimming at a friend's pool, she records her day.

My Rachel in black suit with a colored border around her hem. She is growing more attractive as a social asset every time I see her. Every word she spoke was interesting. Harold is dull and heavy, but a dear. I knitted and the evening rattled by pleasantly but not too excitedly. Rachel and I talked of her visit to her sister—a dismal proceeding. Interesting in all its aspects. A strange institution—semi-prison, semi-sanatarium. Rules about not going too often to the bathroom—a part of self-control! Finally crept to bed late. H. fast asleep.

Ruth's affection for Rachel is clear, even if there was an element of status-hunting involved. Rachel was now quite renowned and successful, and Ruth's life largely revolved around the jockeying for social position that infused her life in Washington. But in Ruth Rachel found, during this time, an outlet for those thoughts and fears she once shared with almost no one but Lyle Saxon.

One week later, back in her East Tenth Street apartment, Rachel sent a bunch of roses to Ruth and wrote a follow-up letter. "I've been meaning to write you before now about my delightful time with you, but I waited till I should have heard from the Doctor. But so far no report, and I'm more than ever convinced that I'm a tough case and I'd better let well enough alone." A month later, on December 7, Rachel writes another heartfelt letter to Ruth, likely the only person at this point with full knowledge of her baby quest. Given this shared intimacy, it seems clear that Ruth has also become the person with whom Rachel allows herself full candor about the other strains in her life.

Things have been rather low with us lately. We've both had trying spells of intestinal "flu" and A. seems pretty weak after his. I know, of course, that what he really needs is a good job, and that if that miracle could happen he'd respond to it and be another person, physically and mentally. O Ruth, you don't know what it is to cope with joblessness and boredom and to be able to do so little about it. . . . The day to day waiting and going rusty is a thing I never thought I'd have to see in anyone I love. So much for that. I didn't mean to get started.

My visit to Dr. Brown had strange results. Whatever he did to me it's entirely stopped menstruation for two months. I'd like to feel hopeful but he and my Dr. here aren't encouraging that anything could have started, so I just go along trying to forget about the possibility. A's test is impossible to achieve normally and we both got in such a mental state over it I decided it wasn't worth trying again <u>ever</u>. I guess nature just put a curse on you and me and a few others because we wanted children too much.

In several of Rachel's poems from that time, her heartache pulses off the page.

PETITION IN SPRING

Heaven help me now,
And every Spring, to bear
These too bright shapes
That throng the earth and air,—
The petal snow on bough,
The scillas' early blue,
The wisps of straw and twigs
That nesting robins strew.
Help me past cowslip's gold
Fringing each marshy pool,
Past other people's children
On the way to school.

"My Neighbor's Fig Tree" makes the point yet more squarely, contemplating the excruciating temptation of a fig branch, its load of ripe fruit "sun-warmed and dark of skin, / Like swelling purses rich within." The laden branch reaches tantalizingly over a

fence, threatening to "make a sinner out of me." The tree is for-
given, though the ache remains:

> My neighbor's fig tree, innocent
> Of boundary, has no intent
> To foster crimes of appetite.
> Ulterior motives, wrong or right
> Concern it less than sun and air
> And that first law—the urge to bear.

Another poem, titled "Not Every Bud . . . ," raises the specter
of May's delicate blossomings as wrenching reminders of nature's
relentless fecundity. Lest "peach trees wrapt in rosy mist / Should
take me unaware," Rachel writes, "I must bind my heart with
sober thoughts." The poem concludes:

> I must remember roots in the dark,
> And, even as I stare,
> Whisper,—"Not every bud that blows,
> Not every bud may bear."

Elizabeth Gilman, who is referenced in Yale's archive library
as a "friend, editor, and general councilor" to Rachel Field, had a
rich correspondence with Rachel from about 1934 to 1942. How
they met is not known, but it appears to be yet another example in
Rachel's life of a professional relationship that evolved into
friendship. In her earliest letters Rachel addresses her as "Dear
Elizabeth Gilman." Later it becomes just "Elizabeth" or "Elizabeth, my dear." In one letter to Elizabeth in February 1938, Rachel
recounts more news of Arthur's difficulties finding and keeping a

job and his problems with depression and anxiety. He is currently working, but in a job that bores him. Any job, however, is better than none, she says. She goes on, as is her habit, by recasting the distressing circumstances in a positive light. "I wouldn't have married A. if he'd been a high pressured, aggressive person and so this other problem comes from that. Not that I care for the work for money's sake, but everyone must have some outlet."

Rachel reports on her own writing work, which is going well. Then she addresses her treatments from Dr. Brown, revealing that Rachel confided in more than one friend about her baby woes.

I was rather miserable after xmas with female jim-jams, the result of that cure thing Dr. B. did. But I seem to be all right again now, but I'm through being tinkered with. I may decide to come on later this spring and see Dr. B. again to check up, though my Dr. here seems to feel as he does and there's really not much they can do. However, if I do come on I'll give you plenty of warning.

That phrase, "I'm through being tinkered with," came from a deep well of emotion in Rachel's heart. The power of that sentiment would later provide the seed that bloomed into her final novel, published in 1942, *And Now Tomorrow*. The novel's heroine contends with deafness rather than infertility, but the scenes of her frustration over countless doctor's visits, all of which lead to disappointment, carry distinct echoes of Rachel's letters about her fertility treatments.

Rachel and Arthur trudged along through 1938 in their New York apartment, Rachel researching and working on her novel, Arthur continuing his search for fulfilling and dependable work.

In May, Rachel received invitations from two Maine institutions—the University of Maine and Colby College—to attend graduation ceremonies and receive honorary degrees on June 13 and June 20 respectively. She refers to the honor in a letter to Ruth.

Of course I'd much prefer having twins conferred upon me, but we seem to have no choice in such matters. Paper babies are not altogether satisfactory, but I'm grateful for them and God knows, Ruth, the more I see of the world and other people the more fortunate I know I am. In spite of terrible spells of discouragement we're tremendously happy in each other and I wonder how I ever put through the years of lone sailing.

Rachel Field outside her Sutton Island home, summer 1938. Two
ceremonies in June of that year, at Colby College and the University of
Maine, awarded her honorary degrees.

By early June, Rachel and Arthur were beginning to plan their trip to Sutton Island for the summer, but Rachel continued her efforts to help her husband find a more steady form of employment. He had already looked into acting, editing, and publishing. A June letter to Louise Seaman Bechtel indicates that he was also exploring library work.

> [Arthur] went over this week and had a very nice interview and somehow talking the library idea over with a <u>man</u> made such a difference. He had seen women before and felt rather dubious at the idea of taking the course next year, but Mr. Stevens gave him encouragement and some new angles and I wouldn't be surprised if he tried it next year. Of course if anything turns up during the summer that seems better, there is no obligation yet and he has not definitely made up his mind but he's considering it very seriously and I think it might work out. Unfortunately he has no college credits at all and while he can get into Pratt [the Pratt Institute, in Brooklyn, which had a renowned library science program] with what training he has, rules are tightening everywhere and it may stand in his way in securing an appointment later. But I believe his personality and experience should count for a lot and there is definitely a dearth of men in the field which is to his advantage. . . .
>
> The main thing is to take the year to study and see. It's inexpensive and certainly is good training, so I'm rather urging him to do it if nothing else turns up.

Rachel and Arthur have been married for three years, but in letters like this one she sounds more like a mother than a wife.

Even if their sincere love for each other was support and balm, the disparity of accomplishment between them must have caused many a sting to Arthur's already vulnerable self-esteem. In that particular month, Rachel was awarded two honorary college degrees, while Arthur faced obstacles to employment due to having no college credit at all. The juxtaposition had to be painful, and one wonders if Rachel's efforts to help Arthur only exacerbated his sense of unworthiness. Still, their New York lives were full and their plans for Maine and Sutton Island gave them something to look forward to, as she reports to Louise in that same June letter.

> Eleanor Farjeon was here and we had her for one evening and found her all and more than a favorite poet should be,—as warm and vivid and grand a person as I've ever met. I wish you could have been with us.
>
> We saw "I Married an Angel" yesterday at the matinee and loved it. Your mother, Mary and Anne were there and I wanted to speak to them, but they were in good seats and A. and I were in standing room and dared not leave our places lest we lose them. . . .
>
> We plan to have about four weeks up there [on Sutton] to ourselves to work on the last chapters of my book and I hope get them done before I go down in July to bring my mother and aunt up for the middle part of the summer. Did I tell you the final title decision? "All This and Heaven Too!" I'm not sure if I like it or not, but H. S. L. [Henry Latham, of Macmillan] and all the salesmen do and that's the important thing. I've just finished chapter 34 and have about seven or eight yet to go.

Rachel did indeed finish her novel that summer, and it was published by Macmillan in the fall. Once again, a book was about to change Rachel's life dramatically.

Dear Rachel,

At the Academy of Motion Picture Arts and Sciences Library and the Warner Brothers archives at USC, I looked at movie memorabilia and photographs of you with stars like Bette Davis, Charles Boyer, and Barbara O'Neil, who had a Scottie dog just like your Trotty. I read about your friendship with Vincent Price and his wife and children—your picnics at the beach, the shared children's birthday parties. It seemed that you became a true Hollywood insider, but the Hollywood you found was the one with real people in it. The stars who came to love you were the ones who wanted to leave the pretense behind and just be. Your sincerity and natural vivacity outshone the Hollywood glitz, at least for those who were drawn to your kind of light. I love to think about the influence you had on that world, and the fact that you never allowed it to change your authenticity. At the same time, I felt so proud of your stalwart business dealings and your confident negotiations with the film industry. Your balance of kindness and toughness never ceases to inspire me.

I should also say—congratulations! You might not have preferred All This and Heaven Too as a title, but the phrase does a good job of representing what life finally laid before you. You came through so much to get to that place where success felt real at last—the success of life, I mean, not fame, although it didn't hurt that you got fame at the same time. I hope you thoroughly enjoyed it; you earned it, Rachel.

Cheers!
Robin

f o u r t e e n

All This and Heaven Too

Rachel and Arthur spent the fall of 1938 wondering where their uncertain star would lead them. By late October, their plans settled into place for another foray into California life. When they pulled out in their Ford with Trotty on their second cross-continental journey together, they didn't know if they'd be gone for a few months or a full year. They had no idea that they were, in fact, leaving the East Coast behind for good. Rachel would never set eyes on her beloved Sutton Island again. Nevertheless, the best of times still lay ahead of her, and the worst of times. In a long letter to Louise in late November, Rachel catches her up with her news. She starts with regrets that she missed Louise's visit to Rachel's mother and Aunt Kitty in Farmington, and gratitude to Louise for her kindness in taking time to see her family. Rachel had recently heard from her mother about Louise's wonderful visit with her husband and dogs.

> It made me feel all the more ashamed that I had not managed to write you for so long and tell you about our plans. But the reason I didn't was that for about six weeks

our plans were changing from day to day. First we decided to come out, then we decided against it and then we waited for a sign from heaven to tell us what to do. It came, in fact, we had three distinct signs pointing the way. First Rosalie Stewart, whom we have known for years, and who has been my agent out here, decided to go into business for herself and she wanted A. to come out and assist her. Then we had a chance to sub-let the sweet little furnished house of some friends of ours, right next door to the one we had two years ago. Then we were able to rent the Tenth St. apartment to a friend of Arthur's, and finally our income tax advisor said we'd be fools not to come and take California residence for a year, thereby saving enough to live on for two. You see out here a married couple may divide on an income, each declaring separate returns on it and that keeps us out of the higher rate class in a good year. My royalties coming all in a bunch in profitable years means that this way we save more by being here than by staying in the East, so that, too, was a big consideration, though the job for A. was the main reason for our coming. Since we started west "All This and Heaven Too" has been sold for motion pictures and so it's a good thing we got our residence established here when we did. Warner's have bought it for Bette Davis and while I wish it might have been for Garbo, still, I'm relieved to have it decided and Bette Davis will be next best, I think.

Rachel's mild remark that her book "has been sold for motion pictures" belies the weight of that news and the forceful battle that Rachel soldiered through to earn herself that sale. Rachel had been working steadily on *All This and Heaven Too* for a couple of years. This was the tale of Rachel's great-aunt Henriette, the Frenchwoman who had married Henry Field after fleeing France to escape a scandal-ridden past. Rachel's aunt had been governess to the royal de Praslin family in Paris when the Duc de Praslin was convicted of murdering his wife. Henriette was implicated in the murder as the suspected mistress of the Duke, but she represented herself with such grace and candor that she was acquitted of any wrongdoing. Nevertheless, the ordeal made it impossible for Henriette to remain in her home country. With *Hitty*, *Calico Bush*, *God's Pocket*, and *Time Out of Mind*, Rachel had cultivated enormous skill at weaving histories into vivid and suspenseful fiction. Through those projects she gained an increasingly formidable reputation as a writer. She was savvy about literary markets and publishing, well read, and well practiced in the art of self-advocacy. Rachel was also a writer on the rise, and she knew it. Even though she might have landed excellent representation in Rosalie Stewart, it was Rachel herself whose powerful confidence and business acumen set the tone for the sale of the film rights for *All This and Heaven Too*.

On September 28, when the book was still in prepublication, Rachel wrote a letter of instruction to Rosalie Stewart that reveals an entirely different Rachel Field from the one we've seen with friends, family, and colleagues. Discussions had already begun with movie studios, and Rachel's confidence in her new book exceeded even her confidence in *Hitty*, which she had rightly predicted would win the Newbery Medal. The humility and grace that Rachel practiced personally gave way to an almost intimidating professional stance as a negotiator. As a businesswoman

Rachel offered no apologies; she took the offensive and became a force to be reckoned with. Though the letter is addressed to "My dear Rosalie Stewart," it is all business thereafter:

I have your letter reporting on what you have been doing with "All This And Heaven Too", but I have been so tied up over at the MacMillan company writing in books that they are sending out in connection with their advance promotion campaign that this is the first moment I could get to write you. I am frankly a little confused as to why if the Studios consider my original price too high, they should still wish to buy the property before publication. I told you in my wire and by letter that I am perfectly willing to wait till after publication for I have faith in the material the book has to offer and I have spent so much time on the research and the writing that I guess I can wait a little longer and put my trust in public reaction to it. I know, as you say, that the situation in Europe is bad for sales at the moment. I am not unaware of that, but don't go and give me a lot of war scare talk. We both know enough about show business to know that at such tense times the public wants and has always wanted to be distracted from present horror. A story like this of mine is just the sort of means of "escape" for people and furthermore it has enough historical significance to tie up to present events without being too close to them. So I am not worrying on that score.

To get down to practical business:—I will accept seventy five thousand for motion picture rights, including radio and television rights, now. For that amount I will sell immediately to any Studio that comes up to that figure. Otherwise I will wait. It is no use to quote smaller figures, for I am definitely not interested in letting it go cheap. I happen to know that Warner Brothers paid $65,000.00 for "Four Daughters" and there was no publication as a book in that case, only the Cosmopolitan serial and no radio or television rights. I also know the figures paid for successful plays such as:—"On Borrowed Time"; "Dead End"; "Boy Meets Girl"; "Having Wonderful Time"; "Stage Door"; and "Room Service" and "You Can't Take It With You". Hit plays, I know, always bring more and I am taking that fact into consideration. But with the campaign the Macmillan Company are starting I know what they think of the book and its appeal to the public. They have given it a larger initial appropriation for advertising than any piece of fiction they have ever published, even more than they gave to "Gone With the Wind". That will give you some idea of the belief they have in it. Even at a conservative estimate the book royalties will be all right. I've lived a good many years without picture sales and if I have to I guess I can again!

All I can say further to you as my agent is this: If you can sell the property now for seventy five thousand, then go ahead. Otherwise we'll wait. But if the book is a hit in the fiction world comparable to twenty or twenty five weeks of sellout houses in a New York theatre for a stage play, then I am going to ask a hundred and fifty thousand for motion picture rights, the same as dramatic authors do. So let me know <u>now</u> what the studios think of this new price figure I have given you.

Always my best and complete confidence in you as my representative,

Sincerely yours,

Rachel Field

P.S. Yesterday I saw some advance trade paper reviews, which are usually the toughest, and they have gone out "big" for the book.

A month later, a story editor who worked for Warner Bros. Pictures sent a confidential airmail letter to producer Walter MacEwen to report on his negotiations for *All This and Heaven Too*. "Had a very long chat recently with Mr. Peterson [*sic*], who is the husband of Rachel Field, regarding 'ALL THIS, AND HEAVEN TOO.' My talk was along the line of getting the authoress to see daylight as to the price that should be quoted on that book."

A week later, from a Western Union telegraph office in Santa Fe, Rachel sent a telegram to Rosalie Stewart. She and Arthur were visiting a Sutton Island friend in Santa Fe on their cross-country drive to Hollywood. These negotiations must have been ongoing during that long trip, but they ended on Saturday, November 5.

1938 Nov 5 AM
ROSALIE STEWART
CHATEAU ELYSEE, FRANKLIN AVE,
HOLLYWOOD, CALIF

THINKING EVERYTHING OVER & CONSIDERING
MY TALK WITH MR. MCEWEN [*sic*] AM
PERFECTLY WILLING TO ACCEPT FIFTY TWO

THOUSAND FIVE HUNDRED IF WARNERS
ACCEPT THIS OFFER BETWEEN NOW AND TIME
MY ARRIVAL IN LOSANGELES [SIC] PROBABLY
WEDNESDAY AM MAKING THIS PROPOSITION
ONLY FOR WARNERS AND I EXPECT IF
GOLDWYN OR COLUMBIA OR ANY OTHER
PROPOSITION COMES THROUGH YOU TO GET
ME SEVENTY FIVE THOUSAND WHICH I FEEL
THAT PROPERTY IS WORTH BUT WARNERS
FIRST INTEREST AND CONSTANT BIDDING
MAKE ME APPRECIATIVE OF THEIR OFFER YOU
CANNOT REACH ME AGAIN UNTIL WEDNESDAY
NEXT IN CASE OF POSSIBLE SALE PLEASE
ARRANGE DISTRIBUTION OF PAYMENTS
ACCORDING TO EARLIER DISCUSSION
RACHEL FIELD PEDERSON

Rachel and Arthur left New York with nothing more concrete in hand than the prospect of Arthur's new job at the Rosalie Stewart Agency. Before they arrived in Los Angeles, they had the promise of $26,250 (the equivalent of more than $478,000 in 2020) to be paid before the end of 1938. Rachel's fortunes appeared to be skyrocketing, but she had seen too much disappointment to be overly optimistic. The rest of her November letter to Louise shows a clear, if tempered, sense of good fortune. There is no mention of the movie royalties. Rachel has already been on a roller coaster of anticipation and disappointment over the movie rights to *Time Out of Mind*. She only gives herself license to celebrate those things which have already come to pass, but her view of even those is ever optimistic.

Personally I am happy to be back here for you know I loved California even though I prefer the northern part to the southern. But I was terribly fed up with New York and the squalor and contrasts and despair of the place really had got on my nerves in the last year. As I grow older I long to be nearer the earth, to be able to step out into a bit of yard and have a detached house, no matter how small. Yet that is so difficult to manage around N.Y. and taxes are so high and going higher. Here we have a perfectly arranged six room bungalow, furnished, with an enclosed garden and garage, all for seventy five dollars and it's in a good neighborhood, just on the edge of the more expensive and stylish Beverly Hills. I simply love it and driving about in the Ford, to market and taking A. back and forth to work usually, though he can take the street car when I don't feel like playing chauffeur. I have just acquired the most miraculous helper, a pretty Norwegian woman who comes three days a week to clean and then cook. . . . You'd laugh to see us, for with our usual inconsistency we are served in style in the dining room one night and on the next we are eating left overs by ourselves in the kitchen.

She goes on to discuss the status of her novel and philosophizes about the vicissitudes of the world's fortune in light of the rumblings of war in Europe. Her closing words about Arthur make it clear that Rachel is by no means counting on any long-term solidity as yet in their California lives.

I am still somewhat dazed by the grand reviews "All This and Heaven Too" got and the wonderful things that the Macmillan Co. are doing for it. It just doesn't seem possible that I did get it written and that it is selling and I feel sure it can't last, or that I will have a law-suit or something will happen to mar the wonder of it. But for the moment I am completely happy and if it weren't for the state of the world and race persecution in Germany and war threats I don't believe I'd be able to stand such good luck coming to me all at once after the despair of last year. But, one does walk in and out of the sun, I find. If we can just hang on while it isn't shining on us that's the trick. It does shift from person to person in a queer inevitable way. It's wonderful to have Arthur working at something he likes again. Of course he wishes he could have had a chance in publishing, as he likes that line better. But this is stimulating and in a way his theatre experience counts for more and he feels it's what he needed to do at the moment whether it continues more than the year or not.

Interestingly, Lyle Saxon remained an influential presence in Rachel's and Arthur's lives. In this November 1938 letter, Arthur seeks Lyle's counsel and connections after beginning his work with Rosalie Stewart's agency.

Rachel and I arrived in Hollywood last Wednesday, and I started work for Rosalie Stewart on Thursday. She has gone in business for herself, and is just handling authors and scripts. She sold ALL THIS AND HEAVEN TOO to

Warner Bros. for Bette Davis. If you hear of some good stuff that you feel will make good picture fare I would appreciate keeping me in mind.

While Rachel was at work on *All This and Heaven Too* she too wrote to Lyle—partly to praise his most recent book, which elicited nostalgia in Rachel about her visit to Melrose Plantation years before. Lyle Saxon exercised a power and pull on both Rachel and Arthur that never lost its strength. Rachel shares with him, author to author, the sense of loss one feels after one's book goes to print; this remains an experience she cannot share with Arthur. Rachel goes on to credit Lyle with the powerful opening of her own book. "I begin as you told me I should by saying that I never knew my great Aunt Henrietta, but I often cracked butternuts on her tombstone."

"I must stop now and fly to get supper," Rachel says in closing, highlighting as always her inclination toward simple home life. "Somehow I always stop the pen with a frying pan or saucepan! A meal seems so much more important to me than getting words on paper. I'm really just a housewife at heart and an author by accident and heredity."

Rachel, dear friend,

This is the apogee of a life. Do we ever know we're in it, when we're in it? You almost seemed to know. It is yet another thing I grew to admire about you, Rachel. In all times, good and bad, you retained such a strong sense of perspective, along with humility and grace.

One of my greatest finds in the Warner Brothers archives was the piano sheet music for "All This and Heaven Too," by Jimmy Van Heusen and Eddie DeLange. It seemed a logical assumption that the song was written in connection with the film based on your book, since it was there in the film archive for All This and Heaven Too and copyrighted right around the time of production (May of 1939). You must have known it! Here was another opportunity to connect with you through music.

In a letter that's housed at Radcliffe I read about an encounter you had once with a friend of yours, who reported that you were filled with gratitude at the good fortune in your life. "All this and Heaven, too," you said to her; "Heaven is Arthur."

When I got home to Maine, I was keen to sit at my piano, play Van Heusen and DeLange's song, and imagine you hearing it in 1939. This was such a different experience from the visceral angst and pain of "Empty Bed Blues." Here was a song of grace, of pure love, serenity, security, and settled bliss. When I get to feeling sad about what you suffered, I sit down and play this gorgeous, romantic song, and I feel your happiness flood through me.

Your inspired follower,
Robin

fifteen

Hannah

For the next three years Rachel's life was a cascade of good fortune. Both personally and professionally she was enjoying her time in the sun, which showed no prospect of clouding over. Arthur was content with steady work at the Rosalie Stewart Agency; Rachel's writing and reputation continued to grow in popularity. With the greatest financial security they'd ever had, Rachel and Arthur had the time and resources to enjoy California's best attributes—beautiful scenery, flowers in constant bloom, fine weather, and a rich theater and film life.

We saw "Ladies and Gentlemen" the new Ben Hecht and Charles MacArthur play with Helen Hayes and Herbert Marshall in Santa Barbara last Saturday night and it was quite thrilling to be in a theater after a year without it. The play was interesting though still full of a good many rough spots and Hayes gave a very fine, sincere performance. Fannie Brice, Zorina, Vincent Price and others from Hollywood sat near us and that is always fun.

Rachel Field, Arthur Pederson, and their dog, Trotty, in their California home, circa 1938.

With the production of *All This and Heaven Too* Rachel stepped into the realm of Hollywood, but she eschewed the glitz and high life. She happily deferred to Warner Brothers's request that someone else write the screenplay, but she made meticulous notes on the script, demanding authenticity and consistency to her novel whenever possible. Business and creative work were her focus, as always, even in Hollywood. The kind of personal friendships she sought and cultivated continued to be those born of true substance. Rachel and Trotty were among the close friends invited for a daily cooldown in the backyard pool of well-known character actress Beulah Bondi, during an unprecedented southern California heat wave. Vincent Price and his wife, Edith Barrett, included Rachel—and Arthur when he was free—in many quiet cookouts and picnics on the beach. When Rachel met Bette Davis on the set of *All This*, the two women discovered an instant liking for each other, due to, among other things, a shared New England background. "She's a most simple and unassuming person, very direct and hard working and I liked her approach," wrote Rachel about Davis after they first met. Davis became a devoted admirer of Rachel's as well, and even wrote an article about an uncanny coincidence that connected her with Rachel Field. In the article, which must have been written some time after the filming of *All This and Heaven Too*, Davis played a bit loose with some details (Rachel was never a newspaper reporter), but the story is charming and worth reprinting here.

A Girl and Her Dog
by Bette Davis

Many years ago—about ten, I suppose—Mother was riding on the train between Boston and New York. The seats were pretty well filled, when a girl got on the train with a dog in her arms. Because of the dog, no one seemed to want her to sit by them. The girl was embarrassed as people quickly filled their seats with packages.

Mother always loved dogs, so she moved over and motioned to the girl to sit by her. Soon they were talking. Mother proudly told her new friend about her daughter, who had just been assigned a small part in a play on Broadway and who, she was sure, was a *great* actress. You know how mothers talk about their fond hopefuls.

The girl told Mother that she had been a newspaper reporter for 12 years, and hoped some day to write a play or a book—something that really mattered.

Before the train got to New York, both Mother and her friend, though they never introduced themselves, had spoken of their dreams and ambitions—the friend for herself, and Mother for me.

Not so long afterward Mother and I left for Holly-wood. At first it was a struggle trying to get a footing, until one day George Arliss picked me for a role in *The Man Who Played God*. Jobs came more easily after that. Mother spent quite a lot of time with me on the sets, especially at first. She had once been a professional photographer, and her advice was often helpful.

One day, while I was making *All This and Heaven Too*, she was visiting me at the studio, and I wanted her to meet Rachel Field, the author. But before I had a chance to introduce her, she walked across the stage to greet an old friend.

"Ever since that day we met on the train I have often thought about you," I heard Mother say. "What are you doing in Hollywood?"

"Well, you see, I did write a book, and the movies bought it. I am here watching it come to life. And, tell me, what ever happened to your daughter?"

"Here she is; I want you to meet her—Bette Davis. But I don't know your name!"

"I am Rachel Field."

I wonder if there isn't some plan or reason behind such chance meetings which, I have found, so often turn out to be very important in the lives of those who are strangely brought together.

Another story about Rachel's unassuming charm was published in a California paper. The reporter recounted her own arrival at the venue for her formal interview. While she was waiting for Rachel (she thought), she encountered a delightful woman who entertained her with conversation for a good half hour or so. "Well, I wonder when Miss Field is going to arrive," the reporter finally said. "Well, whom did you think you've been talking to? I am Rachel Field," said Rachel.

In an undated memo titled "Best Agents' Suggestions for 'Gone with the Wind,'" Rachel Field's name is proposed alongside twenty-three others as a candidate to write the screenplay for the film adaptation of Margaret Mitchell's popular novel. Also on the list are William Faulkner, Sinclair Lewis, and Thornton Wilder, but unlike those other three, Rachel is one of only six that has a large penciled checkmark next to her name. Here is how the memo describes Rachel's qualities:

> Now in Hollywood. Handles her women characters beautifully, as shown in her novels, "All This and Heaven Too" and "Time Out of Mind." Has a nice grasp of period talk and is a very easy person to work with. She used to be a reader at M-G-M in the East, and despite great fame is still humble and pliable.

Rachel's sparkle of life, the twinkle of laughter in her eyes, that sincere, childlike glow that uplifted hearts—all of her innate qualities of inner joy—returned to full strength during these golden years in California, and they were not lost on the people of Hollywood, shopkeepers, journalists, producers, and celebrities alike. There was no pretension in her, and her physical appearance, though sizable, was unglamorous. As a result she was often mistaken for someone else. People were expecting an intimidating celebrity. How could this plain, approachable woman be the renowned author and poet Rachel Field?

Rachel and Arthur encouraged visits from friends and family back east, and many of them took the opportunity. As she always had on Sutton Island, Rachel played the gracious hostess and enjoyed cooking for and sightseeing with guests of all sorts. With those who could not make the trip, Rachel maintained her lifetime practice of prodigious personal correspondence.

In a long letter to Louise Seaman Bechtel in March 1939, Rachel gives a detailed picture of her California life, beginning with reports of the heavy correspondence she is trying to keep up in response to fans of *All This and Heaven Too*. Many of them include personal questions about the genealogy of the illustrious Field family.

I didn't know there were so many people in the world with Field tucked away somewhere in their names, and they all want to know exactly how they are related to Cyrus [Rachel's uncle who was responsible for laying the first transatlantic cable] and Henriette and the rest. One woman even insisted that we must all be related to Marshall Field and thought we were all entitled to share in that fortune. But I had to discourage her firmly.

She invites Louise to make a trip west to visit and to see the Golden Gate International Exposition in San Francisco. Rachel plans to travel north with friends for a few days, then meet Arthur in San Francisco, where he has some business connections to cultivate. She goes on to describe Arthur's work life.

Arthur and Rosalie Stewart make a grand team as she likes to do the high pressured selling end and he likes to read and meet the clients and generally keep up the office end of it. But he gets a commission on any script he brings in and last week he sold an "Anne of Green Gables" book for a series that is starting and so he feels very happy over that.

After describing another Arthur success involving the Disney studio in Hollywood, Rachel reveals her attitude toward the film industry.

Well, it's a lot of fun for me to sit on the side and see the goings-on as long as I needn't get mixed up with the studios and I don't intend to. The only one I could imagine that might set me off would be the Disney one for that is the most happily creative place I have ever been in and I would give a lot to be able to take you over there to see it in action. The musical things they are working on would simply thrill you and I have seen the preliminary sketches for many that are in preparation with Stowkowski [sic] superintending the musical end. "Dance of the Hours", Beethoven's "Pastoral", "Rites of Spring" and "The Sorceror's [*sic*] Apprentice" are all under way. The latter is going to be something. If anything could start me off on another juvenile it would be going over to that studio for the spirit of that place is really infectious.

Then Rachel's report reverts back to the personal.

Trotty had her 11th birthday last month, but she's bearing up nobly though very gray. It's becoming to her only I don't like what the white hairs stand for. . . .

    It is heavenly here with the mimosa and acacia trees in golden-sweet bloom and our little garden has rows of calla lilies so that I can be lavish and have a great white jar of them all the time in the living room. There are roses out, too, and violets and primroses and geraniums rampant along trellises. I love them growing that way in fiercely prodigal clumps of color. We must move next month as the friends who rented us this little place want to come back and so I've been house hunting the last few days. It's rather difficult to find what we want as A. needs to be within walking or bus or car line distance of his office which is in the heart of things. We don't want to take on two cars and A. hates driving in this traffic though I don't mind it much now. But I have a couple of possibilities lined up and one of them has a complete guest room and bath, so we can take in friends who may be coming out for the Fair and whom we can lure here.

In closing her letter, Rachel gets back to the writing life. She tells Louise about her upcoming speaking engagement at the American Library Association's meeting in San Francisco in June, refers to several mutual friends and colleagues who will attend, and wishes Louise could be there. In Rachel's mind, Louise was inextricably tied to her first attendance at an ALA conference, when she flew out with Hitty to receive the Newbery Medal.

How long ago 1930 seems when Hitty took me to California for the first time and you arranged for me to have such a marvelous trip going and coming. So much has happened since then that it fairly frightens me and yet I feel in a queer way that these nine years have been the most important and satisfactory of all the rest. I am almost terrified at all the good fortune that has come to me in them. I know how lucky I've been and I'm grateful from my heart. These last five months have been the happiest of my whole life and I feel almost ashamed to be so happy in a world that is so troubled and despairing. But I don't think it was meant for everyone everywhere to be miserable. It's just my time for being in the sun, or whatever one pleases to call it. I've had the other times and I will again, so I just accept without questioning this interlude that came just when I was most in need of it.

Rachel did, in fact, find a work opportunity with the Disney studio. The musical pieces she referenced were all accompaniments to the animated shorts put together by Disney in the film *Fantasia*. Rachel was hired to write lyrics for "Ave Maria," the background music for one of *Fantasia*'s episodes. Disney later produced a picture book with Rachel's lyrics and scenes from the movie, released at Eastertime because of the religious theme. Her letters continued to report her happiness, in spite of the increasing global tension over the war brewing in Europe. It became clear that she and Arthur would be staying in California through the summer, and if it gave her a pang of longing for Sutton Island, she didn't express it much.

Sutton Island did appear in one letter to her island friend and neighbor, Rosamund Lamb:

> Yes, Arthur and I miss the Western End of Sutton most and you know why! No swims ever equal those in your pool and the happy visits with you there. Your news of the various families amused us. . . .
>
> I am so relieved at your report of dear old Jim Sprague. I told him to do whatever needed to be done to keep our place in repair and I hoped he was equal to it, but had no way of knowing. I am glad Roland can be helpful. They are a grand pair and I miss them.

Though her sentiments about the island were surely sincere, they were likely born more of her generous nature than from any soul-ache of longing. The abundance of Rachel's happiness in California was ever growing, and soon to blossom even more. The Pedersons moved in April into a new home with two extra bedrooms and hosted many visiting guests, including Rachel's mother and Aunt Kitty, who came for three months. In spite of Rachel's disinclination toward cocktail parties, they hosted occasional events to join people together. Alcohol was clearly a presence. "Well, the party was a real success in spite of my fears for I hate cocktail affairs myself," she wrote Louise in June. "It was, however, the only way we could get a number of people together and the combination was good, for all the studio people were thrilled to meet writers and publishers and vice versa. We had about forty five and I'm thankful to say all behaved well and no one was found under a bed or table."

Rachel and Arthur both traveled regularly for work. In Arthur's case, his agency work took him not only around the state of California but also across the country. He sometimes arranged visits to Minnesota en route to visit his father. Rachel's travel decreased during this California period; most of her trips were limited to places within a few hours of Los Angeles, for reasons she did not announce until a few months later. In a letter to her friend Elizabeth, who also experienced frequent travel separations from her husband, Rachel paints a warm picture of her life in California and her relationship with Arthur that summer of 1939.

We thought of you and Malcolm at Watch Hill over the fourth as we drove back from our weekend in Santa Barbara and two days when we escaped and went into hiding at a camp in the woods by some warm sulphur springs where there was a grand pool and a perfect place to relax away from holiday tourists and pops as it was in a national forest preserve and no firecrackers allowed. This was greatly appreciated by Trotty who goes frantic at every pop.

I can imagine what a marvelous reunion you and Malcolm had. When A and I have been separated like that we talk until we drop in the middle of sentences.

After such a time A. always says he feels as if he'd sung Lohengrin at a matinee and Parsifal in the evening!

In late June, one of Rachel's visitors was her old friend Ruth Feis, who was in California with her adopted daughter, Felicia. Her husband, Herbert, was to join them later. In her journals, Ruth's adoration for Rachel is undiminished, and her penchant for detail gives us a view into Rachel's home life, delivered with Ruth's inimitable candor. "Rachel with her hair turned up was coming towards us," she writes, referring to the first moment that she laid eyes on her old friend.

I was so excited I was pounding inside. We steamed away, bags stowed in a yawning baggage place. Then the jacaranda trees in beautiful blossom struck us—lavender but of a plangent lovely quality. A heavy mist lay over the town, burned off later. Rachel and I gossiped and chatted. We got to 1544 Crescent Heights Blvd, a pretty upland street, with a mountain crag looming over us, a mission stucco type of bungalow, quite livable and spreading with a little patio. And Arthur touselled and sleepy. We got freshened up, and had breakfast in the Hollywood breakfast nook in the most spotless kitchen with ruffled curtains. Arthur had to dash to work and we half unpacked—half dawdled, talked endlessly....

After Felicia's nap in which she slept but I didn't—just rested—I got up and found Rachel entertaining a Mr. Morris, an actor, and he is a great friend of Bette Davis. Pleasant, slightly faded, gentleman—in a very fancy soft shirt! I dressed Felicia all in yellow and she was sleepy, and we went out riding up towards some of the swank places in Beverly Hills and up some canyon where we saw Wallace Beery's house, and Dick Powell, and Joan Blondell's lovely place with a swimming pool and open barbecue fireplace—they don't live there, bought it on spec, and want to sell it for $50 or $100,000!

Then home to find Arthur, and a fine "birthday" supper for Felicia. She ate ravenously and loved the cake and ice-cream.

After this initial visit, Rachel drives north toward Santa Barbara with Ruth to "Allegria," a home she has rented for her lengthy stay. Over the subsequent months, Rachel and Arthur make visits to Ruth's place, bearing turkey dinners or oranges and lemons for Ruth and her daughter, and Ruth returns to Rachel's home several times. In July, after Herbert flew in to join Ruth, the Feises left Felicia with a nurse-housekeeper for a few days and drove to Hollywood for a child-free visit with the Pedersons.

Monday, July 24

I took Rachel some lemons and her book "Wickford Point". We scudded away down the inner road—and got to Hollywood about 9:15. Wonderful time. Arthur met us at the door and said Rachel had gone to get Aunt Kitty and Aunt Lucy. And I must say he seemed distrait and strangely worried. Later that was all cleared up—worry over his work. However he asked us to stay then and we decided to. So then we brought our bags in and he left for the office.

She goes on to describe a touristic visit to Hollywood studios, errands she had to run, shopping trips, etc. Then she gets back to Rachel and Arthur's.

> We'd just gotten in when A came in, rather weary and "tight" with Mr. Hall, who stayed a short time only. Arthur began to rave on about Rachel—how he loved her —how he wouldn't let her stay in Hollywood if it were going to affect her, etc. It seems the movies keep offering her huge sums to work for them and she wishes to keep free. But Arthur has to keep turning down offers and it sticks in his throat—sort of—and also he still feels how little he's making—as against her intake! But in spite of his groggy manner I can't help liking him for his evident belief in Rachel, mingled with his almost paternal feeling of her as a little gal! I went to bed hearing him knock over things!

> Tuesday, July 25
> I awoke—made the bed for Aunt Kitty and packed. Then got breakfast. Arthur was thoroughly sober and friendly— he'd already told us about his scare just before we'd arrived. The L. M. Montgomery story which he'd arranged for with RKO was causing some legal tangle and he'd just had word that he was to meet the lawyers at 10. All had gone well, but he'd been scared and worried. He left after breakfast and we went off.

In spite of her clear inclination to find fault, Ruth warmed to Arthur increasingly the more she spent time with her dear old friend and her husband. By the time Ruth had the Pedersons for a visit in late August, she had wrapped Arthur into the effusive enthusiasm she had previously reserved for Rachel alone.

> August 26
>
> Just in time to get home and pick asters and start F's supper when Rachel and Arthur came. They had hot coffee in the garden and F went to bed and then we put on sweaters and walked up over our sunset hill road—they enjoying scents and sights—the brown hills—or golden—with the dark oak trees on them. Then supper and a fine evening of talk on every subject of the world! They are a wonderful couple to me. Rachel is absolutely radiant. They spent the night—hooray.

That fall, Rachel's life took yet another turn upward in an entirely new direction. In early November, she started sending out letters revealing some news she and Arthur had been keeping under wraps for several months, which largely explained her easy dismissal of a trip east that year. Most of her California letters were typed, but this one is covered with Rachel's swoopy scrawl, poured forth in a breathless torrent to a dear old friend.

> Dearest Louise,
>
> Just a hurried line because I can't wait longer to tell you that Arthur and I have adopted a 6 weeks old baby and that I'd give a lot if you were near enough to see her right from the start. It's all happened rather suddenly though we've been on the hunt for some time and we found her out here through Cal. State Child Placement Society. She

is a darling and I saw her first at the age of 2 weeks and she was born Sept. 17th so she and I can celebrate our birthdays together. We have named her Hannah Pederson after Arthur's mother and she weighs 9 lbs. 3 ounces, has fair skin, blue eyes (that may change later) and a lot of wild brown hair that grows like an Indian scalp lock but will change, too, before long. We know all about her background and it is fine, solid American stock on both sides with a flavoring of Scotch-Irish thrown in for good measure.

Arthur left last week for a short business trip East to Minn. and N.Y. and the day after he left word came that we could have the baby, so I now have company to keep me from being too lonely. He saw Hannah while she was at the hospital and approves highly of her. But I can hardly wait for him to get back around Thanksgiving.

Gladys English was one who vouched for us and she has been so interested. We were tempted to name the baby Henrietta and call her "Hitty" for short, but we decided against saddling her with book names and we like Old Testament ones since we are not fortunately living in Germany. Somehow we need her more than ever now with war tragedy all about us and I hope we can do our best for her. I have been able to get a fine practical nurse and thanks to "All This" I need not assume all the care for I'd be pretty awkward with one so young.

Well, this is a crazy letter, but knowing you, my dear, I know you will make allowances for middle-aged foolishness. There's no one I'd rather have share her than you and I only wish you weren't so far. Trot has accepted her very sweetly, but is troubled when the baby cries! Well, my best to you and Ned and so much affection ever and always—Rachel

Gladys English, whom Rachel refers to in the letter, was the founder of the Children's Services Chapter of the California Library Association. She became a dear friend and support to Rachel in California. Her involvement in Rachel's adoption of Hannah was the beginning of a longstanding personal investment into the lives of Rachel, her family, and her friends.

Rachel's reference to a nurse and to her own "middle-aged foolishness" might well make a modern reader take pause (not to mention her comments about "fine, solid American stock"). Yes, she had socialist leanings; she dabbled on the fringes of the "lost generation" writers; she chafed at the restrictive nature of her elitist upbringing and defied conformity in several ways—in her forceful woman's professionalism in a man's world, in her financial independence, in her love life, and in her marriage to an actor. However, she was still a product of her time, of her family, and of her privilege. Women with means commonly employed help with their children. In Rachel's case, it was primarily so that she could continue working, although at age forty-five, she was also understandably intimidated by the prospect of caring for a child for the first time.

Baby Hannah filled the one remaining void in Rachel's longing heart. Rachel's letters overflowed with happiness, photographs of Hannah, and a sense of wonderment at her continuing good fortune. "Today is the nurse's day off and I'm reveling in having her all to myself," she writes to Louise in December. Then she goes on.

It's a curious, but most satisfactory feeling to have her presence here in the household. I long to have you adopt one, too and share the bond. Somehow all the idealization of babies leaves one. I no longer wax sentimental about them—it's like a garden, one is too absorbed and busy to stand off and analyze, but the miracle is no less tremendous before one's eyes.

Then she gets back to the business of writing, an inextricable constant in Rachel's life, especially in her relationship with Louise. Louise Seaman Bechtel would always be Rachel's favorite and most esteemed editor, and she never ceased her gentle urgings to entice Louise back into the business: "I know I shall revert to juveniles again and you not there to advise and inspire me—well, we won't go into that for the moment."

With a child in the house, Rachel's inclination to write "juveniles"—short books and poetry for children—was rekindled. Hannah's baby book became Rachel's labor of love and source not only of personal memories but of material for publication. The scrapbook was meticulously maintained. Rachel wrote notes, addressed to Hannah, in her swoopy handwriting, accompanied by photographs, original poems, hand-drawn and colored illustrations, scraps of memorabilia, records of letters and visits from friends and family, and landmarks in baby Hannah's life.

Dear Hannah—
You were born on a very hot Sunday, September 17th, 1939, at eight forty three in the morning. Los Angeles, California is your native city and you weighed seven and

a half pounds and had blue-gray eyes and a lot of fine dark brown hair that stood up in a crest on your head. I didn't meet you until you were two weeks old and I met you again when you had reached one month, on October 17th. Papa Pederson saw you first then and he liked you as much as I did, especially, he says, your little ears which were nicely flattened to your head. You cried very hard when we left the hospital baby ward and we felt sure that meant that you liked us too!

This is the way you looked on Saturday, November 4th, when Miss Gullett and I brought you home to North Crescent Heights, wrapped in a pink blanket. On the way we stopped at Dr. Newell Jones' office and he examined you all over and we found that you weighed nine pounds and six ounces. You were a Carnation milk baby and that made things nice and easy. The days were so warm that you could take sun-baths in the patio and on the front steps, and when Papa Pederson hurried back from New York on the 18th of November you were just two months old and he watched you having one. Here he is looking at you from under the banana tree. You were on Miss Gullett's lap and I took the picture so I don't show in it.

That afternoon we took you for a long journey in your carriage, a handsome English "Pram" that little Arthur Stewart lent you because he had outgrown it. You began to have lots of telegrams and presents, so many that there isn't room here to write them all down: blankets and sweaters and your first brush and comb from Aunt Rilla and your first dress and shoes from Aunt Molly Boicourt. It kept me busy writing thank-you letters!

When you came to live with us the old tree by the front steps was covered with the most beautiful deep blue morning-glories that I had planted in May. They are the flowers from September and that is the month when you and I have our birthdays, just a day apart. I thought it was a very happy sign that they should still be blooming to welcome you to our house.

Thanksgiving Day came on the 26th of November in 1939 and it was so warm and sunny you could go out in the patio in a little dress just as if it were summer. You seemed to like having me take your picture with Papa Pederson and he liked it even more!

You had two Thanksgiving telegrams and we were more thankful for you than for all the other good things that had come to us. And because it was so warm and sunny and you were so well and safe under the palm tree in the patio, and not sent away with a gas mask to wear like babies across the sea in England and France and Germany and Poland and other countries at war, I wrote this verse for your first Thanksgiving Day.

HANNAH'S FIRST THANKSGIVING

Dear child, be grateful for this sun
Its day-long journey well begun;

Be grateful that it finds you far
From lands where feuds and hatreds are,
Where death wings close, and fear endures
To mask such baby smiles as yours
In shapes grotesque. Be glad and gay
Upon this ancient holiday
For all such benefits as these,
For fertile earth and fruitful trees.
Be one with every hidden seed
That stirs to petalled flower or weed.
Be grateful that you, too, shall know
The selfsame urge that bids them grow
In sun and rain, but never be
Grateful in any wise to me,
Who asks this only—to renew
Acquaintance with the world through you.

Rachel and baby Hannah share a laugh in California, early 1940.

Several of the poems that Rachel wrote by hand into Hannah's baby book were published later on. One of them, "Prayer for a Child," was turned into a book and illustrated by Elizabeth Orton Jones. It won the Caldecott Medal in 1945. The original version was handwritten by Rachel in Hannah's baby book around Christmastime in 1940. It may be Rachel's longest-running book, being still in print in 2020.

The year 1940 rolled past in a flurry of activity for Rachel. She continued to record Hannah's development with delight and wonder, and she kept up with visitors and correspondence. In her fashion, she also maintained a regular routine of writing time; in deference to her new family member, Rachel worked during the two and half hours each day that was Hannah's naptime. Still, given all the other parts of her busy schedule, she had trouble going deeply into her next novel, which had been "knocking around in her mind" for quite some time. Production on *All This and Heaven Too* began early in the year, and the film's opening took place in June, which coincided with yet another move for Rachel and Arthur, this time to an even roomier home on North Camden Drive in Beverly Hills. Their new home allowed them to have a lot of things shipped from New York that had been in storage since they left, as she reports to Prentiss Taylor.

Our New York apartment things came remarkably well, though the dirt of N.Y. appalled me as I tried to get it off in Calif. sunshine. It's been like old home week finding one treasure after another and they all fitted in as if made for this house. We love it even more than we expected to and are gradually getting settled though it was a bit strenuous having "All This" open right on top of our moving. I hardly expected to be presentable when the time came, but it was a big night, though all our hearts were heavy with the news of Paris capitulated. Boyer sat directly behind me and he looked worn and tragic. The picture has had fine critical acclaim, though it's too soon to tell about it commercially. Bette Davis had a tremendous ovation and all consider it her best.

My dear Rachel,

I almost wish you hadn't accepted the relinquishing of Sutton Island with such apparent equanimity, but that's only when I'm being selfish. I'll try to remember what you wrote to Prentiss—"We mustn't have regrets for epochs that are over"—but I'm not always as good at that as you are. I wanted to believe that Sutton Island was your be-all and end-all forever. Certainly you would always cherish it in memory, but with this, as in all things, you took what life handed you with practicality, even the coming of Hannah into your life at last. If only you had followed the path to adoption sooner! It pains me, looking back at your life, to wonder about all the alternate paths that might have led to a different, longer-lasting outcome for your joy. We can never know. You of all people would often say of your dream of motherhood, "Perhaps it is asking too much." Would you have changed anything, had you known? But oh, the elation you found along the way! Can you ever regret it?

All my heart,
Robin

sixteen

Hope and Motherhood

Due to state regulations governing adoption, Rachel and Arthur would not have legal adoptive custody of their child until November of 1940, a year after bringing Hannah into their home. "That will be a red letter day in our lives when the adoption papers go through," she wrote to Elizabeth Gilman in March. "But she seems completely ours and grows more necessary each day of her little existence." Since they could not take Hannah with them out of state, Rachel skipped Sutton Island again that summer of 1940. In fact, although her mother and Aunt Kitty spent time on the island, Rachel began to talk about letting the Playhouse go. In September, she wrote to Prentiss Taylor.

> My mother and Aunt were on Sutton for a couple of months and managed better than I dared think without us, for neighbors were very thoughtful and they drove each way. I want to sell that place there, though so far no one seems to want to take it off my hands. For many reasons I feel the time has come and its cycle for me is over and I wish you had seen it. Of course we may return East,

one never knows, but the place is getting too difficult for older people and if we go back I would like one where I could be more independent of neighbors' boats and piers and where we could make longer summers and be more accessible by car. I hope we can stay on here for the present and that the state of the world will let us continue as things are. But who knows what is ahead—one clings to each sunny, peaceful day with gratitude—I get little time for writing and I can't seem to settle to a long piece of fiction for many reasons, personal and general. But I've done a short xmas story to be in the Dec. American Magazine and a tiny MacMillan xmas juvenile and I tinker at my desk a couple of hours a day while H. naps. Here is her picture to show you how she's changed and to take you much affection with mine—

Hastily—Rachel

As the war marched on in Europe, Rachel's philosophical approach to life served her well. Even now—with a new baby, a new home, continued work opportunities, and a husband content with his work life—she still did not know for certain that she and Arthur would be able to stay in California indefinitely. Nevertheless, she was prepared to take what came: "One clings to each sunny, peaceful day with gratitude." None of her fame and fortune altered her fundamental, simple wish for love in a quiet home.

Dearest Louise,

I can't for the life of me remember if I answered your last good letter or not. I hope I did, but anyway it was a long time ago and I think of you often and wish I could see you and wonder if you've moved back to town and how the place looks now the leaves are gone and your red winter berries showing off by your fields and woods. The days are unbelievably blue and beautiful here and rain has come earlier than usual (We've had two rainy weekends which we loved) so that the brown of summer has changed to dark green on the mountains. You would love our little back yard with its orange and grapefruit and apricot trees and our flowery borders. It is just right for us, not too much to manage and if only affairs foreign and domestic will let us continue to live and work we will be so happy just to go on here as we are doing.

Rachel neither assumed life would be consistently sunny nor fretted that everything would fall apart. The persistence that she had cultivated since childhood kept her going—writing, caring for Hannah, maintaining the bonds of friendship with so many, both through letters and through her revitalizing presence. And there was something else at Rachel's core, something that made her tenacity manifest itself not in grim determination but ebullience. One might even suppose that Rachel's heart, so consistently open to beauty and hopefulness, was the thing that brought her so many opportunities. Even in the worst of times, Rachel never let die that inner spark of excitement that lay ready to be set aflame. Disappointments knocked her down, but she continued to see life for its possibilities. When fortune came her way, she received it with the greatest of joy and gratitude, and even a sense of wonder. Then she wrapped her arms around it and carried on living, working, and loving in full. That was Rachel's own beauty, and it attracted people to her in droves.

One reviewer of *Fear Is the Thorn*, her 1936 collection of poetry, captured Rachel's spirit well in this description of her poems:

> As a whole they have a wistful charm such as she, herself possesses—a lovely trait no public speaking has yet erased from a beautiful picture. Despite the title of the book one finds there is no room in her philosophy for the really morbid; she has no time to waste on the ugly and sordid and macabre; and she does not suspect her mission in life is to pour out upon tolerant readers vials of bitterness to cups of wrath. It is something to find a poet who takes the bitter with the sweet and transmutes all into something glorified!

Earlier in her life, one of Rachel's pinnacle moments of good fortune was discovering the state of Maine and Sutton Island. At that time, Rachel was an insecure, ungainly girl on the cusp of womanhood, who couldn't seem to find where she fit into the world she inhabited. She found her fit on a spruce-tipped, rocky island off the Maine coast, and it became her roots and background. It was her heart home. Even so, Rachel's openness to possibility meant openness to change. She sought love and finally found it in a Broadway actor. She sought writing success and achieved it through years upon years of nail-bitten, persistent, indomitable work. She sought the balm of motherhood and found it in Hannah. All those things took her away from Maine and Sutton Island, but California opened new chambers in Rachel's heart. She didn't just resign herself to this new life, she embraced it fully and was thoroughly happy. "All this and heaven too!"

That fall and winter Rachel celebrated Hannah's first birthday and her second Christmas, dutifully recorded in Hannah's baby book. Arthur's father took ill with complications from diabetes, so Arthur rushed to Minnesota by train some weeks before Christmas. His father improved, and Arthur returned on Christmas Eve. Rachel's mother and Aunt Kitty came west before the holidays, so they were all reunited for Christmas. Lucy Field and Aunt Kitty stayed in a nearby bungalow for three months, enjoying time with Rachel, Arthur, and little Hannah, who was growing to be a lively child. "She's not one of those placid, rock to sleep babies," Rachel writes to Prentiss Taylor in early January 1941.

> There's something in the Cal. air, I guess, that fills them full of spirit and energy, or maybe they take in an excess of vitamins. H. walks everywhere now and has a limited but sufficient vocabulary, which consists of "ma-ma, Arthur, pretty, bye-bye, and 'aw right.'" The latter means both yes and no and so is a bit confusing.
>
> I do hope 1941 is going to be a good year for you, Prentiss, and that fine creative work is ahead in it. For the state of the World one dares not think or predict much. My head reels about the issues. I am not for Roosevelt, but I am not altogether against our joining the war. I mean if we can prevent a second war by going in now, maybe we should, but I'm not entirely convinced.

Rachel's writing routine, using Hannah's afternoon naptime, continued steadily for several months as 1941 marched on. By September of that year Rachel had a new novel well underway, with a December 15 deadline. After Hannah passed her second birthday, Rachel and Arthur found her a preschool, as she explained to Prentiss.

> She seems rather young, but she needed others her own age and the supervised play is better than anything I can do. Arthur drops her at the place on his way to work and I call for her after an early lunch and have her for the afternoon, just reversing my former schedule—So now I write mornings and am on the last chapters of my novel, long delayed. I also have a tiny book of Christmas verse and pictures to be out soon—but I think I wrote you of that. As usual I was sweating and struggling to get myself in the Christmas frame of mind in August.

In the same letter, Rachel shares the news about her house on Sutton Island without fanfare.

> Did I write you that I sold the Sutton Island cottage to Walter Kahn? I was glad to have it go to a friend, not a stranger, & he and his daughter & a Scotch friend had a happy stay there. I wish so much that you could have seen it, but, well, we mustn't have regrets for epochs that are over. If A. and I should return East to live we'll find another place in Maine and I knew the Island was not practical for us any longer, even if we had not come to Ca. I doubt if we could have continued it with my mother and Aunt the ages they are and with the season so short for staying.

She goes on easily about Hannah, visits from friends, and other news, and had this to say about the state of war.

I wonder if you find creative work as difficult to concentrate on as I do in these difficult and confused days? The weight of World Tragedy seems to lay heavy hands on one and what one puts on paper shows the effect of dread and confusion, at least it is so for me and how can it be otherwise? In Washington one must be even more aware of the War and all its implications. I've given up trying to clarify my own views—each day the scene changes so. I just try to go and not be too engulfed by it all. We must keep our courage and not spend it all in panic and vicarious despair—Well, enough of that—

Then came December 1941. The bombing of Pearl Harbor rocked the nation and changed the world. Like all Americans, Rachel was shaken by the news, and yet her life carried on. She still had to fetch Hannah out of bed each morning, dress her, feed her, play with her, tend to household business, keep up with correspondence, and continue writing to meet her manuscript deadline.

Dearest Louise

Your Christmas card is beautiful and I love the latin of "Adeste Fidelis," my favorite verse.

The whole scene has changed in the last two weeks. It has been a shock, but at least now the choice has been made for all of us. Arthur and I hope to get into some home-defense activities, but at present the offices of these organizations are swamped. So we go along in our routines. We're well situated here, not near coast or airplane plants. My mother and Aunt were coming out for xmas in Jan. and Feb. best to postpone the plan for the present at least.

I've been working all Fall under great pressure to finish my novel and at last it's done and turned in. It will be serialized in McCalls beginning Feb. next and Macmillan will publish next summer. They're not keen over having it in a magazine, but it was too good an offer to turn down and cash-in-hand means a lot just now when we don't know what book sales may be in another year. So I was very lucky to have it.

Arthur found these strawberries in San Francisco and they reminded me of your wild ones. Much love goes with them to you and Ned and, oh, dear, how I long to see you! But I can make no plans for coming East. Affectionately always, Rachel

The novel that she finished in December of 1941 was *And Now Tomorrow*, and she dedicated it to her California agent and Arthur's employer, Rosalie Stewart. It was the last work that Rachel ever published.

And Now Tomorrow is the story of Emily Blair, the child of a wealthy New England family. Like Rachel Field, Emily Blair is both protected and shackled by her familial roots, which is made clear from the very first chapter of the book. Rachel told Prentiss that writing this novel during the time of the terrible war in Europe made it difficult to avoid gloom: "What one puts on paper shows the effect of dread and confusion." Indeed, there is a spirit of melancholy that pervades the book, whose action takes place during World War One, beginning with Emily's nostalgic explorations of an old storeroom.

There is a fascination in places that hold our past in safe keeping. We are drawn to them, often against our will. For the past is a shadow grown greater than its substance, and shadows have power to mock and betray us to the end of our days. I knew it yesterday in that hour I spent in the storeroom's dusty chillness, half dreading, half courting the pangs which each well remembered object brought.

"In the life of each of us," Emily continues a page later, "there comes a time when we must pause to look back and see by what straight or twisting ways we have arrived at the place where we find ourselves." Had Rachel gone through a similar self-examination, looking back over her life, leafing through the pages of her past to assess her steps and missteps along the way? Emily's melancholy philosophizing sounds similar enough to Rachel's to make one wonder.

Once I considered myself a very important person in my own world. Now I know that I matter less perhaps than the tireless, pollen-dusted bee; than the mole, delving in darkness; than the inchworm that measures its infinitesimal length on a grass-blade.

I don't pretend to know what I believe beyond this— that nothing which lives and breathes and has its appointed course under the sun can be altogether insignificant. Some trace remains of what we have been, of what we tried to be, even as the star-shaped petals of the apple blossom lie hidden at its core; even as the seed a bird scatters in flight may grow into the tree which shall later shelter other birds.

Emily Blair is a familiar Rachel Field protagonist. She is a good girl, an accommodating, dependable type who aims to please everyone. "Always do what's expected of you, Emily," her father has taught her, and she tries her best to comply. That quality creates a great deal of the tension in the novel, which has as one of its primary themes the conflict between a privileged ruling class and the downtrodden working class. In Blairstown, those two groups are divided by a bridge over the river that powers the mill, owned and operated by generations of Blairs. The river marks the boundary "between secure and precarious living; between the humble and the proud." The marriage between Emily's well-to-do father and her mother, a Polish immigrant from across the bridge, represented the first unconventional crossing of those boundaries, and Emily contends with many more such conflicts in her life. "Some may cross from one side to the other as my mother did . . . and there are a few, like me, who stand on the span of its bridges, knowing that we belong to both—troubled and uncertain because we cannot renounce all of one side for all of the other."

The parallels to Rachel's life are many—the uncomfortable weight of family legacy, the counterpull between a traditional, elitist standard and a more modern, broad-minded inclusiveness. Rachel's writing shows a deeper sensitivity than ever toward the hard life of poor immigrant families. In an early scene at the family mill in Blairstown, the Blairs are passing out Christmas packages to workers and their families, with seven-year-old Emily present. One man hurls his gift basket of food back at the distributors, yelling in broken English that he wants his job back, not a chicken leg and candy. The child Emily—already confused by "gifts" that look like groceries—is haunted by the man's anger. Rachel's socialist friends back in New York had left their mark on her, even though she still didn't seem to always recognize her own collusion with elitism. She was on the cusp of change, but with the past still ingrained in her, as it is in Emily Blair.

More parallels exist between author and protagonist in their family circumstances. Both the author and her protagonist have one sibling, a sister with whom they clash profoundly. Both lose a parent at a young age and live the rest of their lives with an aunt as surrogate parent. Both struggle with math. Both are singled out and sent, contrary to their social standing, to the public high school for a broader education. Both take part in the high school play (Emily Blair's play is named *Everyman*, while the play Rachel wrote at Springfield High School was *Everygirl*). Both fell crazily in love once, only to be spurned; both found love again at last, with a man considered unsuitable. Both love men who feel inadequate. The most powerful parallel between Emily Blair and Rachel Field, how-ever, involves a physical impairment and the struggle to overcome it. In Emily's case, it is deafness following meningitis; in Rachel's, it was her inability to reproduce.

Emily spent years "being tinkered with" by doctors all over the East Coast, in the hopes of regaining her hearing. Rachel went through a similar process in trying to conceive a child—consulting with specialists, taking thyroid, receiving an array of injections and experimental treatments. Some treatments wreaked havoc on her system and her monthly menstrual patterns, but Rachel persisted, driven by tenacious hope. At some point, however, Rachel finally gave up. In Emily's frustration over her medical treatments, I hear Rachel's voice: "There aren't going to be any more doctors and treatments. . . . I've put through two years it's going to take me the rest of my life to forget." The sense of defeat that accompanies that sentiment—for both women—was painful.

Emily Blair finally did get her hearing back. But Rachel's problem was never resolved—that is, not by the time she had turned in her completed manuscript for *And Now Tomorrow*. However, she had reason to keep her hopes alive.

My very dear Rachel,

When I was a graduate student in an MFA program for creative writing—at the age of fifty-three—I expressed bewilderment at my seemingly endless project of writing your story. I was so undisciplined. I continually dropped the project for weeks or even months. I'd think, Maybe it's time I just scrapped that plan and worked on other writing. Then somehow I'd find myself settling back into the story of your life again. I went to my faculty mentor, who was not only a great writer but a keen judge of character with a highly insightful nature. "Why can't I get away from this project?" I asked her. She paused a beat before answering, looking me straight in the eye. "Because you love her," she answered simply. I was stunned, then I wasn't. Oh, I thought, dumbstruck. I suppose that's right.

How is it that your miracle is the part that I can hardly write? Because I love you; maybe that's why.

Once I'd read all your letters to Lyle, I thought I was back on track. Those letters transformed my view of the book. Everything fit now; it made sense. Still, my progress faltered. I kept on writing, but I was still avoiding something, and it took me a while to figure out what it was. As I approached your California years, my efforts dwindled, time and again. It took a major upheaval in my own life to finally reveal to me what was in my way.

Love,
Robin

s e v e n t e e n

Miracle

The sense of relief in Rachel's letters of early January is palpable. There is an atmosphere of suspended uncertainty in the country after Pearl Harbor, which affects everyone's mood. In addition to that, for Rachel, there is that familiar relief that follows the completion of a large project. Her work is done for the time being; her promise of income is secured. She can rest and get caught up with her thank-you notes from Christmastime, which were as warm and profuse as ever. Rachel's swirls of longhand script fill the pages, often with scrawled lines squeezed into the margins to fit in her final remarks.

Sunday, Jan 4, 1942

Dearest Louise,

Your exciting box was the high-light of our Christmas Eve. Arthur and I opened it before the fire after Hannah was in bed and we didn't hurry over a card, a seal or a message. Arthur's unique Santa Claus went immediately on the tree and I sat simply entranced with the exquisite miniature in my hands. You shouldn't have parted with it, my dear, for "The Red Rider" speaks of your countryside and all that you and Ned know and love. But—well—I won't deny that I dote upon it—so perfect to the smallest details and a tiny world caught forever on that little inch square. Only you could have found such a treasure and the only other miniature I love as much is the beautiful little gold album you gave to "Hitty" with the poem years ago and which I keep under lock and key. Really, Louise, you couldn't have found anything I could love more, so your almost super-human generosity must feel rewarded.

If only 1942 can bring us some reassurance of peace in sight. Well, all our thanks and affections always,

Rachel

Elizabeth Gilman had sent a book for Hannah, which Rachel gushed over before continuing with other news.

When I see a small child with books I am more than ever convinced that they are a kind of living miracle—that marks on paper can stir another mind, even a two year old one, surely is akin to the miraculous and to see it is to be made freshly aware.

We've been unusually quiet over the holidays but glad to be. I think few have been able to summon the mood for festivity. One is grateful to be close and to have friends about one. I wish something would bring you out this way again. It would be a joy to see you, but no one can make plans in these times. All goes calmly and with-out apparent panic here after two rehearsal blackouts that tense week of December 7th. Soldiers are on guard along the coast and in open places and oil-wells, etc. Everyone goes on with routine, but there is a queer sense of unreality.

It is no coincidence that Rachel used the term "miraculous" in her letter to Elizabeth, for Rachel had been hoping for her own miracle for some weeks. When it finally came, letters were far too slow for sharing the news, so Rachel made some phone calls around the country. One of them was to Ruth Feis, who was once again spending a good part of her winter nearby in California, with her mother, Mollie Garfield, and her daughter, Felicia. Ruth writes about Rachel's news in her journal sometime in the latter half of January 1942.

Rachel had called me and I told her we would come by for a few minutes. She then told me that she was having a baby!! I was <u>too</u> excited. Rachel said "I think I'd better prepare you—it's not bad it's very pleasant—but you'd perhaps better be prepared—you see <u>I'm expecting</u>!!!" I loved the New England phrase from her—so homely and ugly, really. I can't <u>believe</u> it. We got dressed quickly and started over in Miss Coolidge's car. We got to the Heylers, but Audree wasn't there, so I called Rachel and told her we'd be right over. We did so, and there was bewitching little Hannah running to meet us, calling "Ruth Feis," and "Aunt Mollie," and darling Rachel looking lovelier than I've ever seen her only beginning to have a "tummy"! She told us all the news of her miraculous pregnancy. How they'd all had intestinal flu, and she never seemed to get over it, felt miserable and dopy, was trying to finish her book and it was an agony. Then near Christmas tried to see another doctor and he didn't seem to feel it was a baby, so then Rachel asked for "the rabbit test," injecting a rabbit with urine, and if the rabbit dies, you are sure! A day or so after Christmas the report came that the test was positive! They are all so happy. It does seem the crowning of her life.

For Rachel, the news about Pearl Harbor and the state of the war drifted into the background as she took in the extraordinary events of her personal life, which had been tingling at the back of her mind for some weeks. Chapter 23 of *And Now Tomorrow* begins with this paragraph:

Miracles are out of fashion nowadays. Or perhaps it is only that they have been explained away from us. Radios and newsreels and words have shorn them of their mystery. Yet to each of us, I think, a miracle is given at some time in our lives. We may not choose the moment it shall be revealed or the form it shall take. We may not even realize till long afterward that it was our privilege to be part of one. Our minds may betray the wonder that our hearts accept. I fought against the miracle that was to be mine, but there was no denying it when it came to me.

Whether it was a miracle or a response to the barrage of fertility treatments she had undergone, Rachel conceived a child some time in early November, at the age of forty-seven. She must have sensed something during those final weeks of writing, some stirrings in her body that awakened the stirrings of hope for the impossible. Those rekindled hopes must have flowed through her pen as she wrote about deaf Emily Blair's first faint sensations of detecting sound. The time is early December (for both the heroine and her author), and Emily is returning by train from a Christmas shopping expedition. "I found myself sitting bolt upright on the plush seat with a queer chill at my spine. My bag fell to the floor." Emily discounts the sensation of sound at first, remembering that she has been betrayed before, hurt repeatedly by dashed hopes of her hearing coming back. "I must have dreamed it, I decided; and yet I could not put it from my mind so lightly." Later she detects a vibration of sound a second time, from a blaring horn on a truck that nearly hits her.

I don't know how I made my way across the street. I only know that I was still smiling long after I had reached safety. My knees went weak then, and my hands shook so that I could hardly keep my bundles from scattering. I found the refuge of a bench and sank down on it. I must have made a spectacle of myself, surrounded by gaily wrapped packages, with tears streaming down my cheeks for any passer-by to see. But I didn't care who saw me there. I didn't care what anyone thought. It didn't seem incongruous that a strident motor horn had been the means of revealing the miracle that I could no longer deny.

At what point did Rachel recognize the miracle that she could no longer deny? She clearly felt something that whispered "hope" as she wrote of Emily Blair's miracle, vibrations, perhaps, in the depths of her body that she hardly dared identify as the thing she had longed for for so many years.

With the final confirmation of a pregnancy test in January, Rachel knew it was no mistake. She was going to have a baby. It surely was the "crowning of her life," as Ruth wrote. She was a renowned literary personage with financial security, a loving husband, and a sweet two-year-old child who had joined her family and won her heart. Now her ultimate wish was coming true. She was to experience the miracle of life blossoming within her body. Her bud would bear after all.

Rachel did not share the news with everyone she knew, but her closest friends and family were invited into her circle of joy and amazement. "We do not question miracles," Rachel wrote to one old friend, adding good-humoredly, "I have done everything at strange times in my life and now I am running true to form." She had several visits with Ruth, who reported on their various lunches and outings and little Hannah's charming antics. At the beginning of February she wrote to Louise.

> I still have days of utter incredulity about it all and if the Dr. didn't [confirm] the fact I think I'd just believe I was having "the change" with extra pangs and discomforts. But I've been fortunate so far and I'm doing everything to cooperate and do my part. Oh how I <u>wish</u> you were nearer and we could have a real reunion while we knitted for Red Cross or snatched an hour between activities. I mean you would be the busy one, for I can contribute little except what I can do at home. I'm keeping close to my fireside these days—feel marvelous in the morning and simply <u>miserable</u> by 5 pm. I would have to reverse the usual process, wouldn't I?

But Rachel's instincts were detecting something more insidious than she knew. Those pangs and discomforts were, in fact, more than the normal symptoms of pregnancy—but if a part of her deepest consciousness understood that something was wrong, she surely would have wished desperately not to know. Rachel lived for a few weeks fully immersed in the wonder and amazement of her life's charmed good fortune, until she could no longer ignore what she was feeling.

Dearest Rachel,

I know now why it took me so long to write your life. It was because I couldn't bear to write your death.

I spent several weeks communicating with some of your Field family relatives when I started my research. Before that trip to California in 2009, I contacted one of them for a favor. I had called the LA hospital where you'd been admitted in March 1942 and asked about old medical records. I wanted to learn more about the illness that took your life. The woman on the phone happened to know of an elderly, retired doctor who had studied the history of the Good Samaritan Hospital (known in your day as "the Hospital of the Good Samaritan"). "He might know about old medical records," she said. So I called him. This kind and generous physician—I'll call him Doctor L.—said he might be able to help, but asked me not to use his name. "I'll be in California in March," I told him. "I wonder if you could find the medical records from 1942?" He thought he could, but he would not be able to share them with me without explicit, legal permission from family. That's when I asked for that favor from your distant cousin, many times removed. Sadly, you had no descendants of your own, and that was the best I could do. Thanks to her, I eventually procured a notarized letter of permission and sent it off to Doctor L. in California. He was satisfied with that, and we arranged our appointment.

That is how I happened to be sitting with this white-haired retired oncologist in California one March afternoon in 2009. Black-and-white photographs of physicians from decades past lined the walls of an old doctors' lounge in the Good Samaritan Hospital. Doctor L. carefully hauled open a massive leather-bound tome, the admittance and discharge records from 1942. Page after page was filled with longhand entries written in spidery loops of script. He carefully blocked off the entries on either side of the one I had permission to see. The date read March 15, 1942, and he turned the book solemnly toward me.

In deepest sorrow,
Robin

You'll Never Be Quite the Same

So quickly, in the cruelest turning of fate, the citadel of joyful security that Rachel had constructed over forty-seven years crumbled into rubble. The cancer that they discovered during Rachel's hospital visit had likely been growing for seven or eight years. During that last year of Rachel's life, it is quite likely that she felt poorly, but she might have attributed her discomforts to caring for a toddler, or menopause, or working to meet the deadlines for *And Now Tomorrow*. After learning of her pregnancy, she would have had an easy explanation for any physical symptoms that troubled her. Perhaps it is a blessing that she never knew during those months the real reason she was suffering.

On a Thursday, March 5, 1942, Rachel hurried to Los Angeles's Hospital of the Good Samaritan after a great deal of pain and sleeplessness. She was immediately admitted, with no clear diagnosis, but remained upbeat. During a phone call with her friend Gladys English that Saturday, she asked Gladys to come see her the following week, after her operation that was scheduled for the next day. Ever the optimist, she suggested that Gladys telephone first, because she might be home by then. "Nothing to worry about," she assured Gladys. On Sunday, three days after Rachel's admission, the surgeon Dr. Lawrence Chaffin did a biopsy and found "the most malignant form of cancer of the rectum, far advanced." The only proven cancer treatment at that time was surgical removal, so surgery was scheduled for the next day. Dr. Chaffin was a highly regarded surgeon. Rachel got the best treatment that the medical world had to offer, but it wasn't enough. During the surgery on March 9, Dr. Chaffin found tumors throughout Rachel's lower abdomen, one of them causing a total blockage. He removed both ovaries, performed a colostomy, and removed Rachel's uterus, which carried her four-and-a-half-month fetus. Still, much of the cancerous tissue was left in place; it was too far advanced, inoperable.

Rachel survived the surgery, but shortly thereafter developed postoperative pneumonia. Most likely she never regained consciousness. That knowledge provided a wisp-like thread of silver lining for the very few friends who knew the whole truth. The vast majority of Rachel's friends and fans only learned that she'd died of "pneumonia following surgery." Her sturdy body lasted six more days in room 428 of the Hospital of the Good Samaritan. On March 15, 1942, at one o'clock in the afternoon, Rachel Field Pederson took her last breath.

YOU HAVE ALREADY been witness to some of the aftershock of Rachel's death at the beginning of this book, but it seems appropriate to hear some of these voices again. It is poignant to notice how often those who loved Rachel summoned up her memory in order to bear their sorrow over her death.

The realness of a person such as Rachel can't ever die.

The realness of a person such as Rachel can't ever die.

We shall not look upon her like again.

I felt cut in two when the most unexpected sorrow of all leapt out at me from the air.

Arthur, my very dear friend. This morning by chance I was rereading Rachel's loveliest letter to me, written in August 1940. I was sorting letters and found this like a star. Then the newspapers came and I learned with a blow on my heart that she would write me no more letters. What can I say to you, except that I loved and love her beyond all common love. Life became nobler because I knew her.

Rachel's closest circles of family and friends, for the most part, did not record their raw grief. Indeed, there is an almost sterile aspect to the immediate aftermath of Rachel's death. Local friends rallied around Arthur and Hannah. Gladys English, a local librarian and staunch friend of Rachel's, took particular care over Hannah's well-being from that time forward. She and others apparently made the assumption that Arthur would not be able to handle the child on his own, and perhaps they were right. Arthur soon moved into a second-floor apartment in the home of a local friend, Rilla Palmborg, an older woman who took on much of the care of little Hannah.

Arthur also seemed to abdicate much say in the funeral or

memorial proceedings. A service of some kind took place in California the day after Rachel's death. Her body was cremated, but the remains were not placed where she and Arthur had made their home in California, nor any other place where husband and wife could lie together for eternity. Neither would her former heart home on Sutton Island welcome Rachel back into its mossy embrace. Rachel's ashes went east to be interred in the Field family cemetery in Stockbridge. Lucy Field, Rachel's mother, writes this account to Louise Seaman Bechtel:

> I go on and on, like one in a dream—I simply cannot believe that our one and truly Rachel has gone from us—just a few of us at the old cemetery in Stockbridge, May 9, to lay Rachel by her father whom she never knew, and three darling other children—Rachel was our youngest!

It almost seems as if in death, Rachel's life as a married woman and mother were erased, and she reverted to her status as a member of the Field family, once and for all. However, Lucy and Aunt Kitty remained devoted to Arthur and Hannah, and visited several times in the ensuing year and a half. By August they felt that the two were all right in the care of Mrs. Palmborg, but Lucy clearly worried about Arthur.

> My heart aches for Arthur—they had such a happy 6 years, and Hannah a great joy—but now the changes have come—Arthur was not strong enough to go on, as they had lived—the lovely house has been rented, and Rachel has a devoted friend who has arranged for them in her own home.

As for Rachel Field's professional and artistic standing, accolades abounded for a time. The 1942 summer issue of the *Horn Book Magazine* was dedicated to Rachel Field, including photographs, reprinted letters, Rachel's poetry, and numerous essays of remembrance and admiration. Hollywood produced two more movies based on her novels, *And Now Tomorrow* in 1944 and *Time Out of Mind*, at long last, in 1947. In 1945, Rachel and the illustrator Elizabeth Orton Jones were awarded the Caldecott Medal for *Prayer for a Child*. It seemed, at first, that Rachel's imprint on the film and publishing industries would have staying power.

Unfortunately, neither one of her posthumous films made much of an impression. Without Rachel's energy, her meticulous oversight, and her professional persistence, the heart had gone out of the productions. The heart seemed to leak out of Arthur too. He struggled to do right by Hannah and rise to the task of managing their lives without Rachel, but circumstances conspired against him. Arthur's father died in April, just a month after Rachel, and he spent the summer trying to negotiate his new life with Hannah in the face of this overwhelming grief. By summertime they had moved in with Mrs. Palmborg. Arthur reports most of these facts in a letter to Lyle Saxon in September 1942. "Dear Lyle," it begins. "HAPPY BIRTHDAY. I picked up R's birthday book and there was the date."

News of Arthur after that year became scarce. Some letters amongst Rachel's friends make reference to Arthur's struggles with depression. Several people speculate or "seem to recall" that Arthur was hospitalized for some stretches of time for mental illness. Rachel's mother died a year and a half after Rachel, and Aunt Kitty moved to North Carolina to live with Elizabeth, whose health had improved significantly. Ironically, Elizabeth is the only family member who seemed to find contentment after Rachel's death, even if she never attained anything one might call joy.

One thing we do know is that Arthur kept the copyrights on Rachel's work up to date for many years, and he was protective of her privacy and the privacy of other family members. Ruth Feis and Prentiss Taylor collaborated on continued Rachel Field tributes over the years. Prentiss pushed for a collection of Rachel Field memorabilia to be housed at Yale University, where all of his letters from Rachel remain today. Ruth tried to publish a book of Rachel's birthday greetings, then got to work on a children's biography of Rachel's life. She did extensive research and interviewed many of Rachel's closest friends and family, including her sister Elizabeth. Ruth's letters trace the writing of her book section by section and talk about Rand McNally being her publisher, right up to the very day she sent in the completed manuscript in December 1964. Ruth had several interchanges with Arthur about permissions to publish letters and other archival material, but Arthur was wary; he wanted to protect both Elizabeth and Hannah from public scrutiny. Yet even after that hurdle was surmounted, Ruth's biography never materialized. It seemed to disappear without a trace. One likely explanation is that Ruth called off the project because of yet another tragedy that beset the life of poor Arthur.

Perhaps if Gladys English, with her staunch advocacy and strong-minded directedness, had lived to guide Hannah Pederson into adulthood, things might have been different. For years, Gladys kept an eye on Hannah's well-being to a degree, and she seemed to have some influence. She sent this news to Louise Seaman Bechtel in 1947, just before Hannah's eighth birthday:

Hannah is fine, though right now I should recommend a
good boarding school for her. Arthur finds it very hard
indeed to make up his mind about anything, and any step
as drastic as that simply bowls him over. I keep plugging
away at the idea though. Some day he may do it. Mrs.
Palmborg is devoted to Hannah, but has no idea whatever of discipline, nor of children. Hannah is far above average mentally, most responsive, but she needs guidance
and intelligent care. Neither does she get from Mrs.
Palmborg, who is in a constant state of feeling sorry for
herself. Hannah loves to come to our house because it is
serene and happy. Alice and Hannah did not click at all,
but Bertha [Mahony] and she were immediately drawn to
each other, Hannah even called her Bertha at once.
Strange isn't it how children sense sympathy and friend-
liness at once.

Correspondence after Rachel's death is scarce, but in 1958, a
friend wrote to Louise Seaman Bechtel with the news of Gladys
English's death several years prior.

She never faltered in her devotion to Rachel's Hannah.
She was with her on Hannah's 16th birthday that October. Now Hannah is a freshman at Occidental College
which is just across the road from where I live. She and
Arthur still live at Mrs. Palmbourg's [sic] in Hollywood.
Hannah is a lovely, slender girl—a bit reserved in contrast to her impetuous childhood.

A troubling restlessness and even rebellion grew in Hannah,

who, though proud of Rachel's accomplishments, had no memory of her and disliked being referred to as "Rachel Field's adopted daughter." She clashed with her father and with Rilla Palmborg, who essentially raised her and whom she referred to as "Mom." Mrs. Palmborg died in 1959, removing yet another source of ballast for a precariously anchored young woman. Hannah chafed at her father's urgings that she be more prudent with her money and her behavior. In 1960, Hannah somewhat impetuously married a man a few years older than she. Upon marrying, she inherited a great deal of money from her mother's estate. In an all-too-familiar story, too much money at too young an age was more destructive than helpful to poor Hannah, who did not make sober choices with her finances, her health, or her marriage. The marriage lasted barely over a year, and her father was unable to reason with her to straighten up her life. On July 4, 1965, at the age of twenty-five, Hannah died of alcohol poisoning.

One can only imagine that after such a tragedy, Ruth would have decided to scrap the idea of publishing a biography about Rachel Field, which would only bring attention to Arthur in his grief, and to Hannah's death, heartbreak upon heartbreak.

Rachel, cherished friend,

I hope you never knew that you lost the baby in your womb. I hope you died oblivious to the desolation that was to come after that terrible day, the Ides of March, 1942.

Where do I go from here? Maybe I'll start by telling you a bit more about how you wove yourself into my story.

I wrote a newspaper column in Massachusetts for a couple of years before Jonathan and I moved in 2002 to live full-time in Maine, where I was once again consumed by the job of creating a home for my family, newly uprooted and acclimating to this new place. Then I published my first glossy magazine article in Port City Life magazine in the summer of 2009—thanks to you. It was a major boost to my confidence and my determination to get to a point where I could call myself a writer without blushing, without feeling like a fraud. As 2010 approached, I made a resolution to write every day. Not only did I succeed for 365 days in a row, I also wrote fifty columns for an online media service, then got a job as a regular columnist for the Bangor Daily News, a job I kept up for five years. In 2015, I completed a two-year MFA in creative writing through the wonderful Stonecoast program at the University of Southern Maine. One of my primary goals in applying was to find inspiration to finish my book about you. My Stonecoast degree opened the door to a job as a writing professor at a local university, which I was doing when I finally finished your story —but I'm getting ahead of myself again. The point is, you've been there with me throughout the blossoming of my writing life.

During my first semester at Stonecoast my mom grew seriously ill with two cancers. By February, it became clear that she was nearing the end of her life, and she was discharged from the hospital to go home under hospice care. I left everything behind and went to my parents' home in New York, to help if I could, but mostly just to be with my mother. My attachment to my mom was a constant in my life, even through adolescence. I think you have some sense of this, as a deeply devoted daughter yourself. During those weeks that I spent with my dying mom, and with the encouragement and compassion of that fabulous faculty mentor I told you about, I continued to generate the required twenty-five pages per month required by Stonecoast. The pages were an outpouring of memories, fears, and grief. My time with Mom reignited the adoration I had always felt for her, but had partially tucked away for safekeeping while our lives remained geographically distant. The writing was also therapeutic. It provided a slow release of a panic that threatened to explode me into pieces as I navigated the greatest upheaval of my emotional life.

I took some time off from my newspaper column, and when I started up again, I could think of nothing but my mother to write about, so I wrote a column about her. I got more responses to that column than anything I'd ever written, and I decided to keep going. A year and a half later, I had completed a full-length memoir, including a great deal of exploration into our society's handling of dying and death. It was feverish, impassioned writing, but it also felt important. I had never written like that in my life.

Rachel, a few months after Mom's death, I decided to take a break from working on that highly emotional project and pulled out my notes about your life, for the umpteenth time. It was then that I was reminded of the date you died, a date I *hadn't looked at for several years. When I saw it, I felt a jolt from my stomach to my fingertips. You see, my mother died on March 15—the Ides of March. Just like you.*

This was the final message that smote me on the forehead. I couldn't ignore these signals any longer; I had to finish your story. If I could write my mother's death, I heard a voice inside me say, I must be able to write yours too.

So how do I finish your story, Rachel? Now that I feel a deep, inner assurance of your blessing in writing your story, I am determined to recast your spirit into the world—the best of your spirit. Is that what you've been trying to help me do for all these years? I hope my efforts will please you, at last. I'm sorry it took me so long to hear you. I'm sorry it took me so long to realize how deeply I've come to care about you.

Your spirit has not died, Rachel. You are still here, in the pages of your poetry collections, on the woodsy paths of Sutton Island, maybe even lingering in the Stockbridge cemetery, tempting some little girl to come and crack butternuts on your tombstone, then soar off in her imagination to someplace greenery and whithersoever.

Rachel, this is so hard, finishing. I hadn't anticipated it, but this may be the hardest part of all. I have to say goodbye to you now. I have to let you go back into the world, whatever world that may be. I have to go back into the world too, and get on with everything you have taught me. How can I ever thank you for what you have been in my life, for what you have given me? Thank you for helping me feel that my own life has been just what it needed to be. Thank you for your writing and for offering your best self to the world. Thank you for becoming a deeply important, lifelong friend.

May you be at peace. May your spirit be free to dance and sing—as elves in a magic forest, as a child in bare feet on spring grass, as a woman, wife, and mother in the bliss of fulfillment.

I offer you, always, so much love and admiration, Robin

n i n e t e e n

And Now Tomorrow

In the early years of the twenty-first century there were still occasional tour boats that circled Sutton Island, pointing out the
former summer home of the famous writer Rachel Field. A few of
her books and poems are still in print, and you can find her novels
and films available for sale on Amazon and other websites that
specialize in vintage items. She was a rising star at the time of her
sudden death, and even in spite of the tragic circumstances that
reverberated through her family in the ensuing years, her name
lingered. Like all fame, however, Rachel's has faded to sepia gold,
curling at the edges.

But is fame really the thing that deserves to last? What about
the legacy of a life bravely lived, pulsing with that which inclines
us toward all that we hold most dear? Isn't that worth preserving?
Isn't that the more important thing to be reminded of, to hold on
to? In the voice of Emily Blair, Rachel wrote, "I don't pretend to
know what I believe beyond this—that nothing which lives and
breathes and has its appointed course under the sun can be altogether insignificant." Rachel Field's own story, in spite of its
abrupt ending, is filled with hope, magic, determination, perseverance, delight, reflection, generosity of spirit—all the things

that humans strive for. It was a life worth living and a life worth telling. Once I had slept on her island, I'd never be quite the same. I hope the same might be true for all of you, you readers of her life. I hope that her life—its struggle and triumph, its heartache and ecstasy, its embracing of whatever comes along with a hopeful and practical heart—will change you in some essential way, just as it has me.

Amongst the abundant letters that paid tribute to Rachel Field after her death is this one that I have saved for last. This letter, written by someone who signed only as "Frances," sums up the legacy that I believe Rachel would most cherish. When you remember Rachel Field, remember this:

> There's no denying that we shall miss her welcoming smile, yet no one who has known and loved her is going to feel that she is very far away. Her tenderness and understanding, her capacity for love, her graciousness to the most humble—all this is infinite, a richness that we shall carry with us all our lives. And let us pray, reflecting her spirit, that we shall pass on to others what we have learned from her.

And so we begin.

Hand-drawn and colored illustration on the last page of a tiny
homemade book that Rachel made as a gift for
Louise Seaman Bechtel.

Acknowledgments

I've anticipated writing these acknowledgments with both ardor and apprehension: ardor because I have long awaited the opportunity to thank the legions of people who have supported, guided, and encouraged me through the ten-year process of putting this book together, and apprehension because I'm bound to leave out someone who was instrumental in leading me to a new fount of information or reinvigorating me out of a lull of discouragement, or who generously gave of their time and resources in one way or another. If you are one of those people, please know that your help was greatly appreciated, in spite of my poor record keeping and faulty recall.

As a general note of appreciation, I have to say how many kind and helpful memory keepers I encountered all along the way —archivists, librarians, curators, receptionists, and even a stranger walking her dog on the Hollywood street where Rachel Field's husband and daughter used to live. I am so grateful for their open trust in me and for their willingness to put themselves out on behalf of my research. One curator even bought me a sandwich to sustain me during a long day in the archives. Never underestimate the importance of our history keepers. Next time you see a research librarian, curator, or archivist, say thank you!

To the doll enthusiasts who invited me into the "Hitty" world, sent me invaluable material, shared your passion for Rachel and for Hitty, and offered me the opportunity to speak with you over the phone, in Maine, or in Stockbridge, many thanks. You introduced me to a whole new world connected to Rachel Field.

Sutton Islanders all, you have my gratitude for sharing memories, Rachel Field memorabilia, and your love of our island home. David Audet, when you flew me to Tampa to speak at the Deep Carnivale literature conference, I felt like a real live biographer for the first time.

To other Cranberry Isles and Mount Desert Island residents, your enthusiasm for Rachel's story, your hospitality, and the knowledge and artifacts that you shared were a perpetual inspiration across the years. In particular, I have to thank everyone responsible for initiating and maintaining the Great Cranberry Island Historical Society, not only for your wonderful Rachel and Hitty collections but also for inviting me to share Rachel's story in the charming Cranberry House.

Several Field family descendants were responsible for enriching my knowledge of Rachel's heritage. One in particular arranged for me to gain access to Rachel's medical records in California, and for that I am eternally grateful.

As a biographer with personal Rachel Field connections, Benson Bobrick offered me both artifacts and mentoring. Benson is the one who told me, "The research is never done. Start writing." Thanks for that.

My mentors and classmates at the Stonecoast MFA in Creative Writing all propelled me forward. Cait Johnson, thanks for pointing out what I couldn't see for myself. Thanks also to the Iota Short Prose conference and to Dinty Moore, whose writing prompt inspired the memoir portion of this book.

Three instrumental supporters of my journey did not live to see my book published. I am deeply sad that I didn't get to share it with them, and I honor their memory here. Bruce Komusin, co-founder of the Cranberry House museum, gave me the gift of Rachel's voice on an old radio recording. Russ Carpenter, a generous Field family descendant and historian, shared his time and extensive family histories. "Doctor L.," a retired-oncologist-turned-historian, asked that I not use his name; Doctor L.'s gift was a poignant afternoon discussing Rachel's final days of life at Los Angeles's Good Samaritan Hospital.

Thank you to She Writes Press for believing in publishing good books even if they don't appear to meet "marketable" criteria. To a patient and supportive copyeditor, Molly Lindley Pisani, you'll always have this first-timer's appreciation. To the staff of the Edythe L. Dyer Community Library, thanks for providing a wonderful writing home when home wouldn't do.

To so many friends and acquaintances—including my wonderful book group, the Persian Pickles—thanks for reading Rachel with me, listening to my practice talks, and encouraging me all along the way.

To all my family, for your lifetime of providing much-needed cheerleading from the sidelines, and in particular Tessa, my research assistant extraordinaire. You devoted time to Mom's project graciously, even when she should have been focusing on your move into a new apartment.

And of course, forever appreciation goes to Jonathan, my best editor, best critic, best fan, and best friend, who first brought me to Sutton Island in 1979. Who could have known how far this would take us?

MOST OF THE sources relied on for information in this book are cited in the endnotes. However, I would be remiss not to acknowledge the generous sharing of private collections by Linda Webb and Benson Bobrick (Bobrick's collection is now owned by the

Arne Nixon Center for the Study of Children's Literature), as well as the assistance of several public institutions: the Bangor Public Library in Bangor, Maine; the Portland (Maine) Public Library's Portland Room; the Lyman and Merrie Wood Museum of Springfield History in Springfield, Massachusetts; California's Beverly Hills Public Library; and the Stockbridge Library, Museum and Archives in Stockbridge, Massachusetts.

Notes

Numerous archival sources were consulted in the preparation of this work. The names of these archives are abbreviated throughout these notes as follows:

BRB – Beinecke Rare Book and Manuscript Library, Yale University

GCIHS – Great Cranberry Island Historical Society collection

HFP – Herbert Feis papers, 1916–1971, Manuscript Division, Library of Congress. Ruth Stanley-Brown Feis's papers are located in boxes 37–51.

LARC – Lyle Saxon papers, Manuscripts Collection 4, Box 19, Tulane University Special Collections, Howard-Tilton Memorial Library, Tulane University

MHL – Margaret Herrick Library, Academy of Motion Picture Arts and Sciences

MSL – Maine State Library

MWWC – Rachel Field collection, 1925–1971, Maine Women Writers Collection, University of New England (Portland, ME)

SLAC – Archival collection, Stockbridge Library, Museum & Archives

SLRI – Arthur and Elizabeth Schlesinger Library, Radcliffe Institute for Advanced Study, Harvard University

SC 91: Rachel Field papers, 1924–1942

SC 111: Rachel Field papers, 1845–1942

SML – Sterling Memorial Library, Yale University

USC – Warner Brothers Archives, University of Southern California School of Cinematic Arts

VCSC – Louise Seaman Bechtel collection, Folders 21 and 22, Archives and Special Collections, Vassar College Library

YCAL – Yale Collection of American Literature, Beinecke Rare Book and Manuscript Library

YCAL MSS 407: Lawrence Gilman papers, 1886–1971 (1913–1939)

YCAL MSS 509: Rachel Field collection

YCAL MSS 569: Barrett H. Clark papers, 1905–1953

YCAL MS 630: Field family collection

Names of people who appear regularly in Rachel's correspondence are abbreviated as follows:

ASP – Arthur S. Pederson

BHC – Barrett H. Clark

EG – Elizabeth Gilman

LF – Lucy Field

LS – Lyle Saxon

LSB – Louise Seaman Bechtel

PT – Prentiss Taylor

RLF – Rachel Lyman Field Pederson

RSBF – Ruth Stanley-Brown Feis

WMS – Wilbur Macy Stone

[LETTER #1]

[1] "I met your wife so seldom": Mary W. Cutty(?) to ASP, 16 March 1942, SC 91, box 1, folder 12, SLRI.

[2] "I have been thinking of you and of little Hannah": "Margery" to ASP, 16 March 1942, SC 91, box 1, folder 12, SLRI.

[3] "I felt cut in two": Kate Maclean to ASP, 23 March 1942, SC 91, box 1, folder 12, SLRI.

1: THE ILLUSTRIOUS FIELD FAMILY

[1] "A-field she went": RLF journal, probably 1930s, SC 111, box 2, folder

14, SLRI.

[2] an anecdote about Rachel's childhood: Laura Benét, "Rachel Field— A Memory," *Horn Book Magazine* 18, no. 4 (July–August 1942): 228.

[3] "Well, you've endowed her": RLF to LSB, 27 December 1939, folder 21.280, VCSC.

[4] A colleague reports that Matthew: Stephen Smith, *Memoir of Matthew Dickinson Field, M.D.* (pamphlet, 1895, available in New Hampshire State Library, Concord, NH).

[5] "Dr. Field had an ardent": *Record of the Life of David Dudley Field, His Ancestors and Descendants*, compiled and edited by Emilia R. Field (Denver: privately printed, 1931), 107.

[6] "the Kennedys of the 1800s": Russell Field Carpenter, historian and Field family descendant, 2009 telephone interview with the author.

[7] David Dudley Field Jr. (1805–1894): All summary descriptions of the Field family in this section came from Russell Carpenter's "A Summary Description of the Field Family of Stockbridge, Massachusetts, in the 1800s in Consideration of Producing an Historical Television Documentary about Their Influence on the Nation and the World" (privately printed document, May 15, 2006). Carpenter was a Field family descendant and historian.

[8] "I can just remember Great-Uncle Henry": Rachel Field, *All This and Heaven Too* (New York: American Book-Stratford Press, Inc., 1938), 5.

[9] a poem titled "Family Pew": "Family Pew," in Rachel Field, *Branches Green* (New York: The Macmillan Company, 1934), 43.

[10] her poem "Grandmother's Brook": "Grandmother's Brook," in Field, *Branches Green*, 8.

[11] "It's a judgment on me, I guess": RLF to LSB, 14 March 1939, folder 21.279, VCSC.

[12] "You can see she has the kind of nose": RLF to LSB, 27 December 1939.

[13] "Please tell your father": RLF to RSBF, 23 September 1917, box 1, folder 1936–1939, YCAL MSS 509. Emphasis in original.

[14] "I send you this rather sad looking four leafed clover": RLF to PT, 26 June 1932, box 2, YCAL MSS 509.

[15] "Although I never knew you": This and subsequent quotations in this passage are taken from Field, *All This and Heaven Too*, 1–6.

[16] Elizabeth remembers in her memoir: Elizabeth Field, *A Stockbridge Childhood* (Asheville, NC: The Stephens Press, 1947), 71–72.

[17] her early working title: Bertha E. Mahony, "Of Rachel Field and Letters," *Horn Book Magazine* 18, no. 4 (July–August 1942): 243.

2: INSIDE-SELF AND OUTSIDE-SELF

[1] "High on our dining-room wall": "Great-Uncle Willie," in Rachel Lyman Field, *The Pointed People* (New Haven, CT: Yale University Press, 1924), 61.

[2] "This wish has persisted": Elizabeth Field, *A Stockbridge Childhood* (Asheville, NC: The Stephens Press, 1947), 7.

[3] "Rachel Field tried to recreate the married life": Field, *A Stockbridge Childhood*, 55.

[4] "My sister put this story": *A Stockbridge Childhood*, 72.

[5] "The world of Stockbridge just before": *A Stockbridge Childhood*, 20.

[6] who was once a dinner guest: Article from the Berkshire Web, Pittsfield, MA, archived in the Internet Wayback Machine (https://archive.org/web/) at http://www.berkshireweb.com/themap/stockbridge/history/index.html. No further information is currently available.

[7] "Like many other towns": *A Stockbridge Childhood*, 47.

[8] She never forgot his flashing smile: Margaret Lane, "Rachel Field and Her Contribution to Children's Literature," in *The Hewins Lectures, 1947–1962*, ed. Siri Andrews (Boston: The Horn Book, Inc., 1963), 342–375.

[9] "There at the old wood's edge": "Blue," in Field, *The Pointed People*, 8.

[10] "Christmas trees in ashcans": RLF to PT, 17 January 1928, box 2, YCAL MSS 509.

[11] She "had decided ideas": Field, *A Stockbridge Childhood*, 49.

[12] "Miss Well, the librarian": *A Stockbridge Childhood*, 36.

[13] "Perhaps it was my best book": Gladys St. Clair Morgan, "Realm of Music," *Courier-Gazette*, Rockland, ME, September 14, 1935, MSL.

[14] "I have often thought that I should like": James Gray, "Her First 'Book' Difficult to Fill, Says Rachel Field," unidentified newspaper (possibly *Saint Paul Dispatch*), Saint Paul, MN, January 22, 1936, SC 111, box 3, folder 31, SLRI.

[15] "Literally, I wrote before I could read": Dorothea Lawrance Mann, "Rachel Field the Children's Minstrel," *Boston Transcript*, April 18, 1930, SC 91, box 1, folder 7, SLRI.

[16] "I lazily refused to learn to read myself": Louise W. Bray, *Portland Sunday Telegram*, Portland, ME, January 5, 1930, MSL.

[17] "You see, I liked to make things with my hands": Bray, *Portland Sunday Telegram*, January 5, 1930.

[18] "All I really know about children": This and subsequent quotations are taken from Jean West Maury, "Rachel Field Upholds Belief in Santa Claus," unidentified newspaper and date, SC 111, box 1, SLRI.

[19] The Field girls' daily walk took them: Field, *A Stockbridge Childhood*, 20–21.

[20] "At the end of each day": *A Stockbridge Childhood*, 39.

[21] "The Old Music Box": Handwritten poem, SC 111, box 2, folder 14/15, SLRI. Also published in *Child Life* magazine, Spring 1931.

[22] In a 1932 letter she recounts: RLF to PT, 26 June 1932, box 2, YCAL MSS 509. Emphasis in original.

[23] "Karl Bidwell took the part": Field, *A Stockbridge Childhood*, 41.

[24] "reminisced at a great rate": RLF to PT, 26 June 1932.

[25] "I was given a certain satisfaction": Field, *A Stockbridge Childhood*, 69.

[26] "I don't suppose I shall ever feel": Rachel Field, "History Repeats Itself," *American Girl*, November 1934, SC 111, box 1, SLRI.

[27] "a hidden fairy tune in the bottom": "The Green Fiddler," in Rachel Field, *Taxis and Toadstools* (Garden City, NY: Doubleday, Doran & Company, Inc., 1930), 103.

[28] "My Inside-Self and my Outside-Self": "My Inside-Self," in Field, *The Pointed People*, 74.

3: BEAUTY, LOSS, AND THE EMERGENCE OF A POET'S HEART

[1] rolling bandages for the war effort: Margaret Humberston, Curator of Library and Archives, Lyman and Merrie Wood Museum of Springfield History, telephone and email interviews with the author, September 2011.

[2] should have been a teacher: Elizabeth Field, *A Stockbridge Childhood* (Asheville, NC: The Stephens Press, 1947), 90.

[3] the path toward "conspicuous accomplishments": Field, *A Stockbridge Childhood*, 7.

[4] her poem "Rebellion in September": "Rebellion in September," in Rachel Field, *Poems* (New York: The Macmillan Company, 1957), 10.

[5] her skills in drawing and composition soared: Bertha E. Mahony, "Of Rachel Field and Letters," *Horn Book Magazine* 18, no. 4 (July–August 1942): 246.

[6] perhaps, she once confessed: Louise W. Bray, *Portland Sunday Telegram,* Portland, ME, January 5, 1930, MSL.

[7] "I don't know as I could say I 'enjoyed'": "Of All Her Writings Rachel Field Enjoys Poetry Best," *Lewiston Journal Illustrated Magazine Section,* Lewiston, ME, March 7, 1936, MSL.

[8] "Why do they say that she is dead?": Poem and marginal note from RLF notebook, box 2, folder 15t, SC 111, SLRI.

[9] In a 1931 essay: Rachel Field, "My First Book Friends," *Child Life*, November 1931, box 3, folder 31, SC 111, SLRI.

[10]: "It was written, if I remember rightly": This and subsequently quoted details of the story are found in Rachel Field, "History Repeats Itself," *American Girl*, November 1934, SC 111, box 1, SLRI.

[11] "Johanna sat perfectly still": Rachel Field, *Islanders All*, unpublished manuscript, SC 111, box 2, folders 21–22, SLRI.

[12] "We moved to Springfield after a while": Jean West Maury, "Rachel Field Upholds Belief in Santa Claus," unidentified newspaper and date, SC 111, box 1, SLRI.

4: If Once You Have Slept on an Island

[1] "From the year that I was fifteen": Stanley J. Kunitz and Howard Haycraft, eds., *Junior Book of Authors and Illustrators* (New York: H. W. Wilson Company, 1951), 150.

[2] "One doesn't have to be born in a place": Greta Kerr, "Hitty and Her Chronicler in Maine on Vacation Visit," *Evening Express*, Portland, ME, August 5, 1930, MWWC.

[3] "If I should sit the summer through": "Taking Root," in Rachel Field, *Taxis and Toadstools* (Garden City, NY: Doubleday, Doran & Company, Inc., 1930), 68.

[4] "It was some years after the coming": Rachel Field, introduction to *My Wonderful Visit*, by Elizabeth Hill (New York: Charles Scribner's Sons, 1921).

[5] "her passion for bunchberries, blueberries, the grey rocks": RSBF to LSB, spring 1962, folder 21.285, VCSC.

[6] you can read the youthful swoops: Bunchberry Bungalow guestbook, consulted by the author with permission from the Nevius family.

[7] one friend describes how Rachel: Sophie Goldsmith, "Wish Come True: A Tribute to Rachel Field," *American Girl*, November 1942, folder 22.298, VCSC.

[8]: poems from the summer of 1911: RLF journal, entries dated 2 July 1911 and 23 September 1911, SC 111, box 2, folder 15, SLRI.

[9] "A literary evening enjoyed": Bunchberry Bungalow guestbook.

[10] In the homes of other island friends: Private collections of personal papers and scrapbooks, consulted by the author with permission from the Nussdorfer, Shaw, and Rosenthal families.

[11] "I am truly most myself here": RLF to RSBF, 30 July 1925, box 1, YCAL MSS 509.

[12] all the island staff liked: Margaret Worcester Briggs, *The World Around Me: The Twentieth Century of Margaret Worcester Briggs*, privately printed memoir, undated, 28.

[13] "After the motorboat had chugged us across": Goldsmith, "Wish Come True."

[14] "Trust you to bring the Island closest": RLF to Rosamund Lamb, 22 August 1939, MWWC.

[15] "No other place," she wrote: RLF to PT, 26 June 1932, box 2, YCAL MSS 509.

5: SPECIAL STUDENT

[1] "How could I learn philosophy": "May in Cambridge," in Rachel Lyman Field, *The Pointed People* (New Haven, CT: Yale University Press, 1924), 25.

[2] "The thought of Rachel at Radcliffe": Program from a 1943 memorial service at Radcliffe College for Rachel Field and Ruth Burr Sanborn, SC 111, SLRI.

[3] "The fundamental principle of The 47 Workshop": George Baker, introduction to *Harvard Plays: The 47 Workshop* (New York: Brentanos, 1918), YCAL MSS 509 (formerly catalogued by call number: Za Bi74 918p).

[4] "I've been busy the last two weeks": RLF to RSBF, 21 July 1918, box 1, YCAL MSS 509.

[5] she pours forth an epic: RLF to LF, 8 June 1917, SC 111, box 1, folder 11, SLRI.

[6] "I, too, miss you dreadfully": RLF to RSBF, 16 August 1917, box 1, YCAL MSS 509.

[7] "Wasn't she the most alive": RSBF to PT, 21 September 1964, box 2, YCAL MSS 509.

[8] "When the cake came in, shining": RSBF to LSB, 17 January 1963, folder 21.285, VCSC.

[9] "I just received an unexpected": RLF to RSBF, 16 August 1917, box 1, YCAL MSS 509.

[10] "As for you—well it's a continual marvel": RLF to RSBF, 28 October 1917, box 1, YCAL MSS 509.

[11] "I've written nothing since": RLF to RSBF, 24 November 1917, box 1, YCAL MSS 509.

[12] "I think so much of last summer": RLF to RSBF, 21 July 1918, box 1, YCAL MSS 509.

6: Taxis and Toadstools

[1] "Soon she too would be hurrying along": Rachel Field, *Islanders All*, unpublished manuscript, SC 111, box 2, folders 21–22, SLRI.

[2] "It IS like a Christmas tree": Field, *Islanders All*.

[3] "a big, sunny child bringing in fresh flowers": Laura Benét, "Rachel Field—A Memory," *Horn Book Magazine* 18, no. 4 (July–August 1942): 227.

[4] "I saw that writing was the thing": Dorothea Lawrance Mann, "Rachel Field the Children's Minstrel," *Boston Transcript*, April 18, 1930, SC 91, SLRI.

[5] Historian Jacalyn Eddy wrote: Jacalyn Eddy, *Bookwomen: Creating an Empire in Children's Book Publishing 1919–1939* (Madison: University of Wisconsin Press, 2006).

[6] "My connections have taken me": RLF to George Brett, Jr., 13 January 1934, folder 21.279, VCSC.

[7] "She was one of my very first authors": Louise Seaman Bechtel, "Rachel's Gifts," *Horn Book Magazine* 18, no. 4 (July–August 1942): 230.

[8] "The grand lady is living": Ruth Seinfel, "Dolls of Other Days Spend Quiet Old Age," *New York Evening Post*, December 17, 1931, Za F458+S1, BRB.

[9] correspondence reveals that Mr. Stone: RSBF to PT, 27 February 1963, box 2, YCAL MSS 509.

[10] "Few, if any, of the women of her generation": Laura Benét, "Rachel Field 1894–1942," *Saturday Review*, March 28, 1942, Za F458+S1, BRB.

[11] attached herself instead to a place: Benét, "Rachel Field 1894–1942."

[12] "As Elizabeth undoubtedly told you": RLF to "Frances," 14 July 1922, SC 111, SLRI.

[13] "People become welded to places": Greta Kerr, "Hitty and Her Chronicler in Maine on Vacation Visit," *Evening Express*, Portland, ME, August 5, 1930, MWWC.

[14] "I am truly most myself here": RLF to RSBF, 30 July 1925, box 1, YCAL MSS 509.

[15] her verse has an appeal for all ages: Selected poems from *The Pointed People* (New Haven, CT: Yale University Press, 1924): "Some People," 59; "City Lights," 85; "Rain in the City," 88; "A Summer Morning," 28; "Roads," 33; "Burning Leaves," 22.

[16] She expressed these sentiments: "Something Told the Wild Geese," in Rachel Field, *Branches Green* (New York: The Macmillan Company, 1934), 10.

7: THE LONELY AND DIFFICULT YEARS

[1] "lonely and difficult years": RLF to EG, 13 May 1940, YCAL MSS 407.

[2] "There are many things about the book": George W. Doran Company to RLF, 5 February 1924, SC 111, box 2, folder 30, SLRI.

[3] "You were very reassuring": RLF to BHC, 24 June 1927, YCAL MSS 569.

[4] "She could say in a letter": Josiah Titzell, "Rachel Field, 1894–1942," *Horn Book Magazine* 18, no. 4 (July–August 1942): 222.

[5] She also worked as an illustrator: Margaret Lane, "Rachel Field and Her Contribution to Children's Literature," in *The Hewins Lectures, 1947–1962*, ed. Siri Andrews (Boston: The Horn Book, Inc., 1963), 342–375.

[6] "in a hospital parting with my appendix": RLF to Sarah White Davis (Mrs. Ralf P. Emerson), November 1924, SC 111, SLRI.

[7] "You'll think me a fraud if there ever was one": RLF to BHC, 5 May 1928, YCAL MSS 569.

[8] "Please pardon the messy shape this is in": RLF to BHC, 23 May 1928, YCAL MSS 569.

[9] "My mother also, has been depressed": RLF to RSBF, 3 September 1927, box 1, YCAL MSS 509.

[10] "You are bound to break in sooner or later": RLF to RSBF, 28 Nov 1927, box 1, YCAL MSS 509.

[11] "FOR ANYBODY WHO CARES": Rachel Field, *Eliza and the Elves* (New York: The Macmillan Company, 1926), ix.

[12] "If perchance you should . . . look around for her": Louise W. Bray, *Portland Sunday Telegram*, Portland, ME, January 5, 1930, MSL.

8: SPRIGGIN, THE WHIPPET, AND THE BIRTH OF HITTY

[1] "Spriggin is more enchanting than ever": RLF to PT, 5 November 1927, box 2, YCAL MSS 509.

[2] "Spriggin is very much ashamed": RLF to PT, 17 January 1928, box 2, YCAL MSS 509.

[3] "About Spriggin's name—I really ought": Rachel Field, "All About Spriggin," unidentified and undated article, Za F458+S1, BRB.

[4] "I was so glad to take her to a quiet spot": RLF to PT, 2 April 1930, box 2, YCAL MSS 509.

[5] as in these lines from "Epitaph": Rachel Field, "Epitaph for a Scotch Terrier," first published in The Conning Tower, *New York Herald Tribune*, May 12, 1932. (The Conning Tower was a long-running syndicated column written by Franklin Pierce Adams, which routinely featured contributions from other writers.) Republished in Rachel Field, *Branches Green* (New York: The Macmillan Company, 1934), 17.

[6] "By what sure power": Rachel Field, "For a Dog Chasing Fireflies," first published in *American Girl*, October 1933. Republished in Field, *Branches Green*, 13.

[7] "I finally bought a darling": RLF to PT, 13 June 1928, box 2, YCAL MSS 509.

[8] she found great excitement: Rachel Field, "Song for a Blue Roadster," *St. Nicholas*, 1928 (per an index kept by RLF; no further publication information available). Republished in Rachel Field, *Poems* (New York: The Macmillan Company, 1957), 23.

[9] "Let us stop and say good evening to Hitty": Rachel Field, "The Story About the Story: How Hitty Happened," reprinted with permission from *Friends of Hitty Newsletter*, Spring 1997; originally published in *The Horn Book Magazine*, volume 6, 22–26.

[10] "Dorothy Lathrop, Abbie Evans and I": RLF to PT, 30 August 1928, box 2, YCAL MSS 509.

[11] "In a whaling museum of old Nantucket": "Of All Her Writings, RF Likes Poetry Best," *Lewiston Journal Illustrated Magazine*, Lewiston, ME, March 7, 1936, MSL.

[12] "and there Hitty and Sprig and I": RLF to PT, 4 June 1929, box 2, YCAL MSS 509.

[13] "Hitty is done!": RLF to PT, 10 June 1929, box 2, YCAL MSS 509.

[14] "This will win the Newbery Medal!": RLF quoted in Margaret Lane, "Rachel Field and Her Contribution to Children's Literature," in *The Hewins Lectures 1947–1962*, ed. Siri Andrews (Boston: The Horn Book, Inc., 1963), 342–375.

[15] "that would not do": Lane, "Rachel Field and Her Contribution to Children's Literature."

[16] "I was invited to make a speech": RLF to LS, 31 March 1929, LARC.

[17] "I didn't have a chance to thank you": RLF to WMS, 12 December 1929, MWWC.

[18] "The exquisite little rosary": RLF to WMS, 26 December 1929, MWWC.

[19] "Hitty came alive, became a person": Josiah Titzell, "Rachel Field, 1894–1942," *Horn Book Magazine* 18, no. 4 (July–August 1942): 219.

[LETTER #9]

[1] "Rachel and Lyle all devotion": LF diary, August 1928, author's personal collection.

[2] "This is an astounding coincidence": Chance Harvey, Lyle Saxon biographer, personal interview, email, and telephone correspondence with the author, 2012.

9: MR. MISSISSIPPI

[1] "Love came late to me": Poem handwritten in RLF journal, SC 111, box 2, folder 14/15, SLRI. Later published with the title "Late Spring" in Rachel Field, *Fear Is the Thorn* (New York: The Macmillan Company, 1936), 49.

[2] "Oh Lyle, it is wonderful to feel": RLF to LS, 5 February 1929, LARC.

[3] "Wherever Lyle Saxon lived": Chance Harvey, telephone interview with the author, July 2012.

[4] hobnobbed with the likes of: Chance Harvey, *The Life and Selected Letters of Lyle Saxon* (Gretna, LA: Pelican Publishing, 2003), 131.

[5] "His was a clean, elegant figure": Harvey, *The Life and Selected Letters of Lyle Saxon*, 89.

[6] beginning to attract both gay men and "gawkers": Wayne Hoffman, "The Great Gay Way," *Village Voice*, June 15, 2004, https://www.villagevoice.com/2004/06/15/the-great-gay-way/.

[7] "a pocket edition of a person": RLF to LS, 17(?) March 1929, LARC.

[8] "Lyle Saxon was here for 10 days": RLF to PT, 30 August 1928, box 2, YCAL MSS 509.

[9] "Will you come to dinner": Laura Benét to LS, 8 November 1928, LARC.

[10] Rachel wrote the following poem: RLF journal, SC 111, box 2, folder 14, SLRI.

[11] "Saw Sarah night before last": RLF to LS, 22 April 1929, LARC.

[12] "Your wire came at breakfast": RLF to LS, 1 January 1929, LARC.

[13] "Oh, well, you know the rest of it": RLF to LS, unknown date, LARC.

[14] "You have no idea the effort": RLF to LS, unknown date, LARC.

[15] "They have all gone": RLF to LS, 12 January 1929, LARC.

[16] "Another thirteenth of the month": RLF to LS, 13 March 1929, LARC.

[17] "I must write you today": RLF to LS, 17 March 1929, LARC.

[18] "Your letter came in the last mail": RLF to LS, March 1929, LARC.

[19] "Needless to say I picked your letter clean": RLF to LS, March 1929, LARC.

[20] "I was so glad to see": RLF to LS, unknown date, LARC.

[21] "Your letter was meat and drink": RLF to LS, 14 May 1929, LARC

[22] "Really a horrid little man": RLF to LS, March 1929, LARC.

[23] "Oh how I have been trying": RLF to LS, 31 March 1929, LARC.

[24] "We're still more or less": RLF to LS, 13 April 1929, LARC.

[25] "a year ago this minute": RLF to LS, 26 June 1929, LARC.

[26] "Spriggin would certainly send you": RLF to LS, date unknown, LARC.

[27] "I can't tell you how exciting": RLF to LS, summer 1929, LARC.

[28] "If I have any children": Rachel Field, *Plenty of Time*, unpublished manuscript, SC 111, box 3, folder 28, SLRI, 1.

[29] "Once he had signed it": Field, *Plenty of Time*, 34.

[30] "If Hugh got that advance": *Plenty of Time*, 3.

[31] "She had been the most eager": *Plenty of Time*, 7.

[32] "Why couldn't she just say": *Plenty of Time*, 8.

[33] Similar sentiments appear in poems: "The Busy Body" and "In Defense of Lavishness," RLF poems in private papers, SC 111, box 2, SLRI. Rachel later altered "In Defense of Lavishness" and published it under the title "Apology" in *Fear Is the Thorn*, 23.

[34] "I went on a wild tear the other day": RLF to LS, 19 May 1929, LARC. Emphasis in original.

[35] "Because I know that clocks must tick": "Because I Know," in *Fear Is the Thorn*, 19. The two additional stanzas not printed in *Fear Is the Thorn* are from RLF journal, SC 111, box 2, folder 14/15, SLRI.

[36] "Beauty caught her; stabbed sharp": *Plenty of Time*, 28.

[37] her poet's sensibilities wondered: "Stars Used to Be Enough," "Subtraction (From a Lady's Arithmetic)," and "A Nursery Rhyme," RLF private papers, SC 111, box 2, SLRI. "Subtraction (From a Lady's Arithmetic)" is dated December 31, 1927, but another version in her notes says "Dec. 31, 1928." The first date, I assume, was written in error, since the collection of poems in her papers from that time all coincide with late 1928 and early 1929. A lengthier version of the poem was later published under the title "Higher Mathematics" in *Fear Is the Thorn*, 14.

[38] "To a Certain Gentleman": RLF private papers, SC 111, box 2, SLRI. Later published in *Fear Is the Thorn*, 16.

[39] "Now that her heart was quieting down": Field, *Plenty of Time*, 48.

[40] "Cally felt all her love for Hugh": *Plenty of Time*, 54.

[41] poignant expressions of human longing: "The Pawnshop Window" and "October 14th," RLF private papers, SC 111, box 2, SLRI. An altered version of "The Pawnshop Window" was later published in *Fear Is the Thorn*, 29.

10: THE NEWBERY MEDAL

[1] Instead she dedicated to Lyle: Rachel Field, *Polly Patchwork* (Garden City, NY: Doubleday, Doran and Company, Inc., 1928). In Rachel's letters, Lyle's identity as "Mr. Mississippi" is made clear; see RLF to LS, 19 May 1929, LARC.

[2] "It is one of the days": RLF to LS, 13 April 1929, LARC.

[3] "I am just about frantic": RLF to LS, April 1929, LARC.

[4] "Tomorrow I return to Hitty": RLF to LS, 19 May 1929, LARC.

[5] "I shouldn't be writing you": RLF to LS, May 1929, LARC.

[6] "By doing your little stunt": RLF to LS, June 1929, LARC.

[7] "In Hitty's room the most unusual piece": Quoted in Dottie Baker, "Where Is Hitty," *Doll Reader*, February/March 1986. Rachel's original article is reported to have appeared in *Child Life*, September 1935, 102.

[8] "The lights went out": Rachel Field, *Islanders All*, unpublished manuscript, SC 111, box 2, folders 21–22, SLRI, 113.

[9] Two letters to her mother: RLF to LF, printed with Lucy Field's permission in *The Horn Book Magazine* 18, no. 4 (July–August 1942): 248–250.

[10] "This is to introduce my friend": RLF to BHC, 20 March 1930, YCAL MSS 569.

[11] her first Valentine's Day poem: Poem in RLF private papers, dated February 11, 1933, SC 111, box 2, SLRI.

[12] "In that fraction of time": Rachel Field, *Time Out of Mind* (New York: The Macmillan Company, 1938), 12.

[13] "which isn't a good idea": RLF to PT, 27 January 1928, YCAL, MSS 509.

[14] "Not that Rachel couldn't be difficult": Josiah Titzell, "Rachel Field, 1894–1942," *Horn Book Magazine* 18, no. 4 (July–August 1942): 217.

[15] "whenever I think of John Nelson": Field, *Islanders All*, 452.

[16] "I really feel in grand productive form": RLF to LSB, 29 August 1933, folder 22.309, VCSC.

[17] "Arthur never did get here": RLF to RSBF, 14 September 1934, box 1, YCAL MSS 509.

[18] "I don't want to go off to Rhode Island": RLF to LSB, folder 21.278, VCSC. Rachel's dateline reads only "Friday evening," but a later notation from LSB reads, "After she got Newbery Medal."

11: LOVE AND PAIN, BOUND UP IN TIME

[1] "Since I wrote you last": RLF to LSB, 29 August 1933, folder 22.309, VCSC.

[2] The poem Rachel wrote that night: "North of Time," in Rachel Field, *Fear Is the Thorn* (New York: The Macmillan Company, 1936), 38.

[3] describes Rachel's visit with Mr. Sanford: "And the Place Thereof . . . ," in *Fear Is the Thorn*, 39.

[4] Reviewers wrote, "Here's life masquerading": Unidentified newspaper clipping, advertisement by The Macmillan Company with review testimonials regarding *God's Pocket*, SLRI.

[5] "As we neared Mt. Desert": This and subsequent quotations are from RSBF journal, July 1934, HFP. All emphasis in original.

[6] Rachel, dressed in black coat: RLF private scrapbook of Sutton Island photos, folder 32vf+, SC 111, SLRI.

[7] "The book is rich in passages": Review in *Catholic World*, circa 1936, as seen on a photocopied single page provided the author by a personal friend. Further details unavailable.

[8] "Nat should have anything": Rachel Field, *Time Out of Mind* (New York: The Macmillan Company, 1938), 388.

[9] "He buried his face against me": Field, *Time Out of Mind*, 398–399.

[10] "Shivering there in the dim chillness": *Time Out of Mind*, 399.

[11] "It is a romantic novel of sentiment": Review of *Time Out of Mind*, *New York Times*, April 7, 1935. Found in folder 32vf+, SC 111, SLRI.

[12] "I wonder how many people have read": Eleanor Roosevelt, "My Day, September 1, 1936," *The Eleanor Roosevelt Papers Digital Edition* (2017), accessed 1/23/2020, https://www2.gwu.edu/~erpapers/myday/displaydoc.cfm?_y=1936&_f=md054424.

[13] "Just now I always have the feeling": RLF to RSBF, 3 April 1935, YCAL MSS 509.

[14] "I'm saving a pair to wear at my wedding": RLF to LSB, 25 May 1935, folder 21.279, VCSC. Emphasis in original.

[15] "I wanted to tell you then": RLF to PT, 2 June 1935, YCAL MSS 509.

[16] "Your letter was a joy": RLF to RSBF, 7 June 1935, YCAL MSS 509.

[17] "Your letter broke me all up": RLF to LS, spring 1935, LARC.

[18] "To A. S. P.": Field, *Time Out of Mind*, dedication.

[19] "I am not going to tell you about Sutton": ASP to LS, 30 June 1935, LARC.

[20] "Just as Rachel and her husband left the church": Sophie Goldsmith, "Wish Come True: A Tribute to Rachel Field," *American Girl*, November 1942, folder 22.298, VCSC.

[21] punch holes in colored paper to use as confetti: RSBF to PT, June 1935, YCAL MSS 509.

[22] "Tall and strongly built": Goldsmith, "Wish Come True."

[23] "What a lovely letter from you!": RLF to Rosamund Lamb, 8 July 1935, MWWC.

[24] "Growth is apt to be painful": RLF to LS, spring 1935, LARC.

[25] "on the way to big places": Rachel Field and Arthur Pederson, *To See Ourselves* (New York: The Macmillan Company, 1937), 15.

[26] the following intimate scene: Field and Pederson, *To See Ourselves*, 267–268.

[27] "Interlude: Rachel just telephoned": Joe Titzell to LS, 13 Feb 1929, LARC.

[28] Rachel reveals the lingering power: "A Rhyme for Greenwich Village," in Field, *Fear Is the Thorn*, 28.

[29] "I loved your description of reading": RLF to LS, spring 1935, LARC.

12: NEWLYWEDS AND NOMADS

[1] "I wish now that I'd made you": RLF to EG, 30 June 1935, YCAL MSS 407.

[2] "We've had a perfect trip" RLF to Rosamund Lamb, 8 July 1935, MWWC.

[3] "The summer is slipping away": RLF to EG, 29 July 1935, YCAL MSS 407.

[4] "As things look now": RLF to PT, 2 August 1935, YCAL MSS 509.

[5] "Well, it's terrible and I'm thankful": RLF to PT, 21 August 1935, YCAL MSS 509.

[6] "Rachel Field, a magical name": Gladys St. Clair Morgan, "Realm of Music," *Courier-Gazette*, Rockland, ME, September 14, 1935, MSL.

[7] "In talking of her auctorial adventures": James Gray, "Her First 'Book' Difficult to Fill, Says Rachel Field," unidentified newspaper, possibly *Saint Paul Dispatch*, Saint Paul, MN, January 22, 1936, SC 111, box 3, folder 31, SLRI.

[8] "Miss Field plays many roles": "Cooking Avocation of Rachel Field, Winner Literary Award," *Lewiston Journal*, Lewiston, ME, September 5, 1936, MSL.

[9] "I've been far afield": RLF to PT, 1 March 1936, YCAL MSS 509.

[10] "Rachel is a masterpiece": RSBF journal, 28 October 1937, HFP.

[11] "The coast was so like a higher": RLF to PT, 21 September 1936, YCAL MSS 509.

[12] "I can't tell you how touched": RLF to Rosamund Lamb, 31 August 1936, MWWC.

[13] "We've been here nearly six weeks": RLF to LSB, 13 August 1936, folder 21.279, VCSC.

[14] "The heart of Hollywood is rather": RLF to PT, 21 September 1936, YCAL MSS 509.

[15] "Sprite arrived. She was all agitated": RSBF journal, 1 July 1934, HFP.

[16] "Letters have been almost impossible": RLF to PT, May 1937, YCAL MSS 509.

[17] "If Arthur happens to be visiting": RLF to "Charlotte," 1 September 1937, courtesy of Ann Van Arnum.

[18] "This has not been a summer": RLF to PT, 2 September 1937, YCAL MSS 509.

[19] "We have enjoyed collaborating": RLF to Aimee and Rosamund Lamb, July 1937, MWWC.

[20] "'To See Ourselves' is scheduled": RLF to PT, 24 September 1937, YCAL MSS 509.

[21] "The increasing disposition of people": "Man Plus Typewriter Equals Wealth, to Writer's Child," *Christian Science Monitor*, January 12, 1938, SC 111, box 1, SLRI.

[22] "Arthur has read six mss. in less": RLF to EG, 20 August 1937, YCAL MSS 407.

[23] "Arthur says I mustn't buy anything": RLF to PT, 24 September 1937, YCAL MSS 509.

13: NOT EVERY BUD MAY BEAR

[1] "Warm is my pillow and dreams beguile": "Old Gardener Time," first published in Franklin P. Adams, The Conning Tower, *New York Herald Tribune*, November 16, 1932. Later published in Rachel Field, *Branches Green* (New York: The Macmillan Company, 1934), 3.

[2] "I read at a gallop": RSBF journal, 1 November 1937, HFP.

[3] "I've just been over seeing": RLF to RSBF, 24 April 1933, YCAL MSS 509.

[4] "arrived one afternoon about four": RSBF journal, 25 June 1935, HFP.

[5] "Rachel arrived at 2:30": RSBF journal, October 1937, HFP.

[6] "You remember our talk": RLF to RSBF, 17 October 1937, YCAL MSS 509.

[7] "My Rachel in black suit": RSBF journal, 27 October 1937, HFP.

[8] "I've been meaning to write you": RLF to RSBF, October 1937, YCAL MSS 509.

[9] "Things have been rather low": RLF to RSBF, 7 December 1937, YCAL MSS 509.

[10] her heartache pulses off the page: "Petition in Spring," in RLF private papers, SC 111, box 2, folder 14, SLRI. The poem was published in Adams, The Conning Tower, *New York Herald Tribune*, April 29, 1932.

[11] makes the point yet more squarely: "My Neighbor's Fig Tree," in Rachel Field, *Poems* (New York: The Macmillan Company, 1957), 6.

[12] the specter of May's delicate blossomings: "Not Every Bud . . . ," in Adams, The Conning Tower, *New York Herald Tribune*, May 3, 1933. Later republished in Rachel Field, *Fear Is the Thorn* (New York: The Macmillan Company, 1936), 47.

[13] "I wouldn't have married A. if he'd been": RLF to EG, 10 February 1938, YCAL MSS 407.

[14] "Of course I'd much prefer": RLF to RSBF, 23 May 1938, YCAL MSS 509.

[15] "[Arthur] went over this week": RLF to LSB, June 1938, folder 21.279, VCSC.

14: ALL THIS AND HEAVEN TOO

[1] "It made me feel all the more ashamed": RLF to LSB, 20 November 1938, folder 21.279, VCSC.

[2] "My dear Rosalie Stewart": RLF to Rosalie Stewart, 28 September 1938, USC.

[3] "Had a very long chat recently": Jacob Wilk to Walter MacEwen, 31 October 1938, USC.

[4] "THINKING EVERYTHING OVER": RLF to Rosalie Stewart, telegram, 5 November 1938, USC. Forwarded by Stewart to Walter MacEwen.

[5] "Personally I am happy to be back": RLF to LSB, 20 November 1938.

[6] "Rachel and I arrived in Hollywood": ASP to LS, 15 November 1938, LARC.

[7] "I begin as you told me I should": RLF to LS, August 1937, LARC.

[LETTER #15]

[1] "Heaven is Arthur": "Frances" to ASP, September 1942, SC 111, box 1, folder 12, SLRI.

15: HANNAH

[1] "We saw 'Ladies and Gentlemen'": RLF to EG, 10 July 1939, YCAL MSS 407.

[2] "She's a most simple": RLF to LSB, 14 March 1939, folder 21.279, VCSC.

[3] "Many years ago—about ten": Bette Davis, "A Girl and Her Dog," article clipping, no publication information or date, Za F458 +S1, BRB.

[4] published in a California paper: Circa 1939; further information not found.

[5] "Handles her woman characters": Rebecca Onion, "Memo Evaluating Possible Screenwriters for *Gone With the Wind* Is Frank on the Subject of Faulkner," *Slate*, April 23, 2014, https://slate.com/human-interest/2014/04/gone-with-the-wind-memo-lists-potential-screenwriters-including-william-faulkner.html.

[6] "I didn't know there were so many": RLF to LSB, 14 March 1939, folder 21.279, VCSC.

[7] "Yes, Arthur and I miss": RLF to Rosamund Lamb, 22 August 1939, MWWC.

[8] "Well, the party was a real success": RLF to LSB, 19 June 1939, folder 21.280, VCSC.

[9] "We thought of you and Malcolm": RLF to EG, 10 July 1939, YCAL MSS 407.

[10] "I was so excited I was pounding inside": RSBF journal, 28 June 1939, HFP.

[11] "I took Rachel some lemons": RSBF journal, 24 July 1939, HFP.

[12] "Just in time to get home": RSBF journal, 26 August 1939, HFP.

[13] "Just a hurried line": RLF to LSB, 6 November 1939, folder 21.280, VCSC.

[14] "It's a curious, but most satisfactory": RLF to LSB, 27 December 1939, folder 21.280, VCSC.

[15] Rachel wrote notes, addressed to Hannah: Hannah Pederson baby journal, SC 111, box 2, folder 12, SLRI.

[16] "Our New York apartment things": RLF to PT, 18 June 1940, YCAL MSS 509.

16: HOPE AND MOTHERHOOD

[1] "But she seems completely ours": RLF to EG, 8 March 1940, YCAL MSS 407.

[2] "My mother and Aunt were on Sutton": RLF to PT, 5 September 1940, YCAL MSS 509.

[3] "I can't for the life of me remember": RLF to LSB, 18 November 1940, folder 21.280, VCSC.

[4] "As a whole they have a wistful charm": "A. F. L.," "'Fear Is the Thorn' is Rachel Field's New Title," *Lewiston Journal*, Lewiston, ME, March 14, 1936, SC 111, SLRI.

[5] "There's something in the Cal. air": RLF to PT, 6 January 1941, YCAL MSS 509.

[6] "She seems rather young": RLF to PT, 29 September 1941, YCAL MSS 509.

[7] "Your Christmas card is beautiful": RLF to LSB, December 1941, folder 21.280, VCSC.

[8] "There is a fascination in places": Rachel Field, *And Now Tomorrow* (New York: The Macmillan Company, 1942), 1.

[9] "There aren't going to be any more": Field, *And Now Tomorrow*, 109.

17: MIRACLE

[1] "Your exciting box was the high-light": RLF to LSB, 4 January 1942, folder 21.280, VCSC.

[2] "When I see a small child with books": RLF to EG, 2 January 1942 (written date says "1941," but the error is understandable given that the year is only two days old), YCAL MSS 407.

[3] "Rachel had called me": RSBF journal, January 1942, HFP.

[4] "Miracles are out of fashion nowadays": Rachel Field, *And Now Tomorrow* (New York: The Macmillan Company, 1942), 212.

[5] "I found myself sitting": Field, *And Now Tomorrow*, 216.

[6] "I don't know how I made": *And Now Tomorrow*, 219.

[7] "I have done everything at strange times": RLF as recounted in "Margery" to ASP, 16 March 1942, SC 111, SLRI.

[8] "I still have days of utter incredulity": RLF to LSB, 1 February 1942, folder 21.280, VCSC.

18: You'll Never Be Quite the Same

[1] During a phone call with her friend: Gladys English to EG, 21 March 1942, YCAL MSS 407.

[2] "the most malignant form of cancer": Gladys English to EG, 21 March 1942.

[3] Dr. Chaffin was a highly regarded: Medical details of Rachel Field's hospital stay were obtained through a personal interview with a retired oncologist from Good Samaritan Hospital who requested anonymity, referred to in this book as "Doctor L." The oncologist showed me the handwritten notes entered in a medical record book about Rachel Field's hospital stay and offered an interpretation of the story based on the records.

[4] hear some of these voices again: "The realness of a person": "Ellen" to ASP, 29 May 1942; "We shall not look upon": Mary W. Cutty (?) to ASP, 16 March 1942; "I felt cut in two": Kate Maclean to ASP, 23 March 1942; "Arthur, my very dear friend": Eleanor Farjeon to ASP, 16 March 1942. All of these letters are located in SC 111, box 1, folder 12, SLRI.

[5] "I go on and on, like one in a dream": LF to LSB, 28 May 1942, folder 21.282, VCSC.

[6] "My heart aches for Arthur": LF to LSB, 28 August 1942, folder 21.282, VCSC.

[7] "I picked up R's birthday book": ASP to LS, 4 September 1942, LARC.

[8] "Hannah is fine, though right now": 10 September 1947, folder 21.282, VCSC.

[9] "She never faltered in her devotion": Althea Warren to LSB, 18 February 1958, folder 21.282, VCSC.

[10] A troubling restlessness: My source of information about Hannah's later years was Hannah's ex-husband, who spoke with me by phone on March 3, 2009. He was willing to share what he knew of Hannah's story but preferred not to have his name published.

CHAPTER 19: AND NOW TOMORROW

[1] "There's no denying that we shall miss": "Frances" to ASP, September 1942, SC 111, box 1, folder 12, SLRI.

Credits

Epigraph

Rachel Field, "If Once You Have Slept on an Island," first published in *St. Nicholas*, 1925. Later published in Rachel Field, *Taxis and Toadstools* (Garden City, NY: Doubleday, Doran & Company, Inc., 1930), 62.

Illustrations

Except as noted below, all photos are courtesy of the Arthur and Elizabeth Schlesinger Library, Radcliffe Institute for Advanced Study, Harvard University, SC 111: Rachel Field papers, 1845–1942.

Opposite Contents – Silhouette illustration by Rachel Field: Rachel Lyman Field, *The Pointed People* (New Haven, CT: Yale University Press, 1924), 6.

53 – Rachel Field's high school senior yearbook photograph: *The Pnalka* [yearbook of Central High School, Springfield, MA], 1914, 37. Courtesy of the Library at the Lyman and Merrie Wood Museum of Springfield History, Springfield Museums.

136 – Publicity photo of Rachel Field and Spriggin: Courtesy of Portland [ME] Public Library Special Collections and Archives.

195 – Hand-drawn and colored note from Rachel Field: Reproduced courtesy of Archives and Special Collections, Vassar College Library, Louise Seaman Bechtel collection, folder 21.278.

347 – Hand-drawn and colored illustration: Drawn by Rachel Field. Reproduced courtesy of Archives and Special Collections, Vassar College Library, Louise Seaman Bechtel collection, folder 22.302.

About the Author

Credit: Anna K. Wood

ROBIN CLIFFORD WOOD has a BA from Yale University, an MA in English from the University of Rochester, and an MFA in creative writing from the Stonecoast program at the University of Southern Maine. During twenty-five years as a full-time mom, she published local human-interest features in New Hampshire, New York, and Massachusetts and spent seven years as a regular columnist, first in Massachusetts, then for Maine's *Bangor Daily News*. She began teaching college writing in 2015. Her articles have appeared in *Port City Life* magazine, *Bangor Metro*, and *Solstice Literary Magazine*, which published her powerful essay "How Do You Help Your Parents Die?" in its spring 2019 issue. For more information, visit www.robincliffordwood.com. Wood lives in central Maine with her husband and dogs. *The Field House* is her first book.

SELECTED TITLES FROM SHE WRITES PRESS

She Writes Press is an independent publishing company
founded to serve women writers everywhere.
Visit us at www.shewritespress.com.

Operatic Divas and Naked Irishmen: An Innkeeper's Tale by Nancy R.
Hinchliff. $16.95, 978-1-63152-194-2. At sixty four, divorced, retired, and
with no prior business experience and little start-up money, Nancy Hinchliff
impulsively moves to a new city where she knows only one person, buys a
125-year-old historic mansion, and turns it into a bed and breakfast.

Implosion: Memoir of an Architect's Daughter by Elizabeth W. Garber. $16.95,
978-1-63152-351-9. When Elizabeth Garber, her architect father, and the
rest of their family move into Woodie's modern masterpiece, a glass house, in
1966, they have no idea that over the next few years their family's life will be
shattered—both by Woodie's madness and the turbulent 1970s.

The Butterfly Groove: A Mother's Mystery, A Daughter's Journey by Jessica
Barraco. $16.95, 978-1-63152-800-2. In an attempt to solve the mystery of
her deceased mother's life, Jessica Barraco retraces the older woman's steps
nearly forty years earlier—and finds herself along the way.

There Was a Fire Here: A Memoir by Risa Nye. $16.95, 978-1-63152-045-7.
After a devastating firestorm destroys Risa Nye's Oakland, California home
and neighborhood, she has to dig deep to discover her inner strength and
resilience.

Nothing But Blue by Diane Lowman. $16.95, 978-1-63152-402-8. In the
summer of 1979, Diane Meyer Lowman, a nineteen-year-old Middlebury
College student, embarked on a ten-week working trip aboard a German
container ship with a mostly male crew. The voyage would forever change
her perspective on the world—and her place in it.

Songs My Mother Taught Me: A Story in Progress by Eva Izsak. $16.95,
978-1-63152-551-3. After years of trying to escape her heritage through
constant movement around the globe, middle-aged Eva finds herself in a
poor suburb of Tel Aviv, nursing her dying mother in the house she grew up
in—and is forced to face the ghosts of the past and belatedly cut the
umbilical cord that has had an all-consuming grip on her for more than five
decades.